"I highly recommend *Playing by the Rules* to every male who has a leadership role in an evangelical mission organization. While the monograph meticulously describes and explains women's leadership experiences in evangelical mission organizations, it also makes crystal clear the key to freeing female mission leaders to realize their full potential. Male leaders must work steadily and intentionally to change their organizations' patriarchal cultures. The underutilization of women in missional leadership, apart from issues of injustice, is just bad stewardship."

—**Rich Starcher**, Professor of Intercultural Education & Missiology, Biola University, and Editor-in-Chief of *Missiology: An International Review*

"Sexist organizations are broken organizations, missing out on the leadership gifts of half of humanity. Dr. Dzubinski's research reveals the often subtle ways in which women's leadership is undermined in the unique world of mission organizations. Her work shows that ultimately, 'playing by the rules' means losing the game. For those willing to listen, this book will provide insights to equip the church to more effectively fulfill its mission in an increasingly diverse world."

—**Elizabeth Lewis Hall**, Professor of Psychology, Biola University

"This book comes out of the author's deep love for the evangelical missions community and her conviction that we are limping due to a unseen injury that has been crippling the body of Christ for too long. We can't fix what we don't see. Leanne's discoveries provide a critical path into redemptive, honest partnerships that will bless our God and the world as we take hold of them!"

—**Wendy Wilson**, Mission Advisor for Development of Women, Missio Nexus

"This early yet provocative contribution to the fields of leadership studies and missions represents an important benchmark study that portrays how women leaders in evangelical organizations navigated their leadership journey and made meaning of their leadership experiences. Times have changed, and more change is coming, yet the lessons learned through interviews with the twelve participants in Dzubinski's research have ongoing value in identifying common obstacles and pitfalls that women encounter, and pointing out ways that organizations—far beyond evangelical missions agencies—can ensure support for women leaders to effectively contribute in the roles for which they have been gifted and called."

—**Karen A. Longman**, PhD Program Director and Professor, Department of Higher Education, Azusa Pacific University

"As a woman who served as a missionary overseas for seventeen years, I know well the burden of fulfilling a call to missions in Jesus's name. With that burden also go the restrictions under which many women missionaries must work simply because they are women. Dr. Dzubinski has made an important contribution to understanding the 'dance' many Christian women engage as they attempt to do God's work in mission contexts that limit their ministry because of their sex."

—**Alice Mathews**, retired Professor of Educational Ministries and Women's Ministries, Gordon-Conwell Theological Seminary

Playing by the Rules

American Society of Missiology
Monograph Series

Chair of Series Editorial Committee, James R. Krabill

The ASM Monograph Series provides a forum for publishing quality dissertations and studies in the field of missiology. Collaborating with Pickwick Publications—a division of Wipf and Stock Publishers of Eugene, Oregon—the American Society of Missiology selects high quality dissertations and other monographic studies that offer research materials in mission studies for scholars, mission and church leaders, and the academic community at large. The ASM seeks scholarly work for publication in the series that throws light on issues confronting Christian world mission in its cultural, social, historical, biblical, and theological dimensions.

Missiology is an academic field that brings together scholars whose professional training ranges from doctoral-level preparation in areas such as Scripture, history and sociology of religions, anthropology, theology, international relations, interreligious interchange, mission history, inculturation, and church law. The American Society of Missiology, which sponsors this series, is an ecumenical body drawing members from Independent and Ecumenical Protestant, Catholic, Orthodox, and other traditions. Members of the ASM are united by their commitment to reflect on and do scholarly work relating to both mission history and the present-day mission of the church. The ASM Monograph Series aims to publish works of exceptional merit on specialized topics, with particular attention given to work by younger scholars, the dissemination and publication of which is difficult under the economic pressures of standard publishing models.

Persons seeking information about the ASM or the guidelines for having their dissertations considered for publication in the ASM Monograph Series should consult the Society's website—www.asmweb.org.

Members of the ASM Monograph Committee who approved this book are:

Paul V. Kollman, Associate Professor of Theology and Executive Director Center for Social Concerns (CSC), University of Notre Dame

Robert Gallagher, Chair of the Intercultural Studies department and Director of M.A. (Intercultural Studies), Wheaton College Graduate School

RECENTLY PUBLISHED IN THE ASM MONOGRAPH SERIES

Emily Ralph Servant, *Experiments in Love: An Anabaptist Theology of Risk-Taking in Mission*

Mary Carol Cloutier, *Bridging the Gap, Breaching Barriers: The Presence and Contribution of (Foreign) Persons of African Descent to the Gaboon and Corisco Mission in 19th-century Equatorial Africa*

Playing by the Rules

How Women Lead in Evangelical Mission Organizations

Leanne M. Dzubinski

American Society of Missiology Monograph
Series vol. 52

PICKWICK *Publications* · Eugene, Oregon

PLAYING BY THE RULES
How Women Lead in Evangelical Mission Organizations

American Society of Missiology Monograph Series 52

Pickwick Publications
An Imprint of Wipf and Stock Publishers
199 W. 8th Ave., Suite 3
Eugene, OR 97401

www.wipfandstock.com

PAPERBACK ISBN: 978-1-7252-8514-9
HARDCOVER ISBN: 978-1-7252-8515-6
EBOOK ISBN: 978-1-7252-8516-3

Cataloguing-in-Publication data:

Names: Dzubinski, Leanne M., author.

Title: Playing by the rules : how women lead in evangelical mission organizations / by Leanne M. Dzubinski.

Description: Eugene, OR: Pickwick Publications, 2021 | American Society of Missiology Monograph Series vol. 52 | Includes bibliographical references.

Identifiers: ISBN 978-1-7252-8514-9 (paperback) | ISBN 978-1-7252-8515-6 (hardcover) | ISBN 978-1-7252-8516-3 (ebook)

Subjects: LCSH: Leadership in women. | Women in missionary work. | Women missionaries | Sex role—Religious aspects—Christianity. | Evangelicalism.

Classification: BV2610 D98 2021 (print) | BV2610 (ebook)

Table 2 reprinted with permission from *Missiology: An International Review.* Original publication: Dzubinski, L. M. (2016). Taking on power: Women leaders in evangelical mission organizations. *Missiology: An International Review, 44*(3), 281–295. doi:10.1177/0091829615583732

Dedicated to Paul Dzubinski, my husband and best friend, who has believed in me and supported me unfailingly throughout this process and throughout life. And to Alice Mathews, mentor and friend, who told me to do a PhD. Thanks to you, I did.

Contents

Tables

Acknowledgments

I AM DEEPLY GRATEFUL for the unswerving support I've received in the process of writing this book. Wendy, thank you for walking me through each step and pushing me to be a better scholar. Laura, thank you for helping me keep the goals and purpose clear. Karen, thank you for believing in me from the beginning and giving me courage to believe in myself. April, thank you for adding your voice and teaching perspective to the process. Aliki, thank you for providing support and challenge as I worked through some difficult spots.

1

Introduction

"WE'RE OLD, WE'RE WHITE, and we're male." So began the North American Mission Leaders' Conference in September 2010. Despite the fact that the conference was attended by leaders of almost 200 organizations that work in countries all around the globe, a quick glance around the room showed the truth of the speaker's comment. Only a handful of women were visible. The few men of color were immediately noticeable. And bald and graying heads predominated. That year's conference theme was "Diversity in Mission," with a focus on age, ethnicity, and gender. Still, attendees noticed that gender was barely discussed. Two of the plenary speakers were not white, but all were male. Of about one hundred workshops, only two dealt with issues of gender. Despite the promise inherent in the name, the conference offered little for those looking for gender diversity. In this, however, mission agencies are certainly not alone.

In most fields, including those dominated by women, the top ranks of leadership are solidly male-dominated. This is true in business, where only about 3 percent of Fortune 500 CEOs are women.[1] It is also true in education, where the overwhelming majority of teachers are female yet the bulk of school superintendents and principals are male.[2] In the fields of science, technology, engineering, and math, sometimes known as the STEM fields, the lack of women begins early, with girls vanishing from the classroom in the upper school grades and steadily fewer women pursuing college and advanced degrees in these disciplines.[3] This shortage of women

1. Bosker, "Fortune 500 List Boasts More Female CEOs than Ever Before"; Rosin, "End of Men."

2. Sanchez and Thornton, "Gender Issues in K-12 Educational Leadership."

3. VanLeuvan, "Young Women's Science/Mathematics Career Goals"; Wilson-Jones,

1

at the top of the hierarchy is also true in the realm of religion. On average women comprise more than 60 percent of any religious congregation in the United States, yet Protestant female leadership numbers average only 15 percent and Catholics do not ordain women to the priesthood at all.[4] Social service agencies have similar numbers; in the world of evangelical mission organizations, where the workforce is about two-thirds female, the absence of women leaders is equally noticeable. For example, of the approximately 200 organizations which belong to MissioNexus, the largest professional association of evangelical mission agencies in North America, only five (2.5 percent) have female CEOs.[5]

This absence of women at the top levels of organizations is sometimes called the "female brain drain" and is currently receiving a fair amount of attention in the business literature and in the STEM fields.[6] However, little attention has been paid to the corresponding female brain drain in faith-based organizations, although the numbers are similar. While Protestant evangelical churches are beginning to engage in conversations about embracing women as leaders, the corresponding evangelical mission agencies have barely begun to touch the subject.

Clearly, women in the upper ranks of leadership are scarce. Various factors have been suggested over the years as explanations for this phenomenon but none of them has proven convincing over time. Women do not lack education, since today's women and men earn college degrees in equal numbers; nor do they lack ambition or commitment to work, nor intelligence.[7] There is no shortage of women in the workplace who could be groomed for leadership, since women now make up almost half of the U.S. labor force.[8] In the world of missions, women are educated, committed, effective, and make up fully two-thirds of the work force.[9] The question, then, is what is it about being a woman and being a leader that makes the combination scarce?

In the realm of business, research has been done for more than four decades to explain the lack of women leaders. Various reasons have been

"Undergraduate Females' Viewpoints on the Challenges and Barriers."

4. Lapovsky, "White House Project Report."

5. Wilson, private communication, September 11, 2012

6. Barres, "Does Gender Matter?"; VanLeuvan, "Young Women's Science/Mathematics Career Goals"; Wilson-Jones, "Undergraduate Females' Viewpoints on the Challenges and Barriers."

7. Carli and Eagly, "Gender and Leadership."

8. Carli and Eagly, "Gender and Leadership."

9. Eenigenburg and Bliss, *Expectations and Burnout*; Robert, *American Women in Mission*.

proposed over the years. The earliest was simply the assertion that women could not lead, but that idea proved untenable.[10] Next came the suggestion that there were not enough women in the pipeline to be promoted, but that too was quickly dispelled with women's increasing presence in the workforce.[11] Further suggestions included women's greater involvement with family, lower educational achievements, or lack of ambition as explanations.[12] However, the only factor that continues to impact women is their greater domestic involvement, and this factor alone is not sufficient to account for the decreasing numbers of women approaching the top of organizational hierarchies.[13]

Perhaps the best explanation for the scarcity of women leaders is that of gender-role stereotypes, also known as role congruity theory.[14] The theory proposes that society ascribes certain qualities to women and other, distinct qualities to men.[15] These "unwritten expectations" create a broad, pervasive social understanding of how things are done and who does them. Because our social understanding of what it means to be a leader aligns closely with our expectations for men, we tend to expect that leaders will be males. Because the expectations for leaders do not align with the expectations for women, we may be surprised when women lead, especially if they do it well. Those same expectations may cause us to criticize women who lead in what we believe is a "masculine" way: if a woman is assertive and directive, we may find her to be "bossy" and "domineering," words with decidedly negative connotations. This negativity is because in addition to describing how men and women *do* behave, gender role stereotypes also define how we think men and women *ought* to behave, and lead us to criticize those who break the rules.[16] In fact, women can even

10. Hoyt, "Women and Leadership."

11. Carli and Eagly, "Gender, Hierarchy, and Leadership"; Heilman, "Description and Prescription."

12. Carli and Eagly, "Gender and Leadership."

13. Carli and Eagly, "Gender and Leadership."

14. Eagly and Karau, "Role Congruity Theory of Prejudice toward Female Leaders"; Scott, "Women Leaders in Protestant, Evangelical Nonprofit Institutions."

15. Eagly and Carli, "Women and the Labyrinth of Leadership"; Eagly and Karau, "Role Congruity Theory of Prejudice toward Female Leaders"; Heilman and Eagly, "Gender Stereotypes Are Alive, Well, and Busy Producing Workplace Discrimination"; Schein, "Relationship between Sex Role Stereotypes and Requisite Management Characteristics."

16. Eagly and Karau, "Role Congruity Theory of Prejudice toward Female Leaders."

improve how they are perceived as leaders by increasing their "feminine" behaviors to counterbalance the "masculine" ones.[17]

In the realm of evangelical mission organizations, however, little research has been done into women's leadership. Scott studied employees' perceptions of women leaders in evangelical non-profit organizations, finding that gender-role stereotypes did hamper women's leadership.[18] However, her study did not include mission organizations, nor did she study women leaders themselves. There are no other studies corresponding to the business studies about what helps or hinders women's progress into leadership in mission organizations. We know that only a few women do lead in these organizations, but we do not yet know why. We do not know to what degree gender-role expectations may hinder their progress or what kind of criticism they may encounter when they do lead. We do not know what factors affect women's leadership progress, what behaviors help or hinder them as leaders in mission organizations, or anything about their lived experience.

Part of the challenge in studying this issue is that evangelical religion has constructed a set of gendered expectations for women and men that closely resemble social gender-role stereotypes. In addition to being kind and nurturing, evangelical women are frequently expected to show "gracious submission," meaning that they do not take on leadership roles, but instead willingly follow the lead of their husbands and male spiritual authority figures.[19] Evangelical men, in addition to being independent and taking initiative, are expected to be the leaders in home, church, and society.[20]

What is significant about gender roles in evangelicalism is that they are frequently considered to be God-given and therefore immutable.[21] Where society may recognize them as prejudice and strive to overcome them, evangelical theology upholds them as doctrine and strives to inculcate them in its followers. Still, there is not full agreement on exactly what limitations on women should be enforced, leading to a certain degree of ambiguity regarding the exact parameters of women's roles.[22] Evangelicals may say that male rule is the ideal, yet function in daily life as equals, especially in private.[23] Publicly, however, male rule may be embraced. For example, many churches

---

17. Carli and Eagly, "Gender and Leadership."

18. Scott, "Women Leaders in Protestant, Evangelical Nonprofit Institutions."

19. Shaw, "Gracious Submission."

20. Shaw, "Gracious Submission."

21. Ingersoll, "Engendered Conflict"; Shaw, "Gracious Submission."

22. Bendroth, "Fundamentalism and Femininity."

23. Gallagher and Smith, "Symbolic Traditionalism and Pragmatic Egalitarianism"; Shaw, "Gracious Submission."

exclude women from positions such as pastor or elder which hold direct, public, congregational authority.[24] Women in evangelical organizations may find themselves navigating a narrow space of acceptable behavior, and if they step too far outside those bounds may suffer the consequences.[25] Powerful males may use their authority to intimidate, control, or even dismiss women who do not follow the gendered expectations.[26]

However, no studies have been done to understand how gender-role expectations in evangelical religion affect women's movement into leadership. Further, since leading is outside of the "normal" expectation for women, we do not know how women learn to lead. We know a bit about how women in evangelical colleges learn to lead but we do not know how women in mission organizations gain leadership positions or how they learn to do the job.[27] We also do not know what meaning these women make of functioning in a job that is typically "male." Nor do we know what kinds of consequences they may experience if they step outside the perceived boundaries of appropriate female behavior.

These gender-role stereotypes are even more pronounced in evangelical mission organizations which tend to be characterized by a two-person career model. In this model, one spouse, invariably the husband, has the actual career while his wife serves to support him and maintain the family.[28] Executives, military officers, and high-level politicians tend to function according to this structure.[29] Ministry functions this way as well; several studies have been done showing that pastoral ministry frequently functions as a "two-person career."[30] Clergy wives overwhelmingly consider themselves as contributing directly to their husband's career and as a partner in ministry with him.[31] For many missionary couples this structure is also true. Organizations often assign a position to the husband and expect the wife to support him in his work. If a husband is promoted to leadership, his wife may be expected to contribute to his work as part of the two-person career structure. She might prepare reports, or take on correspondence, or do the budgeting for him, depending on where he needs her help.

24 Scholz, "Christian Right's Discourse on Gender and the Bible."

25. Ingersoll, *Evangelical Christian Women.*

26. Armstrong, "How Evangelical Black Women Learn to Negotiate Power Relations"; Ingersoll, *Evangelical Christian Women.*

27. Dahlvig and Longman, "Women's Leadership Development."

28. Papanek, "Men, Women, and Work."

29. Papanek, "Men, Women, and Work."

30. Frame and Shehan, "Relationship between Work and Well-being in Clergywomen."

31. Pavalko and Elder, "Women behind the Men."

However, we do not know what happens when a woman is promoted to a leadership position. We do not know if she is placed in a job-sharing role with her husband or with another man. We do not know if she is able to function independently as a leader in her own right. We do not know what it means for a woman to lead in an evangelical mission organization, because women leaders in evangelical mission organizations have simply not been studied. Apart from historical studies, the current literature that exists on missionary women focuses primarily on their mental health and well-being. There is a gap in the literature regarding women as leaders in evangelical mission organizations, and we know almost nothing about how they come to their roles, how they learn to lead in a patriarchal structure, what challenges they encounter, and what meaning they make of their presence in that leadership role.

PROBLEM STATEMENT

Despite enormous gains made by women in the last half-century, the upper ranks of many organizations are still male-dominated, even when the majority of the workforce is female. In business, gender-role expectations have been shown to hamper women's upward progress.[32] For women who do achieve leadership positions, strengthening stereotypically female behaviors to balance the stereotypically male ones required of leaders often helps them succeed. However, there is little information about women leaders in evangelical mission organizations. We do not know to what extent gender-role stereotypes help or hinder them in their leadership, or if increasing stereotypically female behaviors benefits them the way it does women in business.

Gender-based role expectations are further complicated by evangelical religion, where gender roles are often constructed as dogma and treated as requirements for faithful women.[33] Little research has been done to discover what happens when a woman accepts a leadership position in an evangelical mission organization which may require her to function somewhat counter to those gendered expectations. Nor do we know how she learns to lead in that setting, or what meaning she makes of leading in a realm often reserved for men.

Ministry adds another layer of complication to gender roles for women. In churches, the pastor's job is often considered a two-person career with wives expected to lead alongside their husbands in a supportive manner.[34] But there is a dearth of studies evaluating to what extent these expectations

32. Carli and Eagly, "Gender and Leadership."
33. Ingersoll, *Evangelical Christian Women*.
34. Pavalko and Elder, "Women behind the Men."

function for women leaders in evangelical mission organizations, or investigating to what extent women leaders there may function as part of a two-person leadership team in a way that supports a male counterpart. We do not know how women are selected for leadership positions, or to what degree their leadership may be framed as part of a two-person model.

Therefore, the purpose of this study is to understand how women lead and make meaning of their leadership in evangelical mission organizations. The research questions are:

1. How have these women become leaders and learned to lead?

2. What if any forms of resistance or subversive behavior do they use in order to lead in a patriarchal culture?

3. How do they and the organizations they work in account for their leadership?

SIGNIFICANCE OF THE STUDY

This study contributes to our knowledge of adult education and HRD on both theoretical and practical levels. Interviewing women leaders in evangelical mission organizations helps us understand more about how adult women learn and make meaning, about how they work within or challenge gender stereotypes and prescriptions, and about how they lead in a patriarchal context. Practically, this study could benefit women leaders in religious organizations, women workers in those organizations, and the organizations themselves in attracting and retaining staff.

Theoretical Significance

This study contributes to the literature on women in leadership, women's learning, and to the literature on evangelical non-profit organizations. First, understanding how women lead and make meaning of their leading in evangelical mission agencies, who mostly adhere to gender-roles as an espoused theory, helps us gain a broader perspective on women's leadership. It helps us understand how women navigate the narrow space of leading by upholding and, perhaps, challenging the gender prescriptions. It helps us understand how to support women who wish to challenge those prescriptions. Further, this study supports, expands, and challenges our understanding of social role-congruity theory.

Second, this study adds to our understanding of adult learning by exploring how women learn to lead in evangelical mission organizations. It sheds light on similarities and differences women in faith-based non-profits face compared to women in business. Anecdotal evidence suggests that women in mission agencies do not move "up the ladder" like women in corporate America, but are placed suddenly in those positions in mid-career. This study helps us understand how they then learn the job. What meaning do they make of taking on a role that is usually reserved for men? This study offers initial findings on those questions.

Third, this study contributes to the scholarship on women in evangelical non-profit agencies. Scott comments that there is little empirical data on evangelical non-profit organizations, and that data regarding women is not readily available.[35] Her study addressed organizational perceptions of women leaders, but it did not study the women leaders themselves nor did it include mission organizations. This study may be the first to directly examine women leaders in evangelical mission organizations. As such it adds one empirical piece to that body of literature on women leaders in evangelical non-profits.

Practical Significance

In the realm of practice, this study is significant on societal, organizational and individual levels. On a societal level, religious leaders are important shapers of "the moral attitudes and behaviors of society," meaning that the lack of women religious leaders represents a serious gap in the formation of our society.[36] Understanding how women succeed as leaders in religious organizations also helps us understand how to retain them, and move towards a healthier society.

At an organizational level, the lack of women leaders is significant to financial and performance levels. First is the replacement cost for lost talent. If families, couples, and women leave their assignments due to unclear or unfulfilled expectations, the financial losses are significant. Employee replacement costs vary by industry, with averages for education and other services running about $14,000 per employee.[37] Second is the financial and performance cost of not having women in top leadership positions. Gender diversity in organizational leadership has been clearly linked to increased organizational performance, including financial performance and decision-making.[38] In today's economic climate, organizations face heightened pressure to reduce avoidable costs while maximizing performance.

35. Scott, "Women Leaders in Protestant, Evangelical Non-profit Institutions."

36. Lapovsky, "White House Project Report."

37. O'Connell and Kung, "Cost of Employee Turnover."

38. Catalyst, *Bottom Line*; Scott, "Women Leaders in Protestant, Evangelical Non-profit Institutions."

In addition to loss of talent and financial loss is the risk that outdated practices could put the continued existence of the organization in jeopardy. Raised in a climate of fundamental gender equality, today's workers may be unwilling to work in overtly patriarchal structures. Without a steady stream of new workers, the organizations may eventually close. So change in this area may well be critical if these organizations want to continue to have a meaningful social and religious impact in the twenty-first century.

Finally, this study is significant at the individual level for the women who work and lead in evangelical mission organizations. A conservative estimate is that the current international missionary workforce includes about 11,000 women. They should receive the same benefits and opportunities as their male colleagues, including opportunities to advance into leadership should they so desire. These are individuals who have dedicated a portion of their lives to overseas service. They are usually highly motivated and idealistic, dedicated to bringing improvement to the world, and willing to do so with little in the way of financial reward. It is unjust to disregard their commitment, passion, and dedication through a lack of organizational support. For these women the issue is one of justice.

DEFINITIONS

For the purposes of this study, the following definitions are used. There is disagreement about terms such as "evangelical" and "feminism," so the ones offered here are not meant to be definitive but rather to reflect the aspects of those words included in this study.

1. Agentic—"Agentic characteristics . . . describe primarily an assertive, controlling, and confident tendency—for example, aggressive, ambitious, dominant, forceful, independent, daring, self-confident, and competitive."[39]

2. Communal—"Communal characteristics . . . describe primarily a concern with the welfare of other people—for example, affectionate, helpful, kind, sympathetic, interpersonally sensitive, nurturant, and gentle."[40]

3. Evangelical—"Adherence to the Bible as the standard for belief and practice, its emphasis on personal conversion, and its missionary fervor."[41]

4. Evangelical mission agency—an organization with an evangelical basis, often belonging to the category of faith missions, which recruits

39. Eagly and Johannesen-Schmidt, "Leadership Styles of Women and Men."
40. Eagly and Johannesen-Schmidt, "Leadership Styles of Women and Men."
41. Bendroth, "Last Gasp Patriarchy."

and deploys workers for religious and humanitarian causes in locations other than their own country or culture.

5. Faith mission—an independent organization not tied to a specific denomination. Workers with a faith mission are typically required to raise their own funding for their work.

6. Feminism—the desire for women to be treated as fully human and fully persons.[42] Feminism includes the understanding that "men have cornered certain rights that should be shared by both men and women."[43] I identify with Tisdell's poststructural feminist who examines and challenges the "connections between individuals and social structures."[44]

7. Gender role—(see also "sex role") Social roles, expectations, and stereotypes that have been constructed for men and women. They are often thought to be based only in biological sex, but in reality are also constructed by society as part of culture.[45] In this book I will use the term "gender" though other authors also use "sex roles" for the same concept.

8. Leadership—"Leadership is a process whereby an individual influences a group of individuals to achieve a common goal."[46]

9. Missionary—a worker for a mission agency. (Note: a missionary is not necessarily an employee of the agency, since they may be classified as a volunteer.)

10. Patriarchy—literally, "male rule" or "rule of the father." For the purposes of this study I define patriarchy as a system of favoritism that gives preference and privilege to men, often at the expense of women.

11. Sex role—(see also "gender role") The terminology used in early writings (1970s) on the concept of social roles based on biological sex.[47] The terminology "sex roles" and "sex role stereotypes" is still used in the literature, but the preference now is to use "gender" instead of "sex" to reflect the constructed nature of these roles and stereotypes.

---

42. Sayers, *Are Women Human?*; Tong, *Feminist Thought*.
43. Groothuis, *Women Caught in the Conflict*, 200.
44. Tisdell, "Poststructural Feminist Pedagogies," 143.
45. Andersen and Hysock, *Thinking about Women*.
46. Northouse, *Leadership Theory and Practice*, 3.
47. Katz, "Sex Roles"; Schein, "Relationship between Sex Role Stereotypes and Requisite Management Characteristics."

2

Review of the Literature: Gender

THE PURPOSE OF THIS literature review is to examine three areas of scholarship that have a bearing on evangelical women in leadership in non-profit mission organizations. First, in this chapter I will consider some aspects of critical feminist scholarship that have particular significance for the topic. What does feminist scholarship say about gender, and about gender essentialist thought? From a feminist perspective, what purpose does gender serve? And what happens when gender constructs are enacted in the workplace as well as the home and family?

In the second chapter I will consider the literature on leadership. Scholars have been studying leadership and trying to discover what makes a good leader for over a century. Early theories sought to understand a leader's traits, skills, or styles to explain leadership. In mid-century the theory of transformational leadership took hold, arguing that good leaders are mindful of their followers' good and development. As the world shifted towards connection through the World Wide Web, post-heroic leadership models moved to the fore. In these theories, leadership is more democratic, being shared among multiple people rather than concentrated in one top person, typically male.

With a leadership framework in place, I will then examine theories of women's leadership. Some strands of thought argue that women make better leaders than men, especially in our newly-flattened world. Yet women are still increasingly scarce the higher we look in the organizational hierarchy. What are the possible explanations for the shortage of women near the top? What information does leadership theory offer for us to understand how women attempt to lead in organizations? What strategies do women adopt in their efforts to lead well? What works for them?

Finally, in the third chapter, I will examine the evangelical worldview regarding women, and what that means for women who lead in evangelical mission organizations. How do evangelicalism's approaches to gender compare with the literature on women in businesses and organizations? What impact do those views have on women who try to lead in evangelical organizations? How do evangelical women fare when attempting to carry out leadership jobs?

The conceptual framework I am using in this study draws from critical feminism, leadership theory, and evangelical theology and practice. Critical feminism provides a lens through which prevailing leadership theory and evangelical theology's gender essentialism can be questioned and potentially refuted.

CRITICAL FEMINISM

I will begin with a broad view of feminist scholarship. In particular, there are three aspects of critical feminist thought that are especially pertinent to my study on women leaders in evangelical mission organizations. First is feminism's assertion that gender is constructed, rather than biologically pre-determined or "hardwired."[1] Much of evangelical religion holds tightly to essentialist views of gender, so understanding how critical feminism evaluates gender determinism can shed light on the world women leaders in evangelical institutions navigate. Second is feminism's conviction that the purpose served by gender construction is power: maintaining power in the hands of males, and thereby strengthening a patriarchal society. Evangelical women leaders in mission organizations are few in number, and encounter challenges to their leadership. Feminism's explanation of power dynamics illuminates some of the struggles that these women face. The third strand of thought comes from the overlap of critical feminism and critical HRD studies, which argues that organizational structures reproduce the power structures of family and society, gendered structures where men are the actors and women the supporting cast. Women leaders in evangelical mission organizations may find themselves paired with their husband or another male in their leadership role, expected to behave in a supportive role even though given a leadership title. This also helps explain why evangelical organizations mostly keep women in supportive or low-level leadership roles with minimal authority. Just as women are expected to be the supportive actors in the home, so they are expected to be the supportive, but not primary, actors in the organization. I will look at each of these three strands of thought in the following sections.

1. Lippert-Rasmussen, "Gender Constructions," 73.

Scholars recognize the eighteenth-century writer and thinker Mary Wollstonecraft as one of the earliest influential feminist authors.[2] Writing in the late 1700s, she argued for an education of girls and women that would be comparable to that which boys and men received.[3] To her, the development of reason was a critical factor in being fully autonomous adult human beings, and this critical skill was best developed through education.[4] What she "most wanted for women is personhood."[5] Although feminism has covered a great deal of ground since Wollstonecraft first wrote in the 1700s, its core as the desire for women to be treated as fully human and fully persons has remained unchanged. As Sayers put it in her 1938 address, "a woman is just as much an ordinary human being as a man."[6]

Almost a century passed before feminism arrived at what scholars refer to as "first-wave feminism."[7] Starting in the 1830s more thinkers began to speak out on the need for women to have the vote and the need for an end to slavery. The list contains many familiar names from the pages of history: John Stuart Mill, Harriet Taylor Mill, Lucretia Mott, Elizabeth Cady Stanton, Angelina and Sarah Grimké, and Lucy Stone, among others.[8] Although many reformers had started out campaigning for women's rights and the abolition of slavery simultaneously, it had become apparent that the two causes would have to be addressed separately, mainly because the abolitionists were not prepared to accept women orators at their conventions.[9] So in 1848 a group of men and women met in Seneca Falls, NY, at what became known as the Seneca Falls Convention, to demand a reform to laws regarding "marriage, divorce, property, and child custody."[10] The Seneca Falls convention was convened as an initial step towards women's rights, though it focused almost exclusively on white, upper-class women and offered little for black women or working-class women, a problem that would continue to plague feminism well into the twentieth century.[11] It was, of course, the Civil War in the United States that ultimately brought about emancipation, and it was the

2. Tong, *Feminist Thought.*

3. Tong, *Feminist Thought.*

4. Tong, *Feminist Thought.*

5. Tong, *Feminist Thought*, 16.

6. Sayers, *Are Women Human?*

7. Evans, *Feminist Theory Today*; Groothuis, *Women Caught in the Conflict.*

8. Groothuis, *Women Caught in the Conflict*; Tong, *Feminist Thought.*

9. Tong, *Feminist Thought.*

10. Tong, *Feminist Thought*, 21.

11. Tong, *Feminist Thought.*

Nineteenth Amendment to the US Constitution passed in 1920 that finally granted women the right to vote.[12]

Another four decades passed before what became known as "second-wave feminism" took root. For a time it had seemed as though, having achieved voting privileges, the stage was set for women's full equality with men. But the early promise did not develop; instead, patriarchal practices continued to prevail. (For the purposes of this study I am defining patriarchy as a system of favoritism that gives preference and privilege to men at the expense of women, rather than the more literal definition of "male rule" or "rule of the father.") Second-wave feminism was sparked in part by the publication in 1963 of Betty Friedan's work, *The Feminine Mystique*.[13] In observing and talking with women around her, Friedan had noticed a certain level of unhappiness even among those who, materially, had everything. That led her to interview and study many women, and eventually to write a book proposing that women suffered from "the problem that has no name."[14] By this she meant the elusive, undefined dissatisfaction that plagued white, middle-class American women in the years from 1945 to 1960, the dissatisfaction that often accompanies women who focus on only one life role.[15] Her conclusion was that the strict construction of the "female role" as centering one's life around caring for a husband, home, and children left women with a deep-seated unease. Friedan explained, "I became aware of a growing body of evidence, much of which has not been reported publicly because it does not fit current modes of thought about women—evidence which throws into question the standards of feminine normality, feminine adjustment, feminine fulfillment, and feminine maturity by which most women are still trying to live."[16] Women, she argued, were taught that their whole purpose was to fulfill this role, and when it left them dissatisfied, they blamed themselves. There was no other framework available to view the issue, and no one questioned the teaching of the "role"—it was simply a given.[17] Although her analysis turned out to be somewhat superficial, ignoring the challenges faced by less prosperous women and saying nothing to men, she did begin to draw public attention by naming an important issue in women's lives.[18] In her suggestions that women simply join the workforce,

12. Tong, *Feminist Thought*.

13. Tong, *Feminist Thought*.

14. Friedan, *Feminine Mystique*, 1.

15. Andersen and Hysock, *Thinking about Women*.

16. Friedan, *Feminine Mystique*, 21.

17. Friedan, *Feminine Mystique*.

18. Reinharz, *Feminist Methods in Social Research*; Tong, *Feminist Thought*.

she reflected a narrow approach to gender issues; it was in her later work, *The Second Stage,* that her thinking took on a more critical stance regarding social structures that harm women.[19]

The 1960s were just the start of the burgeoning push for civil rights, including women's rights. The women's movement and the rapidly expanding field of feminist scholarship quickly began to shed light on history as well as current society. Social institutions, including schools, churches, businesses and other organizations, were shown to be fundamentally androcentric: they were constructed to meet men's needs using men as the standard.[20] Physical sciences like biological and medical sciences had treated men's bodies as the standard for all of humanity.[21] And social sciences, from psychology and developmental theory to sociology, followed the same presuppositions.[22] Men were considered the standard and women, if they were different, were considered deficient.[23] Furthermore, social institutions were also constructed according to these suppositions. Work, family, home, religion, sports—all were constructed to benefit men, frequently at women's expense. And so feminism began tackling these presuppositions, one after another, arguing that different does not equal inferior and contesting the meaning of "different."[24] They insisted that medical research should include women before decisions were made about whether treatments would benefit women.[25] And they argued that women's voices and experiences should be included in designs for everything from education to developmental theory.[26] In short, they fought to move women from being solely in the position of "object" in research to the position of being subject and participant.[27]

Throughout the rest of the twentieth century and into the twenty-first century, the best formula for women and women's advancement continues to be debated. Different strands of feminism have proposed different approaches for women to achieve the full personhood desired since Wollstonecraft and

---

19. Tong, *Feminist Thought.*

20. Evans, *Feminist Theory Today;* Tong, *Feminist Thought.*

21. Hubbard, *Women: The Misunderstood Majority.*

22. Hubbard, *Women: The Misunderstood Majority.*

23. Lippert-Rasmussen, "Gender Constructions."

24. Evans, *Feminist Theory Today.*

25. Hubbard, *Women: The Misunderstood Majority.*

26. Hubbard, *Women: The Misunderstood Majority.*

27. Hesse-Biber and Yaiser, *Feminist Perspectives on Social Research;* Nielsen, *Feminist Research Methods;* Stanley, *Feminist Praxis.*

the earliest feminist thinkers. Is it legal rights?[28] Economic parity?[29] Domestic and family equality?[30] Separation from men entirely?[31] Is it to be treated the same as men?[32] To have differences recognized and celebrated?[33] These and many other ideas have been proposed as ways to affirm women's full humanity and equality with men; answers are still somewhat elusive.

One critical theoretical question lies at the heart of much of the writing, thinking, and practice of feminism, in its many strands. The question is whether it is more helpful to view women as fundamentally the same as men, and suffering inequality due to upbringing and social pressures, or as fundamentally different from men, and therefore suffering from inequality because of that difference.[34] Different strands of feminist thought tend to embrace one view or the other and propose solutions based upon their view of the problem.[35] For example, some strands of feminist thought place a greater degree of emphasis on what they think are women's innate characteristics (such as kindness and nurturance), while other strands reject any idea of innate differences between men and women, attributing apparent differences to socialization.[36] What almost all strands seem to agree on, though, is that an absolute essentialist view of gender is untenable.[37] Yet gender essentialism is one of the most popular and pervasive attitudes in society, functioning particularly strongly in the realms of business leadership and evangelical religion, as we shall see shortly. First I will outline what essentialist thinking entails, and then return to examine how feminism answers gender essentialism.

GENDER ESSENTIALISM

The idea of essentialism can be described as the belief that a thing possesses a "defining essence" which makes that thing be what it is.[38] The concept

28. Evans, *Feminist Theory Today*; Tong, *Feminist Thought*.

29. Evans, *Feminist Theory Today*; Tong, *Feminist Thought*.

30. Evans, *Feminist Theory Today*; Tong, *Feminist Thought*.

31. Evans, *Feminist Theory Today*.

32. Evans, *Feminist Theory Today*; Tong, *Feminist Thought*.

33. Evans, *Feminist Theory Today*; Tong, *Feminist Thought*.

34. Evans, *Feminist Theory Today*.

35. Evans, *Feminist Theory Today*.

36. Evans, *Feminist Theory Today*; Zinn et al., "Sex and Gender through the Prism of Difference."

37. Evans, *Feminist Theory Today*; Zinn et al., "Sex and Gender through the Prism of Difference."

38. Scholz, "Psychologischer Essentialismus als relevantes Konzept für die

is used in multiple disciplines.[39] For example, linguistic essentialism holds that a concept has a defining essence, so that "'tiger', 'gold' and 'water' are properly understood to have essences, in the sense of necessary micro-structures that give rise to their outward properties and that make them the sorts of things they are."[40] Biological essentialism similarly argues that "each species has an eternal, changeless nature shared by all species of its kind."[41] In the social sciences, race, gender, ethnicity, and sexual orientation are sometimes thought of as essentialist qualities. In particular, theories about these categories are considered essentialist "when they claim that these social distinctions have deeply rooted biological underpinnings, that they are historically invariant and culturally universal, or that their boundaries are sharp and not susceptible to sociocultural shaping."[42] So essentialism is the belief in an underlying, unchangeable essence that defines a person, category, or thing.

Haslam, Rothschild, and Ernst name nine factors that typically describe an essentialist category:

1. It is immutable, that is, not easily changed.

2. It has been stable over a long period of time.

3. It is discrete, meaning there are clear boundaries between categories.

4. It is necessary, in that it defines membership in the category.

5. It is uniform, since all members of the category are similar.

6. It is inherent, being an underlying reality rather than a superficial similarity.

7. It is informative, since knowing the category means knowing a great deal about the members of the category.

8. It is characterized by naturalness, since the category appears to be natural rather than artificial or constructed.

9. It is characterized by exclusivity, meaning that membership in one category excludes participation in a complementary category.[43]

Genderforschung."

39. Haslam et al., "Essentialist Beliefs about Social Categories."

40. Haslam et al., "Essentialist Beliefs about Social Categories," 114.

41. Haslam et al., "Essentialist Beliefs about Social Categories," 114.

42. Haslam et al., "Essentialist Beliefs about Social Categories," 114.

43. Haslam et al., "Are Essentialist Beliefs Associated with Prejudice?"; Haslam et al., "Essentialist Beliefs about Social Categories"; Scholz, "Psychologischer Essentialismus als relevantes Konzept für die Genderforschung," 3.

An important factor in understanding these criteria is that each one represents a continuum, rather than an absolute yes-or-no thinking pattern.[44]

In their 2000 study on people's beliefs about social categories as essentialist, Haslam, et al. investigated twenty categories using the nine factors described above. They found that essentialist thinking fell into two categories. The first they called "natural" essentialism, because it encompassed the factors of naturalness, necessity, immutability, discreteness, and stability over time.[45] The second they called "entitativity / reification," meaning belief in a coherent entity. Reification included informativeness, inherence, exclusivity, and uniformity.[46] The distinction is important because they also found that gender, race, and ethnicity belong to the "natural essentialism" viewpoint.[47] Thus to change essentialist thinking about gender or race requires challenging the idea that these categories are natural, unchangeable, and permanent.[48] Challenging reified essentialism requires a different strategy altogether, since it stems from different beliefs. Based on their findings, Scholz argued that "gender categories are seen to be among the strongest essentialist categories in our society."[49]

What Makes Gender Essentialist Categories Intractable?

To many people gender does appear to be entirely natural and based on biological sex; the connection seems completely self-evident and may never be questioned. "Gender essentialists argue that the differences between the sexes are of an intrinsic nature, closely associated with physical, physiological, and/or spiritual differences."[50] Put another way, gender essentialism believes that "gender differences are wholly and directly determined by genetic differences (e.g. the different sex chromosomes) between men and women."[51] Arguing that gender is rooted in biological sex makes gender seem immutable, natural, discrete, necessary, and permanent, and ignores any evidence

44. Haslam et al., "Essentialist Beliefs about Social Categories"; Scholz, "Psychologischer Essentialismus als relevantes Konzept für die Genderforschung."

45. Haslam et al., "Essentialist Beliefs about Social Categories."

46. Haslam et al., "Essentialist Beliefs about Social Categories."

47. Haslam et al., "Essentialist Beliefs about Social Categories."

48. Haslam et al., "Essentialist Beliefs about Social Categories."

49. Scholz, "Psychologischer Essentialismus als relevantes Konzept für die Genderforschung," 8. My translation.

50. Crompton and Lyonette, "New Gender Essentialism," 601.

51. Lippert-Rasmussen, "Gender Constructions," 74.

to the contrary.[52] Further, it can lead to the portrayal of males and females as fundamentally opposite to each other.[53]

What Purpose Does Gender Essentialism Serve?

On a superficial level, the ability to quickly and easily categorize things or people simply makes life easier. It can, for example, dictate who takes care of children and housework and who seeks paid employment in a family.[54] Some think that following gender essentialist prescriptions can lead to increased personal and marital happiness.[55] Still others may find that essentialism offers a sense of order and stability to their lives.[56]

A rather dubious virtue of gender (and racial and ethnic) essentialism is its exculpatory power. If gender is tied to biology then societal inequalities between men and women can be attributed to biology rather than social structures. Inequality between men and women is visible in almost every aspect of society, which I will discuss more a bit later. Essentialists may argue that these inequities are simply the product of biology. Using this reasoning, "theorists make inequalities between the sexes seem natural and inevitable rather than historically constructed and modifiable."[57] Gender essentialism allows social inequalities between men and women to be rationalized as stemming from biological differences, making those inequalities easier to justify and more difficult to challenge.[58]

In this view since inequality is natural and no one is responsible, then no one need do anything to change the situation. Inequalities are inevitable, so there is no reason to try to change them; it would be pointless.[59] In fact the differences are actually seen as legitimate, since "gender conservatism re-affirms the 'naturalness' of gender differences, thus the inequalities which arise as a consequence of these differences are themselves legitimized."[60] And lest anyone argue that in our strongly individualistic societies, it is a breach of rights to assign an entire group of people (women) to a lower-status,

52. Lippert-Rasmussen, "Gender Constructions."

53. Zinn et al., "Sex and Gender through the Prism of Difference."

54. Gaunt, "Biological Essentialism, Gender Ideologies, and Role Attitudes."

55. Crompton and Lyonette, "New Gender Essentialism."

56. Crompton and Lyonette, "New Gender Essentialism."

57. Gaunt, "Biological Essentialism, Gender Ideologies, and Role Attitudes," 524.

58. Bem, "Gender Schema Theory"; Gaunt, "Biological Essentialism, Gender Ideologies, and Role Attitudes."

59. Lippert-Rasmussen, "Gender Constructions"; Scholz, "Psychologischer Essentialismus als relevantes Konzept für die Genderforschung."

60. Crompton and Lyonette, "New Gender Essentialism," 616.

supportive role based on biology, essentialists could argue that woman's role actually reflects the choices she makes *based on* her biology rather than on social structures which constrain her choices. The contradiction between freedom of choice and constrained choice "is resolved if it is asserted that the differences between men and women are 'natural' and that the choices made by women are in accordance with this 'nature' and therefore not constrained by dominant (male) norms and/or inequalities of condition."[61]

In the end, essentialist beliefs can even lead to blaming the women themselves, rather than patriarchal social systems, for women's difficulties.[62] Women's problems become their own inability to fit into the existing social structure, which is characterized as neutral.[63] This leads to the belief that it is up to the women themselves to change; there is no need to challenge the social structures.[64] The problem may be particularly acute for women in ministry. Zikmund, Lummis, and Chang, for example, found that less than one-quarter of female seminary students received any preparation for issues women face in ministry, leading many to "identify their problems as personal failures rather than the limitations of the social or institutional systems in which they are located."[65]

Gender essentialism therefore is appealing because it seems intuitively correct, offers apparent security and stability, is easy, and justifies any existing social inequalities as merely an unavoidable by-product of biology. Feminist scholars, of course, clearly dispute this reading. They assert that "biological difference is exploited by patriarchal society to justify fitness for gender roles, which almost exclusively place women subordinate to men."[66] According to feminist scholars, biology is used as an excuse to create social inequality. But what about today's developments in neuroscience? Do they support the biological argument?

61. Crompton and Lyonette, "New Gender Essentialism," 603.

62. Scholz, "Psychologischer Essentialismus als relevantes Konzept für die Genderforschung."

63. Acker, "Hierarchies, Jobs, Bodies"; Ely et al., *Reader in Gender, Work, and Organization*; Sheppard, "Women Managers' Perceptions of Gender and Organizational Life."

64. Scholz, "Psychologischer Essentialismus als relevantes Konzept für die Genderforschung."

65. Zikmund et al., *Clergy Women: An Uphill Calling*, 131.

66. Fox, "Prototype Theory," 331.

What Does Neuroscience Research Show?

Current scientific research into the brain and its functioning sometimes includes questions about possible differences between male and female brains. A thorough investigation of the subject is far beyond the scope of this chapter, so I will simply mention a few main points for consideration. First, ideas that male and female differences are brain-based have been around for centuries.[67] For example, ideas that women's relatively smaller brain size accounted for their supposedly lower intelligence compared to men were popular in the 1800s.[68] Right- and left-brain theories that attributed different functions to different brain hemispheres, and genders, have also been popular for years, yet they have been so thoroughly disputed that Tokuhama-Espinosa classifies them as "neuromyth."[69] Second, these ideas have a wide popular appeal, as books like Brizendine's *The Female Brain* show.[70] Essentialist views can be appealing, and the wide popularity of these types of books and articles reflects that appeal. Third, although there do appear to be some observable differences between male and female brains "neuroscience has shown that boys' and girls' brains are more than 99 percent alike."[71] Finally, no one is really sure what those differences mean.[72] Diamond argues that "wresting meaning from the multiplicity of similarities and differences between male and female brains presents a considerable challenge in the decades ahead."[73] And Fine cautions that neuroscience is still in its infancy, requiring a great deal more research to determine what brain differences might mean for gender differences. She adds that socialization patterns more than adequately account for observed differences between men and women.[74]

To date, the lack of consistent, verifiable findings about differences between male and female brains, coupled with the strongly supported arguments for the social construction of gender, means that neither neuroscience nor other forms of biological essentialist arguments adequately explain the social differences between men and women. As neuroscience research develops, of course, this could change, but to date there is not

67. Fine, *Delusions of Gender*.

68. Fine, *Delusions of Gender*.

69. Tokuhama-Espinosa, "What Neuroscience Says about Personalized Learning."

70. Brizendine, *Female Brain*.

71. Tokuhama-Espinosa, "What Neuroscience Says about Personalized Learning," n.p.; Diamond, "Male and Female Brains"; Fine, *Delusions of Gender*.

72. Fine, *Delusions of Gender*.

73. Diamond, "Male and Female Brains," para. 19.

74. Fine, *Delusions of Gender*.

enough evidence to argue that gender differences are purely biological, nor is there a proven link between difference—if it exists—and inequitable treatment. In the next section I will talk about feminism's critique of gender essentialism and its argument that gender in reality is socially constructed rather than biologically innate.

GENDER AS A CONSTRUCTED CATEGORY

In order to deconstruct the notion of gender essentialism, we need first to understand that what is presented as originating in some essential female or male nature, tied to biological sex, is generally now accepted as a socially constructed category.[75] Not just gender, but all aspects of a person's identity, including race and class, are constructed by social norms and the context in which one operates.[76] Biological differences between males and females do not account for the differences between what is considered masculine and feminine in society, despite assertions that biology is the only basis for those difference.[77] A much better explanation is that gender identity construction is deeply embedded in our culture; almost everything we can imagine is tied to either male or female identity. Clothes, food, books, and movies are designed and marketed for men or women and education helps train boys and girls to fulfill gender roles.[78] The media too is part of portraying, and teaching, women and men how to be and behave in accordance with gendered identities.[79] Women are socialized to be nurturing, caring, and supportive, while men are socialized to lead.[80] Virtually every aspect of what it means to be "male" and "female" is learned and reinforced repeatedly throughout our culture.

There are also consequences for those who do not fit gendered expectations.[81] There are unkind names for both men and women who fail to conform, and there are social pressures to push people back into the expected

75. Andersen and Hysock, *Thinking about Women*; Hartmann, "Family as Locus of Gender, Class, and Political Struggle"; Maher, "Twisted Privileges"; Misawa, "Queer Race Pedagogy for Educators in Higher Education"; Riehl and Lee, "Gender, Organization, and Leadership"; Stead and Elliott, *Women's Leadership*.

76. Misawa, "Queer Race Pedagogy for Educators in Higher Education."

77. Andersen and Hysock, *Thinking about Women*.

78. Andersen and Hysock, *Thinking about Women*; Sadker and Sadker, *Failing at Fairness*.

79. Andersen and Hysock, *Thinking about Women*; Kilbourne, "Still Killing Us Softly."

80. Tisdell, "Feminism and Adult Learning."

81. Andersen and Hysock, *Thinking about Women*.

molds both in schools and in work settings.[82] These pressures also demonstrate that gender identity is constantly being constructed and reinforced throughout our daily lives.[83] Once these socializations take root and become widely prevalent in a society, they come to seem so "natural" that we forget that they are learned behaviors, and begin to think of them as innate. From here "this form of social construction is . . . described as stereotyping, an oversimplified belief that a certain trait, behavior, or attitude characterizes all members of some identifiable group."[84] Thus the constructed identity is embedded and reified as "natural."[85]

Once a category is thought to be "natural" it becomes quite difficult to challenge. Arguing that what is perceived as "natural" is in reality constructed and learned behavior becomes central to breaking down the myth. For many years "feminists have argued that although there are indeed biological sex differences between men and women, much if not most of the 'difference' between men and women, as expressed in gender hierarchies and patterns of inequality, is in fact socially constructed."[86] Arguing along these lines is precisely the approach recommended by Haslam, et al. to combat a "natural" essentialist view:

> Attempts to modify understandings of social categories as natural kinds must challenge beliefs about their naturalness, immutability, historical stability, discreteness and necessary features. It is precisely these beliefs that social constructionists try to rebut, arguing that social categories are artifactual and arbitrary, rather than natural; historically variant and changeable, rather than stable and immutable; fuzzy, indeterminate or continuous, rather than discrete; and lacking any defining or necessary properties.[87]

Indeed these are the approaches feminist scholars take to challenge the idea of gender as a "natural" or essential category. One way to do this is to examine what purpose gender categories serve in society, and another is to consider who benefits and who suffers under those categories. Feminists

---

82. Eagly and Karau, "Role Congruity Theory of Prejudice toward Female Leaders"; Forsyth et al., "Biases in Appraisals of Women Leaders"; Sadker and Sadker, *Failing at Fairness*.

83. Andersen and Hysock, *Thinking about Women*.

84. Misawa, "Queer Race Pedagogy for Educators in Higher Education," 26.

85. Sheppard, "Women Managers' Perceptions of Gender and Organizational Life."

86. Crompton and Lyonette, "New Gender Essentialism," 601.

87. Haslam et al., "Essentialist Beliefs about Social Categories," 125.

point out that one of the main purposes of gender in our society is power, and that the prime beneficiaries are men.

Gender Construction as Power and Privilege Construction

From the critical feminist perspective, the construction of raced, classed, and gendered identities serves a very specific purpose in our society, a purpose which is tied primarily to power.[88] A close observation of socially constructed gender roles leads almost inevitably to the conclusion that it is usually males who benefit from that construction. In fact it can be argued that roles are deliberately constructed to concentrate power and privilege in the hands of one group—males—at the expense of the other group—females.[89] Gender is tied to power because "gender is rooted in social institutions and results in patterns within society that structure the relationships between women and men and that give them differing positions of advantage and disadvantage within institutions."[90] That difference in advantage or disadvantage describes power—who is privileged and who is burdened by social structures.[91] One example is family and marriage structures in which women still perform proportionately more housework and childcare than men, regardless of employment outside the home.[92] Another is the persistent wage gap between men and women that endures in much of the world, even when all other factors have been taken into consideration.[93]

The root of the power differential between men and women can be found in a tenacious underlying belief that women are somehow inferior to men. In her work on feminism, Tong ties the social and legal structures which limit women and favor men directly to essentialist beliefs about women's inferiority. She explains that at the start of second wave feminism Liberal feminism argued:

> Female subordination is rooted in a set of customary and le-
> gal constraints that blocks women's entrance to and success in
> the so-called public world. To the extent that society holds the
> false belief that women are, by nature, less intellectually and

88. Andersen and Collins, *Race, Class & Gender*; Sheppard, "Women Managers' Perceptions of Gender and Organizational Life"; Maher, "Twisted Privileges."

89. Zinn et al., "Sex and Gender through the Prism of Difference."

90. Andersen and Collins, *Race, Class & Gender*, 80.

91. Andersen and Hysock, *Thinking about Women*.

92. Andersen and Hysock, *Thinking about Women*; Hartmann, "Family as Locus of Gender, Class, and Political Struggle."

93. Andersen and Hysock, *Thinking about Women*; Eagly and Carli, "Women and the Labyrinth of Leadership."

physically capable than men, it tends to discriminate against women in the academy, the forum, and the marketplace.[94]

Men's supposed physical and intellectual superiority, it was thought, gave them the right and the obligation to control women for the good of society; women were best suited for heteronomy, meaning they needed to be ruled or controlled by someone else.

If essentialist beliefs are correct and women are most suited for marriage and motherhood, then the 1950s in America should have been one of the happiest times in prosperous white women's lives, as they left the workforce to make room for men returning from war and embraced the revival of domesticity. Yet we have already seen that Friedan discovered this recipe for female satisfaction to be a myth. Prescribing a domestic role for women did a great deal to concentrate financial power in men's hand and provide them with comfort at home, but as a recipe for female happiness it was a disaster.[95] Women sought help from professional counselors, only to find that "psychotherapists found 'rejection of femininity' in every frustrated or unhappy patient."[96] Counselors prescribed further adherence to the role, and women became increasingly depressed. "Virtually nonexistent in 1955, tranquilizer consumption reached 462,000 pounds in 1958 and soared to 1.15 million pounds merely a year later."[97] Women turned to antidepressants, stimulants, and alcohol, along with counseling, at such a rate that physicians "began to identify a new female malady—'housewife's syndrome,'" which was so severe some argued it was the number one public health problem of the day.[98] There is no doubt that the role, while it may have benefited some men, came at great cost to many women.

Gender and Knowledge Construction

From the 1970s onward the floodgates opened as feminist scholars began writing about every conceivable field.[99] Natural sciences, social sciences, history, philosophy, theology—every discipline was reexamined through a feminist lens to find out if what was known was also true for women.[100] What quickly became apparent was that what counted as knowledge had

94. Tong, *Feminist Thought*, 2.

95. Friedan, *Feminine Mystique*.

96. Ehrenreich and English, *For Her Own Good*, 300.

97. Coontz, *Way We Never Were*, 36.

98. Coontz, *Way We Never Were*; Ehrenreich and English, *For Her Own Good*.

99. Hesse-Biber and Yaiser, *Feminist Perspectives on Social Research*.

100. Nielsen, *Feminist Research Methods*.

been socially constructed by those in positions of power and privilege, typically white males, every bit as much as notions of gender are constructed.[101] Marxist theory had applied this idea to understand class oppression; feminists took another step by

> add[ing] to Marx's perspective on the social construction of ideas, arguing that in general men own the means of production . . . and therefore determine the ruling ideas of any given time. Sexist ideas justify the power of men over women and sanction male domination.[102]

In earlier centuries men forcibly controlled knowledge construction by prohibiting women from studying in universities, schools of medicine, law, theology, and more.[103] Later the barriers became more subtle, simply using men and males as the norm and rendering women's experiences invisible and silent; "dominant forms of knowledge have been constructed largely from the experiences of the most powerful—that is, those who have the most access to systems of education and communication."[104] If men hold power, then men can use that power to determine what is learned and what counts as knowledge, thus enhancing their ability to maintain power, and the cycle continues.[105]

A significant effect on women's lives of the concentration of knowledge and power in the hands of men is that women's work and women's voices become largely invisible.[106] Unpaid housework and child rearing, for example, are rarely considered to be real work and simultaneously, since they are unpaid, support the notion that women's work is less valuable than men's work.[107] Furthermore, since this work takes place privately it is socially invisible. Yet women's work, paid and unpaid, has always been central to survival and to economic production.[108] Essentialism colludes in making women's work invisible since women are seen primarily as supportive of men's work,

---

101. Andersen and Hysock, *Thinking about Women*; Maher, "Toward a Richer Theory of Feminist Pedagogy"; Maher, "Twisted Privileges."

102. Andersen and Hysock, *Thinking about Women*, 73–74.

103. Sadker and Sadker, *Failing at Fairness*.

104. Andersen and Collins, *Race, Class & Gender*, 3; Sheppard, "Women Managers' Perceptions of Gender and Organizational Life."

105. Peters, "Elements of Successful Mentoring of a Female School Leader"; Tisdell, *Creating Inclusive Adult Learning Environments*; Tisdell, "Interlocking Systems of Power, Privilege, and Oppression."

106. Zinn et al., "Sex and Gender through the Prism of Difference."

107. Andersen and Hysock, *Thinking about Women*.

108. Andersen and Hysock, *Thinking about Women*.

rather than contributing in their own right.[109] Revealing and naming these unequal power distributions and social structures that privilege males are central to feminism's mission.[110] In this way, critical feminism attempts to make visible those aspects of women's lives that have been ignored, giving voice and visibility to what was previously hidden.

GENDER, CRITICAL ORGANIZATION STUDIES, AND HRD

A somewhat more recent strand of feminist thought is that represented by critical organization studies and critical Human Resource Development (HRD). The starting point of these studies is the idea that organizations, built as they are in patriarchal societies, represent and promote patriarchal values.[111] Hanscome and Cervero comment that "organizational cultures are little more than mirrors of systems of society [where] men are more highly valued than women."[112] They add that "organizational culture, symbols, work roles and interactions tend to reflect the norms of a wider society in which men are considered the standard."[113] Not only are the organizations themselves patriarchal in their practices, the study and theory about them is too, since "organizational theorising is not neutral but male-gendered."[114]

According to feminist thinking, organizations are more than simply reflections of patriarchal society; they actively participate in creating and reproducing gender in conformity with essentialist notions based on patriarchy.[115] One definition of patriarchy offered by critical feminism is precisely that it is a sex-based structure of power giving preference to males.[116] This describes what critical scholars of organizations draw attention to and challenge. Acker argued that "organizations are one arena in which widely disseminated cultural images of gender are invented and reproduced. . . . some aspects of individual gender identity, perhaps particularly masculinity, are also products of organizational processes and pressures."[117] The images

109. Frame and Shehan, "Relationship between Work and Well-Being in Clergywomen"; Pavalko and Elder, "Women behind the Men."

110. Tisdell, "Poststructural Feminist Pedagogies."

111. Bierema, "Critiquing Human Resource Development's Dominant Masculine Rationality"; Riehl and Lee, "Gender, Organization, and Leadership"; Stead and Elliott, *Women's Leadership*.

112. Hanscome and Cervero, "Impact of Gendered Power Relations in HRD."

113. Hanscome and Cervero, "Impact of Gendered Power Relations in HRD," 509.

114. Brown, "Meetings and Intersections," 197.

115. Acker, "Hierarchies, Jobs, Bodies."

116. Andersen and Hysock, *Thinking about Women*.

117. Acker, "Hierarchies, Jobs, Bodies," 140.

are, of course, those that conform to stereotyped ideas of masculinity and femininity. Women in the workplace then are also subject to the same gender essentialist demands that they encounter in society.[118] Their behavior is expected to conform to the same standards it would in the home, "because it is the 'female' constructed under patriarchy who is given voice and presence, extending the patriarchal family's female role from the private to the public domain."[119] Quoting from a 1930s issue of Fortune which lauded the entry of women into the workplace, Calás and Smircich explain:

> In the field of the office it was not the *work* of the home which was carried over into the industrial setting, but the *setting* of the home which was carried over to the industrial work. The work was new work but it was done by women not because it was new but because they were women. And more importantly, it was the employing male, not the eager female applicant, who was responsible for the result.[120]

Not only do organizations actively reproduce the same power structures of the family and society, they also continue to subsume much of women's work under men's, crediting it to the men even when carried out by the women.

On the other hand, organizations often claim to be neutral territory when it comes to gender issues. By assuming males are the standard, gender issues remain invisible.[121] Acker explains that "since men in organizations take their behavior and perspectives to represent the human, organizational structures and processes are theorized as gender neutral."[122] Recent feminist scholarship has chosen to challenge the supposed neutrality of organizations.[123] Examining the use of language is one approach, since "assumptions of the discourse equated traditional masculine traits (rationality, hierarchy, aggressiveness, objectivity) with value-free and objective knowledge. When 'objective' and 'value-free' knowledge is associated with masculine traits, the discourse is considered a 'gendered' discourse, and knowledge is 'gendered.'"[124] Language that obscures women's experience while promoting men's as the standard also serves to reproduce essentialist

118. Marshall, *Women Managers*.

119. Calás and Smircich, "Dangerous Liaisons," 74.

120. Calás and Smircich, "Dangerous Liaisons," 73.

121. Sheppard, "Women Managers' Perceptions of Gender and Organizational Life."

122. Acker, "Hierarchies, Jobs, Bodies," 142.

123. Ely et al., *Reader in Gender, Work, and Organization*; Sheppard, "Women Managers' Perceptions of Gender and Organizational Life."

124. Storberg-Walker and Bierema, "Historical Analysis of HRD Knowledge," 437.

power structures.[125] Leadership studies are another area where masculine bias is evident. I will discuss leadership at length in the next chapter; for now I will mention that much leadership research has been done using men as the standard.[126]

Given that human resource development is a field that is supposed to represent the value of the workers to the organization, some scholars propose that HRD as a discipline needs an overhaul.[127] Yet this is challenging, since "discrimination in organizations is so deeply embedded culturally that it is practically indiscernible."[128] However, if HRD took seriously its responsibility to represent workers then justice issues such as sexism and racism would need to be addressed.[129]

CHAPTER SUMMARY

From its earliest days, feminism has worked to counter patriarchal systems of favoritism towards males by seeking to elevate women's perspectives, voices, and needs. Feminism is not one systematic way of viewing the world or of diagnosing and proposing solutions to women's, men's, and society's problems; in fact there is quite a lot of discussion and debate about various ways to approach the challenges.[130] Still, the core understanding that women (and others) as a class suffer oppression, and the core desire to end that oppression, thereby transforming women (and others) into fully human, fully participating persons in the fabric of society remains steady.[131] One important way to move towards change has been for feminism to challenge the notion that gender is an innate, unchangeable set of characteristics determined by biological sex and to show instead how gender is a socially constructed category that teaches women to engage in one set of behaviors and men another. Feminism has further demonstrated that these gender categories have served, and continue to serve, to favor men by conferring more power on the social role of "male" than of "female." Through controlling knowledge and social institutions, power is firmly established in male hands, leading to a society that is completely constructed around males as the center and standard, with females given a peripheral and supporting

125. Marshall, *Women Managers.*

126. Brown, "Meetings and Intersections."

127. Bierema, "Critiquing Human Resource Development's Dominant Masculine Rationality"; Callahan, "Gazing into the Crystal Ball."

128. Bierema, "Feminist Approach to HRD Research," 245.

129. Bierema, "Feminist Approach to HRD Research."

130. Evans, *Feminist Theory Today*; Tong, *Feminist Thought.*

131. Tong, *Feminist Thought.*

role only. Feminism seeks to move women to center stage, breaking down and reconstructing ideas as well as structures that oppress women. We have seen that critical HRD studies reveal how organizations are modeled on and simultaneously reproduce patriarchal power structures. In the next chapter I will examine one aspect of organizational life—that of leadership—in greater detail.

3

Review of the Literature: Leadership and Gender

THE FOCUS FOR THIS chapter of the literature review is organizational leadership and women's presence or absence from it. I will begin with a discussion of the history and theories of organizational leadership, and then move to consider women's leadership.

LEADERSHIP THEORY

The study of leadership is a relatively new field, having been with us now for only about a century. The earliest studies concentrated on an individual, typically a white male, who held a prominent leadership position.[1] Known as "great man" theories, they sought to understand the qualities or characteristics of the man that made him into a great leader.[2] As the field of leadership studies grew, more hypotheses were proposed about what made a great leader. Other suggestions included skills, context, relationships with subordinates, and personal styles, among others, all of which seemed to focus primarily on the person and behavior of the leader.[3] The first serious study of women as leaders began in the 1970s, long after the study of leadership was well-established. Not surprisingly, many studies of women have taken a comparison approach, seeking to understand how women's

1. Avolio et al., "Leadership: Current Theories, Research, and Future Directions."
2. Northouse, *Leadership Theory and Practice.*
3. Northouse, *Leadership Theory and Practice.*

leadership differs from men's and what steps can be taken to help women approach male-theorized leadership standards.[4]

Early Studies of Leadership

The earliest studies of leadership used what Stead and Elliott refer to as "leader-centric" theories, meaning that the focus is on the person who occupies a leadership position.[5] Trait, skill, and style approaches to understanding leadership can all be classified as leader-centric, focusing as they do primarily on the person of the leader.[6] The trait theory of leadership was first proposed in the early twentieth century and was based on the assumption that leaders possess some kind of innate quality which enables them to lead; that is, leaders are born, not made.[7] Numerous investigations have led to no clear consensus regarding a specific set of traits, although some common ones seem to reoccur.[8] Many studies suggest that intelligence, self-confidence, determination, integrity, and sociability are key traits for leaders; interestingly, masculinity also shows up as a key trait in various studies.[9] Leader personality traits seem to revolve around extraversion, conscientiousness, and agreeableness, although again there is no definitive consensus.[10]

Similarly, approximately fifty years of studies on leaders' skills have failed to develop a clear consensus on what skills a leader needs to possess.[11] General categories of skill such as technical skills, social skills, and knowledge can be recognized, but they are both general descriptions and not limited to leadership functions.[12] What the skill approach does offer that the trait approach does not is that skills can presumably be learned; leaders are made, not born. This would potentially make leadership more available to women if they learned the correct skills and behaviors.

---

4. Blackmore, "Social Justice and the Study and Practice of Leadership in Education"; Shakeshaft, *Women in Educational Administration*; Stead and Elliott, *Women's Leadership*.

5. Stead and Elliott, *Women's Leadership*.

6. Northouse, *Leadership Theory and Practice*.

7. Ely et al., *Reader in Gender, Work, and Organization*; Northouse, *Leadership Theory and Practice*.

8. Northouse, *Leadership Theory and Practice*.

9. Northouse, *Leadership Theory and Practice*.

10. Northouse, *Leadership Theory and Practice*.

11. Northouse, *Leadership Theory and Practice*.

12. Northouse, *Leadership Theory and Practice*.

Finally, the style approach focuses on the leader's behavior in the contexts of leadership.[13] Since neither the trait nor the skills approach to understanding leadership had been able to offer a definitive explanation of leadership, scholars continued investigating. In the 1950s researchers at Ohio State University began studying leaders' styles—how they interact with their subordinates—and from their research proposed two basic categories: initiating structure, or task-oriented behaviors and consideration, or relationship-oriented ones.[14] Fleishman used their preliminary results to conduct a series of studies among Air Force personnel and his findings agreed with the two categories of structure and consideration.[15] Finally, at about the same time, researchers at the University of Michigan were also establishing the same two types of categories for leadership behavior.[16] From all of these studies, two main styles of leadership behaviors were proposed: task-oriented ones and relationship-oriented ones.[17] The style approach to understanding leadership is particularly significant to an understanding of women's leadership because it is here where the roots of much of the later scholarship regarding the lack of women leaders are found.

Two points are significant here: first, the great degree of overlap in the different studies, and second, the fact that the research was conducted with men. The association of males with task and women with relationship was not part of the original leadership proposition, though it has gained much prominence since the 1970s and can almost be said to have defined studies of women's leadership until very recently, as we will see in the discussion on women's leadership.

Later Studies of Leadership

Throughout the 1960s and 1970s leadership studies continued. The trait, skill, and style approaches to understanding leaders each offered potential and partial explanations, and over the next twenty years more theories were proposed. One idea was called situational leadership, meaning that a leader reads the context and acts in accordance with the needs of the situation.[18]

13. Northouse, *Leadership Theory and Practice*.

14. Northouse, *Leadership Theory and Practice*; Stogdill and Coons, *Ohio Studies in Personnel*; Stogdill and Shartle, *Methods in the Study of Administrative Leadership*.

15. Fleishman, "Description of Supervisory Behavior."

16. Katz et al., *Productivity, Supervision and Morale among Railroad Workers*; Katz et al., *Productivity, Supervision and Morale in an Office Situation*; Northouse, *Leadership Theory and Practice*.

17. Northouse, *Leadership Theory and Practice*.

18. Avolio et al., "Leadership: Current Theories, Research, and Future Directions";

Contingency theory suggested that leadership was based on creating an adequate match between the leader's style and the needs of the context.[19] Path-goal theory argued that the main function of a leader was to motivate followers to accomplish a goal, and leader-member exchange (LMX) theory focused on the interaction between a leader and followers, recognizing that some followers are treated as an "in-group" and thus tend to succeed, whereas others are treated as an "out-group" and do not do as well.[20] While each of these theories added a nuance of understanding to the existing leadership models, none of them seriously challenged the trait, skill, and style approaches to understanding leadership. Then, in 1978, James MacGregor Burns proposed the idea of transformational leadership, suggesting a rather different view of leadership than anyone up to that time.[21]

Transformational Leadership. Burns argued that there were two approaches to leadership: transactional and transformational.[22] Transactional leadership is the most common approach and operates on a system of exchanges between leaders and followers, such as financial rewards or promotions for performance, and punishment for failure.[23] Transformational leaders, however, operate relationally. "Transformational leadership is the process whereby a person engages with others and creates a connection that raises the level of motivation and morality in both the leader and the follower."[24] Transformational leaders focus as much on the followers' good as on their own; transformational leadership occurs when leaders connect with their followers in such a way as to inspire and motivate them, and actually seek the employees' good.[25] Transformational leadership focuses on improvement, values, and the collective good, not just the good of the leader.[26]

Northouse, *Leadership Theory and Practice.*

19. Avolio et al., "Leadership: Current Theories, Research, and Future Directions"; Northouse, *Leadership Theory and Practice.*

20. Avolio et al., "Leadership: Current Theories, Research, and Future Directions"; Northouse, *Leadership Theory and Practice.*

21. Northouse, *Leadership Theory and Practice.*

22. Northouse, *Leadership Theory and Practice.*

23. Eagly and Carli, "Women and the Labyrinth of Leadership"; Northouse, *Leadership Theory and Practice.*

24. Northouse, *Leadership Theory and Practice,* 176.

25. Northouse, *Leadership Theory and Practice*; Vinkenburg et al., "Exploration of Stereotypical Beliefs about Leadership Styles."

26. Northouse, *Leadership Theory and Practice*; Yoder, "Making Leadership Work More Effectively for Women."

Building on Burns' work, in the 1980s Bass developed a four-part scale to measure transformational leadership qualities. The four factors he deemed central to transformational leadership were idealized influence or charisma, inspirational motivation, intellectual stimulation, and individualized consideration.[27] Kouzes and Posner further developed the concept of transformational leadership in their best-selling leadership study *The Leadership Challenge.*[28] Although there are some cautions about the transformational approach to leadership, mainly its potential for abuse in the hands of a charismatic but unprincipled leader, the general concept has been well-studied and appears to be—when used well—a relatively healthy leadership model.[29]

Post-Heroic Leadership: Democratic and Shared. As the twentieth century progressed and North American culture continued to change, additional theories on leadership began to emerge. The emergence of the World Wide Web and the age of the internet meant that information which used to be hard to access was suddenly available to anyone with an internet connection anywhere in the world, with the click of a mouse button. Leaders and officials were no longer the only ones with access to knowledge and information, and society and organizations began to undergo a profound shift towards what has come to be known as flattened organizational structures.[30] Technological proficiency has become an important component of leadership, as has collaboration.[31] Leadership began to lose some of its mystique and leaders were less often seen as the absolute authorities that they had been in the past.[32] Put another way, "'Capital-L' leadership is making way for 'small-l' leadership as hierarchy makes way for collaboration."[33]

Early models of leadership—those based on traits, styles, or skills—focused almost exclusively on the person of the (male) leader: what he was and did. They have become known as "heroic" leadership models with their focus on one central figure who determines the direction and outcome for everyone.[34] Transformational leadership theory is also sometimes consid-

27. Bass et al., "Transformational and Transactional Leadership of Men and Women," 9; Bass and Avolio, "Shatter the Glass Ceiling."

28. Kouzes and Posner, *Leadership Challenge.*

29. Avolio et al., "Leadership: Current Theories, Research, and Future Directions."

30. Anderson, *Organization Development.*

31. Penney, "Voices of the Future."

32. Penney, "Voices of the Future."

33. Penney, "Voices of the Future," 56.

34. Ely et al., *Reader in Gender, Work, and Organization.*

ered a heroic model, since the transformational power depends totally on the will to good or evil of the leader.[35] Others consider it post-heroic since it focuses strongly on followers.[36] Democratic, distributed, and shared leadership practices, with their focus on the interactions between leaders and followers and the way they appear to share responsibility, power, and authority, are considered post-heroic.[37] Replacing the "great man theories" of the early- and mid-twentieth century, theories regarding democratic leadership styles have been gaining ground.[38] Democratic leadership is the idea of leadership by consensus-building rather than by autocratic decision-making.[39] Usually called shared, collective, or distributed leadership, the point is that the function of leading is distributed throughout members of a work unit or team, not located in one individual.[40] Like transformational leadership, women are often thought to be naturally better at shared and democratic leadership styles, and are in fact found to use those styles more often than men do.[41] These styles are contrasted with autocratic or command-and-control leadership which tends to be hierarchical and non-relational, and usually associated with men.[42]

Over the years leadership studies have focused first on the personal characteristics of the leader, then on the style of the leader's behavior, and eventually on the context and interactions of the leader and followers. Over time the focus has shifted from the person of the leader to the behaviors and interactions the leader has with followers. Since the late twentieth century, both transformational leadership theory and democratic leadership theory have drawn a great deal of attention and research, and it is these leadership theories that have been connected with women's styles. Still, as we will see in the section on women's leadership, their supposed ability at these types of leadership has only partially served to increase the numbers of women in organizational leadership.

35. Northouse, *Leadership Theory and Practice.*

36. Stead and Elliott, *Women's Leadership.*

37. Blackmore, "Social Justice and the Study and Practice of Leadership in Education."

38. Avolio et al., "Leadership: Current Theories, Research, and Future Directions"; Penney, "Voices of the Future."

39. Eagly and Johnson, "Gender and Leadership Style."

40. Avolio et al., "Leadership: Current Theories, Research, and Future Directions."

41. Eagly and Johannesen-Schmidt, "Leadership Styles of Women and Men"; Eagly and Johnson, "Gender and Leadership Style."

42. Rosener, "Ways Women Lead"; Weikart et al., "Democratic Sex."

WOMEN IN ORGANIZATIONAL LEADERSHIP

Since the 1960s women's movement, women have moved steadily into the realm of public work, so that today women comprise 60 percent of the workforce, whereas in 1970 they accounted for only 30 percent.[43] However, women's movement into leadership and management positions has not kept pace with their movement into the workforce. According to the United Nations, women continue to be underrepresented in "jobs with status, power and authority" as well as "legislators, senior officials and managers."[44] The report states that the "glass ceiling has hindered women's access to leadership in private companies . . . especially the largest corporations which remain male-dominated."[45] Reports in the popular press also discuss the absence of women at top levels of leadership. Both *Forbes* and the *Huffington Post* published articles discussing the issue and seeking explanations and solutions.[46] *Business Week* ran a gripping slideshow presentation of twenty-nine major U.S. companies with no women at the top.[47]

This discrepancy between women's labor participation and their representation in management has generated research and theorizing as scholars have sought explanations for the gap. Early ideas that there simply were not enough women in the pipeline to be promoted were quickly dispelled as more women entered the labor force.[48] The next idea was that of a "glass ceiling."[49] The glass ceiling is conceived as an invisible barrier that prevents women from rising to the top levels of organizational leadership.[50] Over time additional popular versions of the "glass" idea have been added to the lexicon, including:

- Glass escalator—giving men a smooth ride to the top[51]

- Glass cliff—putting women in precarious or difficult leadership positions with an increased likelihood of failure.[52]

43. "Women in the Labor Force, 1970–2009."

44. *World's Women 2010: Trends and Statistics.*

45. *World's Women 2010: Trends and Statistics.*

46. Rosener, "'Terrible Truth' about Women on Corporate Boards." Keefe and Zehner, "Saying 'No' to All-Male Corporate Boards."

47. "No Women at the Table."

48. Carli and Eagly, "Gender, Hierarchy, and Leadership"; Heilman, "Description and Prescription."

49. Carli and Eagly, "Gender, Hierarchy, and Leadership"; Eagly and Carli, "Women and the Labyrinth of Leadership."

50. Carli and Eagly, "Gender, Hierarchy, and Leadership."

51. Northouse, *Leadership Theory and Practice.*

52. Ryan and Haslam, "Glass Cliff."

- Stained-glass ceiling—the lack of women in religious leadership.[53]

More recently, scholars have suggested that the barriers for women actually resemble a labyrinth more than an absolute barrier.[54] The paths to leadership for women, unlike those for men, are filled with obstacles all along the way, leading to the steady disappearance of women the higher one looks up the corporate ladder.[55] Overall there is widespread agreement that something continues to hinder women's access to leadership roles, and research continues to attempt to understand its causes and find strategies to break it. The purpose of this part of the literature review is to explore the current thinking about the obstacles to women's leadership and the effects on women's career progress. Specifically, I have asked two questions: first, how does the literature describe women's leadership, particularly compared to men's leadership? and second, what reasons are proposed to account for the low numbers of women at top levels of leadership?

The approach I take here is to consider the question from two diametrically opposite perspectives. I start by looking at the recently popularized idea that women make better leaders than men. This idea was suggested in the 1990s as work structures moved towards team focus and lessened hierarchies. However, despite its appeal, it has not really borne the fruit we would expect if it were true, or if society had truly come to believe it. There are more women in positions of leadership now than thirty years ago, but women's supposed advantage has not materialized to the degree that early theorists hoped. Then I will move on to consider the idea that women are simply unsuited for leadership. This belief has been part of social thinking since leadership studies began, and although today it would be politically incorrect to say it in so many words, it still seems to persist in an unspoken yet powerful way. Because of its persistence over time and across industries, it seems to be the more salient way of understanding women's leadership. I will also include discussions of types of leadership and the observed leadership styles of men and women, along with the proposed explanations for apparent differences. Finally, I will delineate and evaluate some of the proposed strategies for women who wish to lead in the twenty-first-century American workplace.

53. Adams, "Stained Glass Makes the Ceiling Visible."
54. Eagly and Carli, "Women and the Labyrinth of Leadership."
55. Eagly and Carli, "Women and the Labyrinth of Leadership."

Theory 1: Women Make Better Leaders Than Men

An idea that has been steadily gaining popularity and attention over the last few decades is the belief that women actually make better leaders than men.[56] Changes in the workforce and the way work is done cause some to think that women are actually now more suited to meet the leadership needs of the twenty-first century. In this line of thought, women are seen to have innate abilities for democratic leadership styles, community building, nurturing of employees, networking, and strong interpersonal skills.[57] Eagly and Carli argue that men's and women's leadership styles differ and that "women's approaches are the more generally effective," and Eagly documents a number of newspaper and magazine articles which support the idea that what the world needs today in a leader is women's people skills.[58]

The roots of this idea can be traced back to two significant developments in leadership theory from the mid-1900s: first, the Ohio State studies and second, the development of transformational leadership theory. In the late 1940s researchers at Ohio State began studying leadership behaviors.[59] They found that leaders basically rely on two categories of behavior: initiating structure and consideration. Those two basic ideas are also sometimes thought of as "task behaviors" and "people behaviors."[60] Fundamentally, a leader needs to pay attention to the tasks and goals that need to be accomplished and simultaneously pay attention to the wellbeing of the people working on those tasks and goals. It is worth noting that the identification of these findings with gendered behaviors was not part of the initial assessment.

A second key development in leadership theory that seemed to support the idea that women make better leaders than men was Burns' transformational leadership theory. Bass and Avolio continued to develop the study of transformational leadership, and in 1994 they published an article called "Shatter the glass ceiling: Women may make better managers."[61] They cited items from the popular press of the time that claimed better leadership

56. Helgesen, "Female Advantage"; Helgesen, *Female Advantage*; Regan and Brooks, *Out of Women's Experience*; Rosener, "'Terrible Truth' about Women on Corporate Boards"; Rosener, "Ways Women Lead."

57. Greenberg and Sweeney, "Leadership: Qualities that Distinguish Women."

58. Eagly and Carli, "Women and the Labyrinth of Leadership"; Eagly, "Female Leadership Advantage and Disadvantage."

59. Northouse, *Leadership Theory and Practice*; Stogdill and Coons, *Ohio Studies in Personnel*; Stogdill and Shartle, *Ohio Studies in Personnel*.

60. Northouse, *Leadership Theory and Practice*; Stogdill and Coons, *Ohio Studies in Personnel*; Stogdill and Shartle, *Ohio Studies in Personnel*.

61. Bass and Avolio, "Shatter the Glass Ceiling."

qualities were inherently female, and went on to propose that "women exhibit behaviors and characteristics that have been related to higher levels of effort, performance, and advancement across organizations."[62]

The roots of their work lie in the transformational leadership theory proposed by Burns in 1978.[63] Using an instrument they had developed, they measured men's and women's use of transformational leadership styles. When they compared men's and women's scores they found that women ranked higher than men on all four measures of transformational leadership.[64] They concluded that this happened because of women's "tendencies to be more nurturing, interested in others, and more socially sensitive."[65] Transformational leadership can be measured in four aspects: charisma, inspiration, intellectual stimulation, and individual consideration, and it is thought to improve individual and organizational performance.[66] These qualities seem to align with women's nurturing, caring, and relational nature, creating the possibility that women are better able to use transformational leadership styles and find the style suits them better as leaders.[67] Men, on the other hand, scored higher than women on transactional factors such as active and passive management by exception, meaning correction, and on laissez-faire approaches involving a lack of leadership.[68] In the transactional factor of contingent reward, or reward for performance, women also outperformed men.[69] Finally, Bass and Avolio also found that followers performed better under transformational leaders than transactional ones.[70]

After considering possible explanations such as extreme female competence to understand these results, they concluded, "We think a better and more plausible explanation for the observed differences regarding transformational leadership ratings may lie in the tendencies of women to be more

62. Bass and Avolio, "Shatter the Glass Ceiling," 550.

63. Northouse, *Leadership Theory and Practice.*

64. Bass and Avolio, "Shatter the Glass Ceiling."

65. Bass and Avolio, "Shatter the Glass Ceiling," 556.

66. Bass et al., "Transformational and Transactional Leadership of Men and Women"; Eagly, "Female Leadership Advantage and Disadvantage"; Northouse, *Leadership Theory and Practice.*

67. Bass et al., "Transformational and Transactional Leadership of Men and Women"; Powell et al., "Sex Effects in Evaluations of Transformational and Transactional Leaders."

68. Bass and Avolio, "Shatter the Glass Ceiling"; Northouse, *Leadership Theory and Practice.*

69. Bass and Avolio, "Shatter the Glass Ceiling."

70. Bass and Avolio, "Shatter the Glass Ceiling."

nurturing, interested in others, and more socially sensitive."[71] Because of the growth of team-oriented workplaces and consensus styles of decision-making, they believed that women's transformational qualities would make them increasingly suited to organizational leadership, leading to the end of the glass ceiling.[72] The qualities they emphasized are similar to the "consideration" behaviors defined in the Ohio State studies. Since organizations now value these types of behaviors, they argued, organizations should recognize these innate qualities in women, "shatter the glass ceiling" as their title suggests, and move women into leadership positions. Interestingly, they explicitly caution readers that these behaviors should not be labeled "feminine" but rather "good leadership behaviors."[73] They seemed to think that dichotomizing behaviors based on gender is undesirable.

A handful of scholars followed Bass and Avolio's lead in proposing that women offer better leadership skills for twentieth- and twenty-first-century organizations. Rosener found that women tend to use a leadership style she called "interactive" because they focus attention on the leader's interactions with her followers through participation, and she argued that this approach was just as effective, if different, from men's more hierarchical styles.[74] Regan and Brooks found women used what they called "relational leadership" very effectively.[75] And Helgesen also argued that women's use of "webs of inclusion" make for better leadership in today's world.[76] All of these authors argue that women prefer to use consensus forms of decision-making by inviting participation from followers and that this involvement, though it may take longer, leads to better decisions and fewer challenges in the end.[77] Women using these approaches to leadership also tend to minimize status differences between leaders and followers.[78] In today's "flattened" organizations, therefore, women's democratic styles yield better results.

A somewhat related argument is that women are simply different in their leadership than men, and should be evaluated separately. Two emerging approaches to theorizing women's leadership along these lines have appeared in recent scholarship, taking a deconstructionist approach to the issue. Stead and

71. Bass and Avolio, "Shatter the Glass Ceiling," 556.

72. Bass and Avolio, "Shatter the Glass Ceiling."

73. Bass and Avolio, "Shatter the Glass Ceiling," 558.

74. Rosener, "'Terrible Truth' about Women on Corporate Boards"; Rosener, "Ways Women Lead."

75. Regan and Brooks, *Out of Women's Experience.*

76. Helgesen, "Female Advantage"; Helgesen, *Female Advantage.*

77. Helgesen, *Female Advantage*; Rosener, "Ways Women Lead."

78. Helgesen, "Female Advantage"; Regan and Brooks, *Out of Women's Experience*; Rosener, "Ways Women Lead."

Elliot argue that focusing on women's leadership without comparing them to men, and taking into account the varying contexts of women's leadership, may help us understand and appreciate what women's successful leadership looks like.[79] More importantly they hope to open space for more and varied dialogue about the nature of leadership and why it is so challenging to move beyond our present, heroic conceptions. Second, Calás and Smircich deconstruct the notion of women's supposed leadership advantage which only serves male interests, and suggest instead a complete reversal of perspectives.[80] Perhaps tongue-in-cheek, they suggest that women's "gossip" is sharing information, women's "hysteria" is outrage at injustice, and the "frugal housewife" is the best manager of limited resources.[81]

Despite the popularity of the idea that women should be better leaders than men in late-twentieth-century organizations, the predictions made by these theorists do not seem to have come to pass, as the numbers given earlier show. Evidence is somewhat mixed about women leaders' progress: there are more women leaders now than fifty years ago, yet the top levels remain solidly male.[82] Although some studies do seem to indicate that women tend to use transformational leadership styles more often and more effectively than men do, the results are not necessarily as clear-cut as Bass and Avolio suggested.[83] Nor is it obvious that the differences that do exist can be attributed to "female nature"; they may have more to do with women using styles that work for them, such as moderating task-oriented behaviors through the use of communal ones.[84] Context matters as well, since organizations that are more amenable to transformational leadership styles may also be more woman-leader friendly.[85] It is worth noting, too, that the argument that women make better leaders than men is, at heart, an essentialist argument. Those who make this claim appeal to women's "innate" qualities or attributes, such as their relational and nurturing nature,

79. Elliott and Stead, "Learning from Leading Women's Experience"; Stead and Elliott, *Women's Leadership*.

80. Calás and Smircich, "Dangerous Liaisons"; Calás and Smircich, "Voicing Seduction to Silence Leadership."

81. Calás and Smircich, "Dangerous Liaisons."

82. Baumgartner and Schneider, "Perceptions of Women in Management."

83. Eagly, "Female Leadership Advantage and Disadvantage"; Eagly and Karau, "Role Congruity Theory of Prejudice toward Female Leaders"; Rosener, "Ways Women Lead"; Vinkenburg et al., "Exploration of Stereotypical Beliefs about Leadership Styles"; Powell et al., "Sex Effects in Evaluations of Transformational and Transactional Leaders."

84. Hoyt, "Women and Leadership"; Powell et al., "Sex Effects in Evaluations of Transformational and Transactional Leaders"; Vinkenburg et al., "Exploration of Stereotypical Beliefs about Leadership Styles."

85. Yoder, "Making Leadership Work More Effectively for Women."

to support their position.[86] Yet if gender is constructed, as feminists maintain, then these are qualities that women have learned to use rather than unchangeable female attributes possessed by all women.

Generally, however, researchers have not continued to argue for the proposition that women are better, but have concentrated on investigating the differences between men and women. So at present we cannot argue convincingly that women actually do make better leaders than men, however much theories lead us to think that this ought to be so. Now I will turn to consider the opposite proposition, that women are somehow inherently unsuited for leadership and that this unsuitability accounts for their absence at top levels.

Theory 2: Women Are Unsuited for Leadership

The idea that women are unsuited for leadership was expressed openly and blatantly up through the middle of the twentieth century.[87] Bartol and Butterfield give two examples in the introduction to their study.

> For example, in a Bowman, Worthy, and Greyser (1965) study that sought managerial opinions about women executives, 51% of the male respondents agreed that women are "temperamentally unfit for management." Gilmer (1961) found that over 65% of the male managers in his study felt that women would be inferior to men in a supervisory position.[88]

Another study they cite found that respondents recommended female job candidates for clerical positions and male candidates for management positions thus indicating a belief that women were not suited for leadership positions.[89] *Harvard Business Review* in 1965 reported the results of a survey of 2,000 executives who believed that women were not qualified to be executives.[90]

This attitude is consistent with prevailing leadership theories of the first half of the twentieth century. Until the Ohio State studies and the styles studies of the 1950s, theories about leaders focused on their supposed innate traits that made them into leaders.[91] Trait theories were also known as "great man"

86. Bass and Avolio, "Shatter the Glass Ceiling"; Helgesen, *Female Advantage*; Regan and Brooks, *Out of Women's Experience*; Rosener, "Ways Women Lead."

87. Northouse, *Leadership Theory and Practice*.

88. Bartol and Butterfield, "Sex Effects in Evaluating Leaders," 446.

89. Bartol and Butterfield, "Sex Effects in Evaluating Leaders."

90. Cited in Denmark, "Styles of Leadership," 101.

91. Northouse, *Leadership Theory and Practice*.

theories because they searched for the "innate qualities and characteristics possessed by great social, political, and military leaders."[92] Notably, the great leaders who were studied were male, and males were seen as the standard of leadership; masculinity was frequently cited as a desirable leadership trait. Women were not even considered as potential leaders.

With the women's movement of the 1960s and the steady entrance of women into the workforce, changes in society meant that the blatant view of women as not suited to lead disappeared, or seemed to.[93] A better explanation is that the increasing push for equality brought by the women's movement caused the idea to move underground and become invisible. The fifty-year search for what makes women different from men, including the ways they lead, seems to hold an underlying, unspoken assumption that there is in fact an essential difference between men as males and women as females, and that these differences can account for the shortage of women leaders. I will return to this point later in the discussion.

Differences between Male and Female Leaders

In 1973 Virginia Schein published an article called "The relationship between sex role stereotypes and requisite management characteristics."[94] She set out to analyze the reasons women were seen as lacking leadership ability. Citing current studies about the prevalence of gender role stereotypes in society, she hypothesized that since most leadership positions were occupied by males, "then managerial position would seem to require personal attributes often thought to be more characteristic of men than women."[95] Those same stereotypes, she thought, would prevent some women from aspiring to leadership in order to avoid the cognitive dissonance of potentially conflicting roles. Her study of 300 insurance company managers showed that, in fact, the qualities of a manager and a male were closely aligned, while the qualities of a female and a manager were almost mutually exclusive.[96] She posited that this lack of alignment could account for the shortage of women in positions of leadership. She also thought that since the Ohio State framework valued both structure and consideration behaviors, women ought to be able

92. Northouse, *Leadership Theory and Practice*, 15.

93. Northouse, *Leadership Theory and Practice*.

94. Schein, "Relationship between Sex Role Stereotypes and Requisite Management Characteristics."

95. Schein, "Relationship between Sex Role Stereotypes and Requisite Management Characteristics," 95.

96. Schein, "Relationship between Sex Role Stereotypes and Requisite Management Characteristics."

to move into leadership positions by using their "stereotypical female" qualities. However, progress did not occur as she had hoped. Fifteen years later, after affirmative action policies had been in place for some time, she and two colleagues repeated the study to see what might have changed regarding perceptions of women's management. They found that although women's views of what made a successful manager had moderated to include both "male" and "female" characteristics, "male managers have not changed their attitudes over the last fifteen years," a discovery they found "disquieting."[97] This time, rather than concluding on a positive note that the situation should be improving for women, they commented that since male attitudes had not changed toward women, legal and structural measures were likely needed to improve women's access to leadership.[98]

At about the same time Bartol and Butterfield proposed the idea that the fundamental difference between male and female leaders lay not in how they led, but in how their leadership was evaluated.[99] In their study, participants rated males more highly than females when they used "initiating structure" behaviors and females more highly when they used "consideration" behaviors. Over the years a plethora of studies has continued to support the idea that males are viewed as effective leaders when they use task-oriented approaches to leadership, but that those same behaviors are not viewed favorably when used by women; instead women are viewed positively when they use relationship-oriented behaviors.[100] In fact this idea that men and women are evaluated on different standards is the most widely-accepted theory on the lack of women in leadership positions today. Since the 1970s a great deal more research has been done and the theory has been amplified, combining the two ideas of gender role stereotypes and leadership evaluations.

97. Brenner et al., "Relationship between Sex Role Stereotypes and Requisite Management Characteristics Revisited," 668.

98. Brenner et al., "Relationship between Sex Role Stereotypes and Requisite Management Characteristics Revisited."

99. Bartol and Butterfield, "Sex Effects in Evaluating Leaders."

100. Bartol and Butterfield, "Sex Effects in Evaluating Leaders"; Denmark, "Styles of Leadership"; Forsyth et al., "Biases in Appraisals of Women Leaders"; Heilman, "Description and Prescription"; Koenig et al., "Are Leader Stereotypes Masculine?"; Powell et al., "Sex Effects in Evaluations of Transformational and Transactional Leaders"; Schein, "Relationship between Sex Role Stereotypes and Requisite Management Characteristics."

Basic Gender Role Stereotypes

Many authors discuss the impact of social role expectations, or gender-role stereotypes, on both the behavior and the evaluation of leaders. Society is permeated with gender-role stereotypes which assign "agentic" behaviors to men and "communal" behaviors to women. Agentic behavior is that of an agent: one who gets things done. Communal behavior is that which focuses on the community, caring for the needs of others. Translated into a work setting, the expectations become closely aligned with the "initiating structure" and "consideration" behaviors that were defined by the Ohio State studies.[101]

> Agentic characteristics, which are ascribed more strongly to men than women, describe primarily an assertive, controlling, and confident tendency—for example, aggressive, ambitious, dominant, forceful, independent, daring, self-confident, and competitive. In employment settings, agentic behaviors might include speaking assertively, competing for attention, influencing others, initiating activity directed to assigned tasks, and making problem-focused suggestions.
>
> Communal characteristics, which are ascribed more strongly to women than men, describe primarily a concern with the welfare of other people—for example, affectionate, helpful, kind, sympathetic, interpersonally sensitive, nurturant, and gentle. In employment settings, communal behaviors might include speaking tentatively, not drawing attention to oneself, accepting others' direction, supporting and soothing others, and contributing to the solution of relational and interpersonal problems.[102]

It is important to notice that these behaviors are "ascribed" to men and women; that is, they are taken for granted as the ways men and women do, and should, behave. Further, although both consideration and structure have been considered to be part of the leader role since the Ohio State studies, the tendency is to value task accomplishment over relationship as the bottom line analysis of performance.[103] Thus leader behaviors are more congruent with male gender stereotypes than with female gender

---

101. Johanson, "Perceptions of Femininity in Leadership."

102. Eagly and Johannesen-Schmidt, "Leadership Styles of Women and Men," 783.

103. Hale, *Performance Consultant's Fieldbook*; Johanson, "Perceptions of Femininity in Leadership"; Robinson and Robinson, *Performance Consulting*; Swanson and Holton, *Foundations of Human Resource Development*; Stolovitch and Keeps, *Training Ain't Performance*.

stereotypes.[104] This connection is so strong that Schein referred to it as the "think manager—think male" effect.[105] According to Koenig's research, "the masculinity of the cultural stereotype of leadership is a large effect that is robust across variation in many aspects of leaders' social contexts."[106] The current performance focus in human resource development is one indication of how strongly task accomplishment is valued in organizations, and by extension, in organizational leaders.[107] Thus there is great congruence between expectations of men and leaders: the stereotyped behaviors coincide and men are therefore assumed to be qualified to lead. For women, the story is different: there is little congruence between the stereotyped expectations of women and those of leaders. See Table 1 for a comparison of men, women, and leader stereotypes. At best what women are believed to offer is a secondary, supporting-type of leadership skill, but not the primary one of getting things done.

Table 1: *Gender-role stereotypes and leader stereotypes*

MEN	LEADERS	WOMEN
Assertive	Set vision & direction	Affectionate
Controlling	Accomplish jobs & tasks	Helpful
Confident	Be an expert	Nurturing
Task-Oriented	Influence others	Kind
Independent	Be assertive	Sympathetic
Initiators	Solve problems	Followers, supporters
AGENTIC = **Get things done**	**AGENTIC =** **Get things done**	**COMMUNAL =** **Care for others**

104. Carli and Eagly, "Gender and Leadership"; Vinkenburg et al., "Exploration of Stereotypical Beliefs about Leadership Styles."

105. Schein, "Relationship between Sex Role Stereotypes and Requisite Management Characteristics."

106. Koenig et al., "Are Leader Stereotypes Masculine?," 637.

107. Robinson and Robinson, *Performance Consulting*; Swanson and Holton, *Foundations of Human Resource Development*; Stolovitch and Keeps, *Training Ain't Performance*.

DESCRIPTIVE AND PRESCRIPTIVE NORMS:
THE DOUBLE BIND

There is a second layer to the problem of expectations for men's and women's behavior when it comes to functioning in a leadership role. Stereotypes carry a double power, both describing how people do behave and defining how they ought to behave. Eagly and Karau define stereotypes as both descriptive and injunctive norms. Descriptive norms describe behaviors that a group of people do, while injunctive norms add a layer of "should" or "ought" to the description, thus obliging people to conform to expectations.[108]

Injunctive norms are doubly powerful, because they allow for censure of those who depart from the requirements. In the realm of women's leadership, injunctive norms mean that women, who often use some agentic behaviors to fulfill their responsibilities, encounter disapproval for using those very behaviors that good leaders are expected to use.[109] For example, many studies show that women leaders tend to adopt and use somewhat "masculine" behaviors, becoming task-oriented and directive.[110] This choice is logical in that these are the types of behaviors expected, even required, of leaders. Yet for women, by exhibiting these task-oriented behaviors they are violating the stereotypical expectations of women to behave communally and thus suffer disapprobation for departing from the injunctive norms.[111] When they violate that norm and engage in "masculine" behavior, they are devalued as not being feminine, or not behaving properly as a female.[112]

This situation is known as a double-bind: neither choice has wholly positive outcomes for the woman.[113] She can choose to behave in a "masculine" way and violate feminine role expectations, or she can choose to behave in a "feminine" way and violate leader role expectations. Because

108. Eagly and Karau, "Role Congruity Theory of Prejudice toward Female Leaders."

109. Carli and Eagly, "Gender, Hierarchy, and Leadership: An Introduction"; Eagly, "Female Leadership Advantage and Disadvantage"; Eagly and Johannesen-Schmidt, "Leadership Styles of Women and Men"; Gregory, "Are Women Different and Why Are Women Thought to be Different?"; Heilman, "Description and Prescription"; Yoder, "Making Leadership Work More Effectively for Women"; Eagly and Karau, "Role Congruity Theory of Prejudice toward Female Leaders."

110. Carli and Eagly, "Gender, Hierarchy, and Leadership: An Introduction"; Eagly, "Female Leadership Advantage and Disadvantage"; Eagly and Johannesen-Schmidt, "Leadership Styles of Women and Men"; Gregory, "Are Women Different and Why Are Women Thought to be Different?"; Heilman, "Description and Prescription."

111. Bowles et al., "Social Incentives for Gender Differences."

112. Bowles et al., "Social Incentives for Gender Differences."

113. Eagly, "Female Leadership Advantage and Disadvantage"; Gregory, "Are Women Different and Why Are Women Thought to be Different?"; Koenig et al., "Are Leader Stereotypes Masculine?"; Korabik, "Androgyny and Leadership Style."

the two types of behavior are viewed as mutually exclusive, it is impossible for her to simultaneously conform to both sets of expectations. It could be argued that men also face these norms but since male norms align with leader behaviors, men are rarely penalized for exhibiting agentic, leader-type behaviors.[114]

Context plays a role in determining how severely the woman leader is judged. Organizational context varies widely, from heavily masculinized, command-and-control situations where performance is everything (for example, the military) to service-oriented ones where supporting followers matters most (for example, some social service organizations).[115] Generally, the more masculine the environment both in terms of male workers and task-orientation, the more difficult it is for a woman leader to succeed.[116]

One obvious issue underlying this problem is the tendency to bifurcate behaviors into male-only and female-only categories.[117] The more strongly these bifurcations are seen as valid, meaning the more essentialist the viewpoint, the greater the opprobrium for someone who violates either side of the scale. Scholars point out that healthy adult behavior is typically quite androgynous, with adults being able to use different behaviors in accordance with the demands of the circumstances.[118] In theory this type of androgynous behavior as flexibility should be quite beneficial to the work place, and is a recommended approach.[119] But in practice it can be damaging to women in strongly stereotyped environments.

Another issue underlying this problem is one of performance versus perception.[120] No authors argue that the woman's actual performance is an issue; to the contrary, study after study shows that women's performance is comparable to that of men's.[121] Rather, the problem is one of perception.[122]

114. Andersen and Hysock, *Thinking about Women.*

115. Yoder, "Making Leadership Work More Effectively for Women."

116. Yoder, "Making Leadership Work More Effectively for Women."

117. Heilman and Okimoto, "Why Are Women Penalized for Success at Male Tasks?"

118. Korabik, "Androgyny and Leadership Style."

119. Korabik, "Androgyny and Leadership Style."

120. Bass et al., "Transformational and Transactional Leadership of Men and Women"; Gregory, "Are Women Different and Why Are Women Thought to Be Different?"; Heilman and Eagly, "Gender Stereotypes Are Alive, Well, and Busy Producing Workplace Discrimination"; Heilman, "Description and Prescription"; Lyness and Heilman, "When Fit Is Fundamental."

121. Eagly et al., "Gender and the Effectiveness of Leaders"; Gregory, "Are Women Different and Why Are Women Thought to Be Different?"

122. Gregory, "Are Women Different and Why Are Women Thought to Be Different?"; Heilman and Eagly, "Gender Stereotypes Are Alive, Well, and Busy Producing

When they perform well according to the "masculine" model, women are often perceived negatively *as women* by colleagues and their work contributions are devalued accordingly.[123] The relationship is corollary: "To the extent that female leaders violate their associates' gender expectancies, they may be subjected to prejudiced reactions which may include biased performance evaluations and negative preconceptions about future performance."[124] So, comparable performance does not lead to comparable evaluation, but to the perception of lower performance by women, just because they are women.

The strength and consistency of these findings over a period of forty-plus years, especially when combined with the prevalence and strength of gender essentialist attitudes already discussed, seems to indicate that the diagnosis of the problem is valid. Eagly, Carli, Heilman, and other researchers offered a major step forward with their gender-role theories in understanding and explaining the shortage of women leaders. However, other than repeating that attitudes need to change, there is little in the way of corrective suggestions for moving towards a full inclusion of women in leadership. Also, to a large degree, all of these studies have continued to focus on "essential" qualities, even though the qualities may be ascribed to socialization rather than tied to biological sex. Gender-role stereotypes are simply another way of describing the belief that men are characterized one way and women another, and of reinforcing the idea that there is little or no overlap between the two. We are back to a definition of gender as primarily "difference" and that is exactly what these studies have examined. Since males were the standard for original leadership studies, studies of women intentionally or unintentionally wind up seeking to understand women's shortcomings, rather than expanding existing models or creating new ones.[125]

In a situation such as this, where women are condemned if they perform well by male standards and equally condemned if they perform well by female standards, what are the options for women? What workable strategies have researchers found to support women in their leadership efforts?

SUCCEEDING IN A MAN'S WORLD: STRATEGIES FOR WOMEN LEADERS

In a world where women continue to encounter stereotypes and prejudice against their successful leadership contributions, choosing to forge ahead

---

Workplace Discrimination"; Heilman, "Description and Prescription."

123. Gregory, "Are Women Different and Why Are Women Thought to Be Different?"; Yoder, "Making Leadership Work More Effectively for Women."

124. Eagly et al., "Gender and the Effectiveness of Leaders," 126.

125. Elliott and Stead, "Learning from Leading Women's Experience."

as a leader requires some choices on the part of a woman. One choice she may make regards the type of leadership she will practice. There is some evidence that women tend to use transformational, democratic, and post-heroic leadership models with reasonable success. Another choice she may make is what kinds of strategies she uses in pursuing leadership. I will look at each of these areas in turn.

Leadership Style

The review of the literature suggests that women do tend to prefer post-heroic leadership styles to the more authoritative, hierarchical styles frequently used by men. For example, Bass and Avolio found that women outperformed men on all four measures of transformational leadership. They believed women were "naturally" better at transformational leadership because of their more "nurturing nature."[126] Women are often thought to be naturally better at shared and democratic leadership styles as well. The evidence for women's use of democratic leadership styles is quite strong. For example, Eagly and Johnson's meta-analysis of 162 studies showed women favoring democratic styles.[127] Twelve years later Eagly and Karau reported "a tendency for women to lead in a more democratic and participative style than men."[128] In general multiple studies show that women do in fact use democratic styles more often than men do.[129] These styles contrast strikingly with autocratic or command-and-control leadership which tends to be hierarchical and non-relational, and usually associated with men.[130]

Although at first glance the post-heroic models appear to favor women as leaders, the persistence of gender-role stereotypes means that women are rarely rewarded for what is presumed to be their "natural" way of behaving and the newer forms of democratic leadership may share the responsibility while maintaining power squarely in the hands of a few at the top of the hierarchy.[131] Thus even the most recent developments in leadership theory

126. Bass and Avolio, "Shatter the Glass Ceiling."

127. Eagly and Johnson, "Gender and Leadership Style."

128. Eagly and Karau, "Role Congruity Theory of Prejudice toward Female Leaders," 590.

129. Eagly and Johannesen-Schmidt, "Leadership Styles of Women and Men"; Eagly and Johnson, "Gender and Leadership Style"; Hoyt, "Women and Leadership."

130. Rosener, "Ways Women Lead"; Weikart et al., "Democratic Sex."

131. Blackmore, "Social Justice and the Study and Practice of Leadership in Education"; Calás and Smircich, "Dangerous Liaisons"; Fletcher, "Greatly Exaggerated Demise of Heroic Leadership."

continue to leave women at a disadvantage compared to men, regardless of the skills that women may offer to their organizations.

A question we need to consider is whether post-heroic leadership styles actually represent something innate about women, or represent a learned behavior that they choose to use to function as women in leadership. It is quite possible that women learn to use these styles because the styles work better for them *as women*. One possible explanation is that "democratic relationships, participatory decision making, delegation, and team-based leadership skills . . . are consistent with . . . the communal characteristics typically ascribed to women."[132] Another possibility is that women use these behaviors because they work well for women, leading to more positive evaluations.[133] In that sense women have learned to "be adaptive in that they are using the style that produces the most favorable evaluations for women."[134] Eagly, Karau, and Makhijani found that women were evaluated positively for using democratic styles that suit the female gender-role stereotype, but negatively for using more autocratic, masculine styles.[135] They too think that women may choose to behave this way to minimize the negative consequences of violating the gender-role stereotypes, rather than because of any innate leaning toward participatory leadership. If we accept that leadership is at least partially learned, then women are learning which leadership skills and behaviors will help them succeed and choosing to use them.

The fundamental problem with associating transformational, democratic, or post-heroic styles of leadership with women is that it takes us right back into essentialist ideas of gender. Proponents of the idea that women's leadership is fundamentally different from men's are likely responding to a common thread in much of the writing about how women "ought" to succeed as leaders, and that is simply to become more like men.[136] Studies of women's leadership repeatedly show that using "masculine" behaviors, even to the point of changing dress and speech patterns, can help women succeed as leaders and that many women make these adjustments.[137]

---

132. Eagly and Karau, "Role Congruity Theory of Prejudice toward Female Leaders," 592.

133. Yoder, "Making Leadership Work More Effectively for Women."

134. Hoyt, "Women and Leadership," 267.

135. Eagly et al., "Gender and the Effectiveness of Leaders."

136. Helgesen, *Female Advantage*.

137. Baumgartner and Schneider, "Perceptions of Women in Management"; Carli and Eagly, "Gender, Hierarchy, and Leadership"; Eagly, "Female Leadership Advantage and Disadvantage"; Eagly and Johannesen-Schmidt, "Leadership Styles of Women and Men"; Gregory, "Are Women Different and Why Are Women Thought to Be Different?";

Given the prevalence of women using such strategies, taking a "stand up for women" approach makes a certain amount of sense. The problem is that it only serves to reinforce essentialist notions of gender difference by stressing the value of female behaviors as contrasted to male ones. Labeling women's leadership as better than men's for certain times or contexts places men and women in competition with one another, which also serves to reinforce the essentialist notions of difference.[138] The problem lies not in calling attention to women's contributions, but in insisting that they make those contributions solely because they are women.

Early leadership theories concentrated on the person of the leader—usually a male—and conceptualized leadership based on the traits, skills, and behaviors used by that person in their leadership position.[139] Shakeshaft called attention to the tautology inherent in conceiving "of leadership as that which men who are designated as leaders do."[140] Among other things, she argued, it left out what women leaders do and any "possible female conceptualizations of leadership behavior."[141] If leadership is what leading men do, then leadership is by definition male. Later theories of leadership tried to move away from this problem by studying women's leadership, usually with a view to finding out how they differed from men. Once that was known, then either the women could learn to be more masculine, or the construction of leadership could be broadened to include women's strengths. In all of these approaches to leadership, however, the fundamental assumption of gender essentialism still prevails.

Leadership Strategies

Researchers find women using a variety of fairly healthy strategies to function in a male world; they have also found evidence of some less healthy strategies that women may embrace to cope with the stress created by the dissonance between female roles and leader roles that they encounter.

First, many successful female leaders use styles that seem very "masculine" as they work. They may dress and speak in ways that resemble their male colleagues and use more task-oriented behaviors.[142] Although in 1982 Peters proclaimed that "the days of women succeeding by learning to play men's games are gone. Instead men now have to learn to play women's

---

Heilman, "Description and Prescription."

138. Elliott and Stead, "Learning from Leading Women's Experience."

139. Brown, "Meetings and Intersections."

140. Shakeshaft, *Women in Educational Administration*, 154.

141. Shakeshaft, *Women in Educational Administration*, 154.

142. Baumgartner and Schneider, "Perceptions of Women in Management."

games" the truth seems to be that those days are far from gone.[143] Studies continue to show that one effective strategy used by women leaders is to rank high on the "masculinity" scale: to exhibit behaviors that blend in with the dominant male leadership culture of the organization.

A second strategy that successful women leaders use is extreme competence. Researchers repeatedly found that women displayed more competence and greater achievement than their male colleagues.[144] Higher achievement can serve women well, but it carries a hidden risk of the woman being devalued: she may be disliked for her competence or judged as unfeminine if competence looks like assertiveness.[145] It can also increase stress and demand a higher investment of time at work. Thus it is also a risky strategy for women, yet not one that they can afford to ignore.

A compensating strategy that many women use is to increase their communal or relational behaviors. Since this aligns with female stereotypes, it can serve to diminish the negative consequences brought about by task-oriented behaviors and competence.[146] Another aspect of increasing communal behaviors that seems to work well for women is that of minimizing the status differential between herself as a female leader and her subordinates.[147] Again, this strategy aligns with stereotypes: women are consistently viewed as having lower status than men, so embracing this seems to work to a woman's advantage when she is leading.[148]

A fourth strategy that women may be able to use is to choose to work in a female-friendly environment. Typically this means choosing a work context with a high percentage of female employees and leaders already

143. Bass and Avolio, "Shatter the Glass Ceiling," 558.

144. Baumgartner and Schneider, "Perceptions of Women in Management"; Bierema, "Model of Executive Women's Learning and Development"; Yoder, "Making Leadership Work More Effectively for Women."

145. Eagly and Karau, "Role Congruity Theory of Prejudice toward Female Leaders"; Gregory, "Are Women Different and Why Are Women Thought to Be Different?"

146. Baumgartner and Schneider, "Perceptions of Women in Management"; Bowles et al., "Social Incentives for Gender Differences in the Propensity to Initiate Negotiations"; Eagly and Karau, "Role Congruity Theory of Prejudice toward Female Leaders"; Heilman and Okimoto, "Why Are Women Penalized for Success at Male Tasks?"; Schein, "Relationship between Sex Role Stereotypes and Requisite Management Characteristics."

147. Baumgartner and Schneider, "Perceptions of Women in Management"; Yoder, "Making Leadership Work More Effectively for Women."

148. Bowles et al., "Social Incentives for Gender Differences in the Propensity to Initiate Negotiations"; Powell et al., "Sex Effects in Evaluations of Transformational and Transactional Leaders."

present.[149] A similar strategy is to work in a middle-level leadership position. Lower levels are seen as task oriented, middle levels as about managing relationships, and upper levels as requiring visionary, big-picture skills. Thus the middle level seems most compatible with female stereotypes and women seem to do better there.[150]

Researchers have found evidence of several more behaviors women leaders may use that might be viewed more as coping mechanisms than healthy strategies. The first could be called turf protection. In some cases successful women leaders may feel the need to protect their hard-won position, and may display a tendency to block the aspirations of other women. This happens "when a woman who has made it to the top finds a reason not to help other women aspiring to break through the glass ceiling."[151] Baumgartner and Schneider refer to this behavior as the "queen bee effect."[152]

A second mechanism women may use is to deny that there are, or were, any barriers at all to women's success.[153] Having suffered and struggled to the top, they may think it natural and even necessary for other women to prove themselves in the same way.[154] Or they may think that although others have suffered discrimination, they themselves have not, and that they have no responsibility either to help other women or to challenge the organization.[155]

Finally, Sloan and Krone found women using a number of truly negative, even self-defeating behaviors to cope with their jobs. These included black humor, subversive resistance, rejection of power, and a willingness to stand up for injustice towards others but not themselves.[156] Although these behaviors function as coping strategies to give temporary relief to women leaders, especially those in extremely patriarchal structures, they are not recommended as healthy strategies for women leaders in general, since they may lead to depression and hopelessness.[157] Sloan and Krone's study reflects the pessimism and depression felt by women who, half a century

149. Eagly and Carli, "Women and the Labyrinth of Leadership"; Eagly et al., "Gender and the Effectiveness of Leaders."

150. Eagly et al., "Gender and the Effectiveness of Leaders."

151. Baumgartner and Schneider, "Perceptions of Women in Management," 561; Trinidad and Normore, "Leadership and Gender."

152. Baumgartner and Schneider, "Perceptions of Women in Management."

153. Baumgartner and Schneider, "Perceptions of Women in Management."

154. Baumgartner and Schneider, "Perceptions of Women in Management."

155. Rowney and Cahoon, "Individual and Organizational Characteristics of Women in Managerial Leadership."

156. Sloan and Krone, "Women Managers and Gendered Values."

157. Sloan and Krone, "Women Managers and Gendered Values."

after the women's movement of the 1960s, still find themselves personally devalued at work because of their gender. These findings remind us that addressing the issues discussed here is about more than research for understanding; it is also about hope, health, and healing for significant numbers of women in the workplace today.

Organizational Strategies for Change

Another way to think about the problem is to consider what types of strategies can help women leaders succeed. The strategies just mentioned are for individual women, and they fit within the first of Kolb et al.'s four-part framework for understanding organizational approaches to women, which they call "fix the women." The second is "celebrate differences," the third "create equal opportunity," and the fourth "revise work culture."[158] We have seen that many of the theories of women's leadership fall into the first three categories. We have also seen how these approaches fall short of addressing structural inequities. Finally, we know that the passage of time and the steady application of these ideas has not led to the expected increase of women leaders that we would have seen, if these truly addressed the root of the problem.[159] Each of the three approaches has helped women make progress, yet none of them has yet brought a state of equity between men and women.[160] So the authors suggest seeking to revise the culture of work and organizations, which can strengthen the gains brought by each of the three previous approaches. This approach, they argue, is more radical, more difficult, and potentially more promising than any of the others both for women and for organizations.[161]

To achieve such change, we must remember that work and organizational culture are inherently gendered.[162] Organizations have, for the most part, been created by men with men's lives and values in mind.[163] They function to maintain and perpetuate gendered structures even while presenting a façade of neutrality under the belief that "male" equals "human."[164] Therefore,

158. Kolb et al., "Making Change," 10–13.

159. Fletcher, "Greatly Exaggerated Demise of Heroic Leadership."

160. Kolb et al., "Making Change."

161. Kolb et al., "Making Change."

162. Sheppard, "Women Managers' Perceptions of Gender and Organizational Life"; Yoder, "Making Leadership Work More Effectively for Women."

163. Acker, "Hierarchies, Jobs, Bodies"; Kolb et al., "Making Change."

164. Acker, "Hierarchies, Jobs, Bodies"; Brown, "Meetings and Intersections"; Calás and Smircich, "Dangerous Liaisons"; Sheppard, "Women Managers' Perceptions of Gender and Organizational Life."

the best way to improve women's participation in leadership, and improve organizational performance by not limiting people's contributions based on gender, is to seek to deconstruct these gendered approaches to work. To do this requires changing the organizational culture, which is notoriously difficult and time consuming.[165] An organization, perhaps with the support of an organization development consultant, could certainly choose to pursue this strategy to support its women leaders. Individual women alone, however, are not likely to effect this level of change on their own.

A few other authors made concrete suggestions about how organizational changes can begin to come about. Both Bierema and Eagly mentioned that HR departments need to adjust, without making specific recommendations.[166] Others offered two main categories for change: move more women into leadership and legitimate their work. The simple presence of more women in leadership roles helps to overcome tokenism and make the presence of women seem more normal.[167] The more women there are functioning in a given role, the more they are seen as qualified to fulfill that role. So the simple act of seeing women lead makes others think that women can lead.[168] Second, organizations must support the women leaders they select.[169] A job without the resources or authority to do that job will certainly be perceived as tokenism, or worse, a hidden disbelief in the woman's qualifications. Organizations that truly want to embrace and benefit from women's leadership abilities need to have significant numbers of competent women leaders and support them in their work. By moving more women into leadership, supporting those women, and seeking to change the organizational culture organizations may begin to embrace their own female leadership talent.

Unresolved Issues Regarding Women's Leadership

Despite the enormous gains for women in the workplace in the last half of the twentieth century and the first decade of the twenty-first, women still continue to face significant obstacles to functioning as respected, contributing members of leadership in many organizations. Gender stereotypes,

165. Burke, *Organization Change.*

166. Bierema, "Model of Executive Women's Learning and Development"; Eagly, "Female Leadership Advantage and Disadvantage."

167. Yoder, "Making Leadership Work More Effectively for Women."

168. Bartol and Butterfield, "Sex Effects in Evaluating Leaders"; Powell et al., "Sex Effects in Evaluations of Transformational and Transactional Leaders"; Schein, "Relationship between Sex Role Stereotypes and Requisite Management Characteristics."

169. Yoder, "Making Leadership Work More Effectively for Women."

discrimination, and the hidden belief that women are still somehow "unsuited" to lead run rampant, if hidden below the surface, in our society.[170] Having reviewed the relevant literature and the suggestions for women leaders and organizations, in the end I am troubled by the relative lack of good ideas to bring change, and by some of the hidden problems still evident in the existing studies.

The first problem is that there is still somewhat of a "blame the victim" mentality. This is seen in the paucity of suggestions for organizational change and the plethora of suggestions for how women can change to meet the standards. As Yoder points out, "Relying on women themselves to compensate for structural inequities is inherently unfair, even to successful women, and makes less successful women vulnerable to self-blame and victim blaming from others."[171] Yet current research devotes almost no attention to structural inequities, and instead focuses on researching the women themselves, as if they were the problem. If the stereotypes and gender role theory is correct, the solution lies not in changing the women but in changing the stereotypes and the system. If we cannot do this, we are left with a double injustice: we have put "the responsibility for effective leadership solely on the shoulders of women and accept[ed] the corollary of blaming women for failed leadership."[172] But if the problem is structural, not personal, the theory has diagnosed the problem yet has still to provide workable solutions.

Closely tied to the first problem is a distressing tendency to discuss ways in which women can please or appease the men.[173] This is particularly evident in recommendations that women change their styles of dress, demeanor, speaking, decision-making, and use of power. In making these suggestions, the underlying assumption is that since men hold the power and women are the supplicants, it is up to the women to position themselves in such a way as to gain approval.[174]

Third is the cyclical nature of the problem. If we need more women leaders in order to see that women can lead, and if the prevailing view is that women cannot lead, therefore they are not given an opportunity, then what hope is there for women? The corollary of the suggestion to put more women into leadership to relieve tokenism is that having few women there

170. Brenner et al., "Relationship between Sex Role Stereotypes and Requisite Management Characteristics Revisited."

171. Yoder, "Making Leadership Work More Effectively for Women," 819.

172. Yoder, "Making Leadership Work More Effectively for Women," 817.

173. Bierema, "Model of Executive Women's Learning and Development."

174. Ingersoll, "Engendered Conflict."

leads to a belief that women cannot lead.[175] This can easily become a vicious cycle. The suggestion that an organization simply put some more women in leadership could easily backfire if an organization, in haste and without sufficient thought, were to place untrained or unqualified women into positions, and if those women then performed poorly. The outcome could be more detrimental to the future of women in that organization than it was before the intervention. How can we break this cycle?

Finally, these analyses are heavily based on the trait and styles view of leadership. Some of the authors acknowledge this, and mention other types of leadership that have not been studied regarding women's practices.[176] In a globalized world where context and situation can be critical, simply focusing on the traits and styles of a leader may not be enough. Trait theories of leadership were already being challenged by the middle of the twentieth century. Yet most of these studies seem to focus almost exclusively on the traits of women that make them good leaders or not. In this way they present an essentialist view of males and females. If the trait theory of leadership is no longer uncontested, then surely the traits of women are no longer of central relevance to women's leadership abilities.[177] Perhaps it is time to move the conversation to focus more on skills, abilities, training, and other styles of leadership, rather than staying mired in a potentially fruitless discussion of what men and women are like.

In the end, much of the literature focuses more on the nature of women than on the organizational context where she works. While centering the debate here is helpful to bring understanding of the current situation and how we got here, it offers little in terms of transformational approaches for the future. Worse, most of the strategies suggested for women reproduce male power structures rather than challenging them.[178] More research needs to be done not just with women who have broken through the glass ceiling, but on ways organizations can dismantle that ceiling and give everyone equal access to the escalator.

CHAPTER SUMMARY

Understanding women's leadership is both challenging and discouraging. From their inception, leadership studies have conceived of leadership as a male function. Men have been studied and used as the standard, with

175. Trinidad and Normore, "Leadership and Gender."

176. Eagly et al., "Gender and the Effectiveness of Leaders."

177. Northouse, *Leadership Theory and Practice.*

178. Bierema, "Model of Executive Women's Learning and Development"; Marshall, *Women Managers.*

women either accommodating or falling short of the male model. Women can learn leadership, yet if they learn it well and practice it in a masculine way, they may be penalized. This is mainly because essentialist views are still incredibly strong in our culture and society, as we have seen. Leadership for women is still an uphill battle.

The literature is still not clear about what helps women succeed at leading. From "be like men" to "be different from men" to "fight for equality" women have tried to succeed in a male world. We have made progress, but success is slow. Change has been incremental, and the expected boom for women leaders has yet to materialize. Ely et al. assert that "leadership is perhaps the most prized activity in Western organizations today."[179] If leadership is still fundamentally about power, and gender is still fundamentally about power, then the link between gender and leadership will continue to prove extremely difficult to break.

179. Ely et al., *Reader in Gender, Work, and Organization*, 153.

4

Review of the Literature: Evangelicalism and Gender

THE FIRST TWO CHAPTERS of this literature review considered current thinking on the role of women in society and in organizational leadership in the U.S. Despite great gains in the workplace women continue to lag significantly in terms of leadership. Furthermore, we have seen that there are ingrained underlying assumptions about males and females that color our expectations of who is suited to lead, with women falling short. Next I turn to an examination of evangelical religion, and its worldview which states outright that women should not hold positions of authority over men.[1] The gender essentialist idea that is being challenged in mainstream society continues to function openly as an espoused value in much of the evangelical subculture. In order to understand the lack of women in leadership positions in evangelical mission agencies that draw much of their funding and recruiting from the evangelical subculture, understanding the philosophical framework that discourages or outright prohibits women from leadership roles is also necessary.

WOMEN IN EVANGELICAL RELIGION: THE POWER OF GENDER ESSENTIALISM

Evangelicalism is typically defined in terms of a specific set of theological beliefs; thus, someone who holds to the literal truth and authority of the Bible, the virgin birth of Jesus, salvation only through faith in Jesus' death, burial,

1. Barclay, "Are Mission Agencies 'Institutionally Sexist'?"; Bendroth, "Last Gasp Patriarchy"; Gallagher and Smith, "Symbolic Traditionalism and Pragmatic Egalitarianism"; Sowinska, "Ambiguous Women."

and resurrection, a transformed life, and sharing this message with others would typically be considered an evangelical.[2] However, Ingersoll points out that defining evangelicalism in terms of theological beliefs rather than practices has the effect of focusing primarily on men's concerns.

> Scholars have also defined religion in terms that captured the dimensions controlled by elites (mostly men) and underplayed the dimensions that shape the living of religion by lay people (a majority of whom are women). Thus we end up with definitions of evangelicalism that are rooted in theological disputes and pertain only indirectly to the tradition as it is experienced by believers.[3]

One of the most noticeable aspects of the evangelical tradition as it is experienced by believers is gender essentialism. Gender essentialism, or the idea that men and women are fundamentally different by virtue of their biology, is a well-established phenomenon in evangelical religion that has held sway for roughly a century.[4] Since biology is thought to be determined by God, it is used to define separate roles for men and women based on biological differences and tied to religious requirements.[5] Fundamentally, men are assigned to the public realm of work, and women are assigned to the private realm of home and family, with a supportive and nurturing role. A brief look at history helps explain how evangelical religion came to embrace gender essentialism as a core tenet of its belief system.

Roots of Gender Essentialism in Evangelicalism

In assessing the literature, there is broad agreement that a hallmark of both historic and current evangelicalism in the United States and the United Kingdom is gender essentialism. In this view, males and females are seen to have "essential" differences based on their biological sex and these differences are taken as foundational for defining acceptable roles and behaviors for men and women. In this view, the tendency is to see men as suited for leadership, employment outside the home, and religious authority and women as suited for domestic tasks, emotional nurturing of the family, private religious practice, and relational work.[6] Since gender is determined by biology, and biology is determined by God, the prescribed gender roles are also considered to be ordained by God, immutable, and incontestable. However, a close look at evangelical gender roles shows that they align almost seamlessly with the social

2. Armstrong, "How Evangelical Black Women Learn to Negotiate Power Relations."

3. Ingersoll, "Engendered Conflict," 47.

4. Bendroth, *Fundamentalism & Gender*; Zinn et al., "Sex and Gender through the Prism of Difference."

5. Gallagher and Smith, "Symbolic Traditionalism and Pragmatic Egalitarianism."

6. Brereton and Bendroth, "Secularization and Gender."

gender-role stereotypes discussed in chapter 3. See Table 2 for a comparison of the social and religious role prescriptions. What evangelicalism prescribes as appropriate roles for men and women are precisely those roles defined by the general culture's gender-role stereotypes. In evangelical religion one result of the role requirements is that, although more women than men are active in churches, men are still primarily the leaders in those churches.[7]

The role gender plays in evangelical religion in the United States has slowly gained attention in the scholarly literature over the past 30 years. Historian Margaret Bendroth, for example, traced the development of gender ideologies in evangelical religion from the late 1800s through the twentieth century.[8] She argued that over time, gender roles became increasingly idealized, though the actual practice regarding women has differed in different settings.[9] Ingersoll has also studied the phenomenon of gender roles in evangelicalism, concluding that they have become constructed as part of the culture, to the point of being no longer negotiable, but considered as doctrine.[10]

Table 2: *Comparison of social gender-role stereotypes with evangelical gender roles*

SOCIAL GENDER-ROLE STEREOTYPES		EVANGELICAL GENDER ROLES	
MEN	**WOMEN**	**MAN'S ROLE**	**WOMAN'S ROLE**
Assertive	Affectionate	Lead	Submit
Controlling	Nurturing	Make decisions	Support decisions
Confident	Kind	Spiritual authority	Caretaker
Task oriented	Relational	Get things done	Relational
Independent	Dependent	Independent	Dependent
Initiators	Followers/ supporters	Initiator	Responder
AGENTIC	**COMMUNAL**	**AGENTIC**	**COMMUNAL**

Leanne M. Dzubinski, "Taking on Power: Women Leaders in Evangelical Mission Organizations." *Missiology: An International Review* 44.3 (2016), 283. Reproduced with permission.

7. Adams, "Stained Glass Makes the Ceiling Visible," 81, 100.

8. Bendroth, "Fundamentalism and Femininity"; Bendroth, "Last Gasp Patriarchy"; Bendroth, *Fundamentalism & Gender*; Brereton and Bendroth, "Secularization and Gender."

9. Bendroth, "Fundamentalism and Femininity"; Bendroth, "Last Gasp Patriarchy"; Brereton and Bendroth, "Secularization and Gender."

10. Ingersoll, *Evangelical Christian Women*; Ingersoll, "Engendered Conflict."

The development of gender essentialism, or the belief that males and females have "essential" differences based on their biological sex and that these differences are foundational to defining acceptable roles and behaviors for men and women, can be traced historically to the Victorian age and increasing prosperity for a few in the wake of the Industrial Revolution.[11] As work increasingly moved outside the home to locations in factories, the split between work and domestic life grew.[12] Men were identified with the world of paid work and women with the world of domesticity, located in the home.[13] Thus the concept of "separate spheres" for men and women developed with women assigned to the private sphere and men to the public sphere.[14] Evangelical religion of that day accepted and promoted this idealized view of men identified with work and women with family, and incorporated it into their teachings and practices, where it has remained to this day.[15]

Inherent in the separate spheres is also the idea of a hierarchy between males and females:

> One hallmark of traditional evangelical Protestantism has been the adherence to neotraditionalism in which women are seen as subordinate to men. This particular gender ideology focuses on gender differences in family responsibilities and has its roots in the ideal of separate spheres for women and men that emerged during the late nineteenth century. Natural, even God-given essences were argued to be the basis of masculine aggression, worldly wisdom, and rationality and its complement, feminine submission, purity, piety, and domesticity—an argument that continues to be presented by a number of contemporary evangelical writers today.[16]

Essentialism and hierarchy were tied together inextricably, placing men in authority over women in a "natural, even God-given" structure.

In the wake of the women's movement in the mid-twentieth century, evangelicalism again faced a choice about whether to embrace the culture's views of women. The debate was quite strong. But this time the tide turned against society, with much of evangelicalism choosing to follow the earlier

11. Ross, "Separate Spheres or Shared Dominions?"; Gallagher and Smith, "Symbolic Traditionalism and Pragmatic Egalitarianism."

12. DeBerg, *Ungodly Women.*

13. Andersen and Hysock, *Thinking about Women.*

14. Ross, "Separate Spheres or Shared Dominions?"

15. Bendroth, "Last Gasp Patriarchy"; Ingersoll, "Engendered Conflict"; Ross, "Separate Spheres or Shared Dominions?"

16. Gallagher and Smith, "Symbolic Traditionalism and Pragmatic Egalitarianism," 212–13.

path of essentialist thought.[17] Both Ross and Ingersoll argue that gender essentialism has become entrenched within evangelicalism to the point that it now serves as a boundary marker and a test of orthodoxy for many.[18] Despite ongoing discussions, for many within evangelicalism today, essentialism, at least as an espoused theory, is non-negotiable. The belief in gender essentialism is both prevalent and persistent in evangelical religion, and the rest of this section seeks to understand why that is so, why women support it, whether any successful opposition exists, and what the implications may be for women in mission organizations today.

What Purpose Does Gender Essentialism Serve in Evangelical Religion?

Knowledge production, power, voice, and visibility are central themes in critical feminist research, and understanding how they function helps shed light on the strength of gender essentialism's hold on evangelical religion as well.[19] The first major function of gender essentialism in conservative protestant religion is that of preserving male power by controlling women, keeping them in a position of obedience to and dependence on men.[20] According to the essentialist view, men are responsible to provide materially for their families and lead them, both spiritually and in decision-making; women are to accept men's leadership and provision, and care for the family's needs by staying at home.[21] Leadership in home, church, and society is assigned to men, while nurturing husband and children is assigned to women.[22] So male rule and female submission are at the heart of the definitions of male and female roles.[23] According to Shaw, it is a need for order, hierarchy, and control over the women near them since they cannot control the external world that motivates men to maintain power over women in evangelical circles.[24]

---

17. Gallagher, "Marginalization of Evangelical Feminism"; Groothuis, *Women Caught in the Conflict.*

18. Ingersoll, *Evangelical Christian Women*; Ross, "Separate Spheres or Shared Dominions?"

19. Tisdell, "Poststructural Feminist Pedagogies."

20. Sowinska, "Ambiguous Women."

21. Gallagher and Smith, "Symbolic Traditionalism and Pragmatic Egalitarianism."

22. Sowinska, "Ambiguous Women."

23. Gallagher, "Marginalization of Evangelical Feminism"; Gallagher and Smith, "Symbolic Traditionalism and Pragmatic Egalitarianism."

24. Shaw, "Gracious Submission."

By assigning men the responsibility of providing materially for their families, of course, women are maintained in a position of economic dependence and are thus less likely to resist male power.[25] By assigning men spiritual authority over wives (and children) women are also maintained in a position of dependence, in a way that is both more subtle and potentially more powerful. If staying faithful to their religion means obeying men, some women will acquiesce in their pursuit of spirituality. Current rhetoric in evangelicalism says that women are equal in worth "before God" yet should "submit graciously" to male rule.[26] This vocabulary is an attempt to remove some of the sting of inequality while maintaining male power in structures that "disadvantage and control women."[27] Levitt and Ware point out that "distinct gender roles [are] often fashioned as comparable, but this perspective masks the fact that the division of responsibility assigned power, decision making, and economic freedom to one member of the marriage while self-negation is meted to the other."[28] The "equal in being but different in role" rhetoric is nonsense, of course, on two counts.[29] First, the myth of "separate but equal" has already been completely debunked in the area of race relations, since separate was found to be inherently unequal by the Supreme Court in 1947.[30] Second, proclaiming that women are of equal value spiritually before God while requiring them to submit to male spiritual authority is fundamentally senseless in that it claims women are simultaneously equal and unequal to men.[31] Yet for some the rhetoric may serve to soften the blow and make the relative positions of men and women more palatable.[32] The religious injunctions for women to be obedient, submissive, quiet homemakers aligns well with an unchallenged essentialist view, and helps explain why much of evangelical religion resists feminism—precisely because it challenges the very things essentialism and evangelicalism promote as values for women.[33]

25. Levitt and Ware, "Anything with Two Heads Is a Monster"; Shaw, "Gracious Submission."

26. Shaw, "Gracious Submission."

27. Shaw, "Gracious Submission," 64.

28. Levitt and Ware, "Anything with Two Heads Is a Monster," 1178.

29. Groothuis, "Equal in Being, Unequal in Role."

30. Goff, "Playing with the Boys"; Johnson et al., "African Americans and the Struggle for Opportunity in Florida."

31. Groothuis, "Equal in Being, Unequal in Role."

32. Gallagher and Smith, "Symbolic Traditionalism and Pragmatic Egalitarianism."

33. Gallagher, "Marginalization of Evangelical Feminism."

A second function of gender essentialism in evangelicalism is to serve as a boundary control between "the world" and "the believers."[34] Traditional attitudes toward gender can serve as a quickly-discernible indicator of a person's status as in or out of the community.[35] Gender essentialism, "which would be called sexism in a secular context is often seen as being endorsed by God in a religious context," making it a litmus test for orthodoxy.[36] Both Sowinska and Gallagher discuss how feminism in the evangelical church was successfully linked with perceptions of excesses of feminism in society, and thus discredited.[37] Further, it was also tied to theological liberalism and disbelief of the Bible, which would lead to a loss of true faith. Gallagher explains, "Evangelical authors . . . have successfully defined evangelical feminism as a version of theological liberalism, teetering on the edge of biblical relativism's slippery slope."[38] By equating feminism with a disbelief of the Bible, evangelical gender essentialists are able to prevent any further discussion on the topic.[39]

This function, especially when connected with male spiritual authority, also serves the purposes of strengthening male power. If males are the ones with spiritual authority, then they are also the ones who define the boundaries of "in" and "out." Bendroth noted that men became the defenders and definers of orthodoxy as evangelicalism was established.[40] Furthermore, from the 1930s on, men have limited women's access to theological education, thus limiting their ability to lead spiritually or to enter the clergy as professionals.[41] On the other hand, if women wanted to work overseas in missions, they faced fewer obstacles, since "historically, even the most conservative fundamentalists and evangelicals have permitted women to preach to the 'unsaved' in foreign lands. Limitations on women's preaching have almost always centered on women preaching to white, middle-class, American men."[42] Such an attitude is both racist and sexist, and clearly serves to protect the power of those who promote it. Yet challenging the structure is considered subversive and

---

34. Gallagher, "Marginalization of Evangelical Feminism"; Gallagher and Smith, "Symbolic Traditionalism and Pragmatic Egalitarianism."

35. Gallagher, "Marginalization of Evangelical Feminism."

36. Ingersoll, *Evangelical Christian Women*, 94.

37. Gallagher, "Marginalization of Evangelical Feminism"; Sowinska, "Ambiguous Women."

38. Gallagher, "Marginalization of Evangelical Feminism," 232.

39. Bendroth, *Fundamentalism & Gender*; Ingersoll, *Evangelical Christian Women*.

40. Bendroth, *Fundamentalism & Gender*.

41. Bendroth, *Fundamentalism & Gender*.

42. Ingersoll, *Evangelical Christian Women*, 130.

women who do so may find themselves quickly ostracized from the community.[43] English and Tisdell define religion as "an organized community of faith, with an official creed and codes of behavior (determined by those with the most power in these institutions)."[44] From this discussion, it is clear that evangelicalism is a religion, and that its "creeds and codes" related to gender are defined by men to maintain male power.

A third possible explanation for the current strength of gender essentialism in the evangelical world may be that women and men who no longer subscribe to gender essentialism simply leave the evangelical church. As women enter the workforce and are increasingly in contact with social gender norms of equality, they may begin to question and then leave the churches where they no longer fit.[45] Aune documents the shrinking membership of the evangelical church in the UK, noting that between 1985 and 2005 UK evangelical churches lost three times the number women as men, representing a departure rate double that of men given the higher numbers of female church membership.[46] These findings could possibly be substantiated by *The White House Project Report: Benchmarking Women's Leadership*, which studied the presence of female leaders in 10 sectors of American life. In the section on religion, the authors report that although women have always been the majority of religious followers, averaging 60 percent of any religious community, in a study done in 2007 by the Pew Forum on Religion & Public Life, they found that some groups with a stronger emphasis on gender essentialism have more male than female followers.[47] Neither Aune nor the White House report offers explicit data that women are leaving gender essentialist religions, but the theory is intriguing and both numbers and incidental evidence support that conclusion. If it is true that women and men who disagree with gender essentialist views simply leave, that could explain why gender essentialism still prevails in parts of the evangelical world.

Why Do Women Support Gender Essentialist Views?

Another important question to consider in searching the literature on gender essentialism among evangelicals is why women, in the largely egalitarian, equality-based societies of North America and the UK, would support gender essentialist views and their accompanying limitations on female personhood. The main reason for women's continued support is that accepting

43. Ingersoll, *Evangelical Christian Women*.
44. English and Tisdell, "Spirituality and Adult Education," 287.
45. Aune, "Evangelical Christianity and Women's Changing Lives."
46. Aune, "Evangelical Christianity and Women's Changing Lives."
47. Lapovsky, "White House Project Report."

gender roles equals being faithful, since the roles have become codified as doctrine.[48] Evangelicals believe that "the Bible delineated clear distinctions between men and women" meaning men and women show obedience to God by conforming to those roles.[49] Rejecting those roles would mean rejecting God's plan for humanity, because any "rejection of gender essentialism challenged the created order. God had ordained certain roles for men and women."[50] Because of the connection of gender roles with doctrine, any other perspective, such as the feminist perspective of gender as constructed, and indeed feminism as a movement itself, has been thoroughly demonized within the evangelical faith.[51] Feminism has been portrayed as the enemy of faith, of the family, and of society to such an extent that many evangelical women reject it outright.[52] Bendroth explains that evangelicals have become utterly opposed to feminism in all its forms.[53] And Sowinska adds that "the word 'feminism' carries with it an image of enormous negative energy . . . in the church."[54] Kidd makes an explicit link between demonizing feminism and supporting male power: portraying a negative image of feminism has become a successful way of controlling church women.[55] So evangelicals, and evangelical women, are strongly discouraged from reading any writings on women, particularly feminist scholarship that is produced outside the bounds of the evangelical community.

A few other authors offer other, more pragmatic reasons for women's acceptance of gender essentialism. Some suggest that women may actually benefit from these beliefs, and others think that women have learned to give verbal assent without actually following the demands of the belief system.

One suggested reason women may collude in these structures is that such hierarchy schemes may also be beneficial to women in some ways. For example, they may gain love, security, and respect and have husbands who are strongly committed to the family and children.[56] Gallagher and Smith further argue that by giving verbal support to the idea of the husband as leader, married women gain economic stability in a world where women continue to be

48. Ingersoll, *Evangelical Christian Women*; Ingersoll, "Engendered Conflict."

49. Dowland, "'Family Values' and the Formation of a Christian Right Agenda," 623.

50. Dowland, "'Family Values' and the Formation of a Christian Right Agenda," 623.

51. Dowland, "'Family Values' and the Formation of a Christian Right Agenda."

52. Wilcox, "Feminism and Anti-Feminism among Evangelical Women." Dowland, "'Family Values' and the Formation of a Christian Right Agenda."

53. Bendroth, "Last Gasp Patriarchy."

54. Sowinska, "Ambiguous Women," 170.

55. Kidd, *Dance of the Dissident Daughter*.

56. Gallagher and Smith, "Symbolic Traditionalism and Pragmatic Egalitarianism"; Woodberry and Smith, "Fundamentalism Et Al."

economically dependent on men.[57] Levitt and Ware also note the financial dependence of women on men, and the threat of poverty, as a significant reason women stay even in unsafe relationships.[58] Aune hypothesizes that women who desire "defined roles and the patriarchal bargain of male protection may gravitate towards evangelical religion."[59] After all, such churches support the idea of women at home, raising children and caring for the house, so women who desire that lifestyle find their ideals supported in these churches.[60] Thus emotionally, relationally, and financially, women may gain by giving at least symbolic support to notions of gender essentialism.

Another possible explanation for women's collusion is suggested by Pevey, Williams, and Ellison.[61] In an attempt to discover how women maintain happiness and self-esteem within a strongly patriarchal structure, they too found that women had pragmatic reasons for accepting a masculine God. They argue that "conservative religion can enhance women's relationships with their husbands by making the men more communicative, sensitive, and caring" and husbands may be more likely to obey a male rather than a female god.[62] They also found that a verbal assent to male rule was usually accompanied by a description of egalitarian marriage practices. Multiple studies have found a similar disjuncture between espoused theories and theories-in-use among women in conservative evangelical churches. The entire focus of Gallagher's earlier work, aptly titled, "Symbolic traditionalism and pragmatic egalitarianism" is the distinction between espoused theories and theories in use among evangelical women.[63] Bendroth also draws attention the inconsistencies between rhetoric and practice in evangelical gender relationships.[64] Though she does not propose a framework to understand the inconsistencies, she does argue that their prevalence should prevent scholars from viewing evangelicalism and gender constructs as either monolithic or simplistic.[65]

57. Gallagher and Smith, "Symbolic Traditionalism and Pragmatic Egalitarianism."

58. Levitt and Ware, "Anything with Two Heads Is a Monster."

59. Aune, "Evangelical Christianity and Women's Changing Lives," 285.

60. Aune, "Evangelical Christianity and Women's Changing Lives."

61. Pevey et al., "Male God Imagery and Female Submission."

62. Pevey et al., "Male God Imagery and Female Submission," 184.

63. Gallagher and Smith, "Symbolic Traditionalism and Pragmatic Egalitarianism."

64. Bendroth, "Last Gasp Patriarchy."

65. Bendroth, "Last Gasp Patriarchy."

Can a Feminist Ethos Exist in an Evangelical Setting?

Several scholars have examined attempts to introduce an egalitarian ethos to the evangelical subculture in the last generation. "Christian feminism," sometimes known as "egalitarianism" rejects "any restrictions based on gender alone."[66] Sowinska and Gallagher have both written on the issue. Sowinska theorizes that egalitarianism is making some impact on evangelicalism, though she also recognizes that many women have been ostracized and eventually left their faith over the issue, while others may have successfully negotiated a middle space between evangelicalism and feminism where they can comfortably live.[67] Gallagher has a somewhat less hopeful view. She argues that the weight of patriarchy has been enough to keep an egalitarian ethos on the margins of the subculture. Among critical factors she cites are the weight of evangelical academic institutions and publishing houses, which are largely controlled by gender essentialists.[68] Ingersoll also examines attempts to hold "middle ground" by those who want to remain evangelicals yet not accept patriarchy. "Maintaining the middle ground is not easy" seems like an understatement, especially given that the subtitle of her book is "war stories in the gender battles."[69] She supplies plenty of war stories, including significant defeats, for those who seek to incorporate feminist equality beliefs within the religious structures of evangelicalism. There is also some evidence that women are socialized into accepting gender views when they join conservative churches, rather than bringing change.[70]

Both Sowinska and Gallagher trace the history of the two main opposing groups which write and publish within evangelicalism on their respective positions.[71] The Council of Biblical Manhood and Womanhood (CBMW) was founded in 1987 to promote gender essentialism throughout the evangelical world.[72] In contrast, Christians for Biblical Equality (CBE) was founded in 1986 to write and publish material on gender parity and be a resource for churches and people wanting to examine the issue from within evangelical scholarship.[73] Both of these groups attempt to write on the issue in terms that will appeal to the evangelical constituency. This means that

66. Sowinska, "Ambiguous Women," 173.

67. Sowinska, "Ambiguous Women."

68. Gallagher, "Marginalization of Evangelical Feminism."

69. Ingersoll, *Evangelical Christian Women*, 44.

70. Cooley, "Discipling Sisters."

71. Gallagher, "Marginalization of Evangelical Feminism"; Sowinska, "Ambiguous Women."

72. Gallagher, "Marginalization of Evangelical Feminism."

73. Gallagher, "Marginalization of Evangelical Feminism."

they concentrate on each other's arguments, and mainly quote from and refute each other. As one reviewer wryly commented, "One notices in both of the books under review that evangelicals quote mostly evangelicals."[74] Partly because of this, and partly because the Christian feminist writers tend to focus on theological rather than practical issues, the influence of the egalitarian viewpoint has remained small.[75]

Results of Gender Essentialism in Evangelicalism

Some of the results of gender essentialism have already been mentioned, such as the possibility that evangelical churches are losing women members, particularly those who do not conform to the traditional homemaker paradigm, at a faster rate than they are losing men. Part of the problem is that the debate stays centered within evangelical scholarship, meaning that information such as that found for this study is not often discussed. By debating the meaning of Greek words and phrases, the exegesis of ancient texts, and the proper hermeneutical methods of interpretation, gender essentialists have managed to restrict the conversation to issues of little importance to most church members today.[76] In contrast, issues of sexism, justice, abuse of power, domestic violence, and social transformation, which might well be of interest to the larger population, are barely addressed. By repeated charges that non-essentialists do not believe the Bible, essentialists have managed to keep the debate focused in the areas that appear most favorable to themselves and most threatening to the subculture's identity.

IMPLICATIONS FOR MISSION ORGANIZATIONS

Gender essentialism confronts a cognitive dissonance problem in missions with the participation of married women in the work at all. Fitzgerald studied the work of single Irish Protestant missionary women in the eighteenth and nineteenth centuries. In explaining how single women, who were initially not sent out to work, eventually made inroads she notes:

> Married women presented a dilemma for evangelical societies such as the CMS. While on the one hand the CMS relied on married women to play an adjunct role and epitomise the "ideal" Christian wife and mother, on the other hand, missionary work took women away from the home, their sphere of influence.[77]

74. Bishop, "Book Reviews," 5.
75. Ingersoll, *Evangelical Christian Women*; Sowinska, "Ambiguous Women."
76. Bendroth, *Fundamentalism & Gender*.
77. Fitzgerald, "To Unite Their Strength with Ours," 150.

The discrepancy between gender essentialist ideals for married women and the demands of the work was a significant factor in mission organizations agreeing to send single women to help with the work. In part the perceived need for women to participate in the work at all came as an unexpected consequence of the Victorian ideal of separate spheres.[78] Since the ideal assigned actions of love and compassion to women, it also became the basis for women to exercise that love and compassion outside the home as well as inside, in works of reform and moral improvement in the wider society.[79]

Gender essentialism may account for the overall silence in the literature regarding missionary women. By the end of the nineteenth century, women accounted for more than two-thirds of the Protestant missionary force worldwide and that number remains constant today.[80] Yet very little has been written about current missionary women's work, and it mainly focuses on mental health and well-being. Two psychological studies on the well-being of missionary women have been published. The first, by Hall and Duvall found that women classified as "homemakers" and "support workers" were happier than their counterparts who were actively involved in ministry alongside their husbands.[81] The authors note that this finding is contrary to most other research on married women. A later study by Crawford and DeVries found the opposite to be true, but only marginally so.[82] They suggest that subculture expectations of gender essentialism combined with a tendency to "put their best foot forward" in representing their lives and work may account for this discrepancy between studies of married missionary women and the general population.[83] Two more studies focused on missionaries' marital satisfaction. The first, by Rosik and Pandzic was a longitudinal study of marital function in missionary couples.[84] The second, by Bikos, et al. compared missionary wives to other expatriate wives in the areas of mental health and well-being.[85] Both of these studies found that women's satisfaction was lower than men's, that it declined over time, and that women were nevertheless still tightly tied to gender-essentialist roles. Bikos, et al. found

---

78. Ross, "Separate Spheres or Shared Dominions?"

79. Ross, "Separate Spheres or Shared Dominions?"

80. Robert, *American Women in Mission.*

81. Hall and Duvall, "Married Women in Missions."

82. Crawford and DeVries, "Relationship between Role Perception and Well-Being in Married Female Missionaries."

83. Crawford and DeVries, "Relationship between Role Perception and Well-Being in Married Female Missionaries," 195.

84. Rosik and Pandzic, "Marital Satisfaction among Christian Missionaries."

85. Bikos et al., "First-Year Adaptation of Female, Expatriate Religious and Humanitarian Aid Workers."

the loss of mental health and functioning in the wives of faith workers to be "alarming" and were puzzled that the women continue to endorse the life role while sustaining such low mental health and marital satisfaction. Yet beyond history and psychology, the literature is silent on missionary women. Gender essentialism may lie behind this silence, since women are presumed to be in the home rather than active workers.

This assumption reflects yet another aspect of missionary women's lives, the fact that they are frequently structured as part of a two-person career, which is another aspect of gender essentialism as it is lived by believers. The concept was first named in 1973 by sociologist Hanna Papanek, who described it as:

> a special combination of roles which I call the "two-person single career." This combination of formal and informal institutional demands . . . is placed on both members of a married couple of whom only the man is employed by the institution.[86]

She explained that the two-person career was often seen among corporate executives, high-level politicians, academicians, and government agencies, particularly in the military and diplomatic services.[87] The two-person career, she argued, fit perfectly with "the stereotype of the wife as supporter, comforter, backstage manager, home maintainer, and main rearer of children."[88] It begins "before the career itself . . . when the husband it interviewed for a job . . . and is called 'finding out whether the wife is suitable.'"[89] It includes activities such as volunteer work, hospitality, and children's parties, which appear to be optional but in reality are highly expected.[90] The woman is expected to be "satisfied with knowing the extent of her contribution to her husband's work and to the growth and development of her children."[91] Finally, Papanek commented, "needless to say, the wife's contribution is usually not directly acknowledged, nor is it directly remunerated."[92] That this description also applies to clergy marriages is clear.[93] In the Protestant faith,

---

86. Papanek, "Men, Women, and Work," 852.

87. Papanek, "Men, Women, and Work."

88. Papanek, "Men, Women, and Work," 853.

89. Papanek, "Men, Women, and Work," 858–59.

90. Papanek, "Men, Women, and Work."

91. Papanek, "Men, Women, and Work."

92. Papanek, "Men, Women, and Work," 863.

93. Frame and Shehan, "Relationship between Work and Well-Being in Clergywomen"; Frame and Shehan, "Care for the Caregiver"; Frame and Shehan, "Work and Well-Being in the Two-Person Career"; Murphy-Geiss, "Married to the Minister."

"hiring a minister has long been a two-for-one deal."[94] Mission work functions similarly to the clergy marriage and is almost always characterized by the two-person career structure.[95]

Gender essentialist ideas also have an impact on leadership within mission organizations. Farley notes that male and female missionaries differ in their preference for thinking (T) and feeling (F) on the Meyers-Briggs inventory in ways comparable to the general population. He describes the connection between women missionaries and male leadership this way:

> However, whereas most missionaries serving overseas are female, UK-based mission agency executive staff are predominately (72%) male (Brierley, 2008). If these leaders are typical male missionaries, then their decision making process differs from that of many of their overseas personnel, and their personal development plan should aim to raise awareness of and strengthen their less preferred decision-making function.[96]

Although she does not refer to the idea of gender essentialism as such, Robert notes both the resistance to women's leadership and women's voices in missiology, and the bias against what mission organizations perceive as "women's work."[97] These two threads, she argues, have caused women to perform the bulk of mission work while having little say in its direction. She maintains that changing global realities require mission organizations

> to take seriously the centrality of women in the mission of the church, to recognize their contributions, to develop missiologies that put gender analysis back into mission theory, and to respond to the needs of women for social justice, security, healing, and hope.[98]

According to these authors confronting gender essentialism is significant to the work of missionary women for a number of reasons: their participation in the work, their psychological and emotional well-being, leadership, and having a voice in the theoretical work in the field of missiology.

---

94. Murphy-Geiss, "Married to the Minister," 933.

95. Hall and Duvall, "Married Women in Missions."

96. Farley, "Psychological Type Preferences of Female Missionaries from the United Kingdom," 668.

97. Robert, "Women in World Mission."

98. Robert, "Women in World Mission," 61.

Section Summary

The connection between gender essentialism and evangelicalism is well-documented in the literature. The main reasons for the connection are thought to be boundary control, male power, and the loss of members who do not subscribe to such views. Whether evangelicalism can open itself to include non-essentialist views of gender is yet to be seen. The implications for faith-based non-profits working around the world, and the women in those agencies, seem discouraging. If the agencies and the women themselves hold to the same views as the subculture from which they come, then a change in organizational practices might require a serious change in philosophy that these agencies are afraid to undergo. On the other hand, it is possible that the need to recruit new workers, the continual need for engagement in social profit endeavors worldwide, and a philosophical commitment to charity could be enough to push mission organizations into the vanguard of a new approach to gender within the evangelical tradition. In the end the question may revolve around which forces are stronger: the ones driving change or the ones resisting it.[99]

THE GAP

The common thread running through both the leadership studies and the religious studies is one of determinism. It may be called "gender-role stereotypes" or "gender essentialism," but regardless of the name it reflects a deterministic view of the nature of humanity. However much society strives to correct deterministic imbalances due to gender (and race and ethnicity) they continue to plague us today. Many studies have been conducted in the last forty years demonstrating the strength of gender-role expectations on women in the workplace, and the effects on women's advancement to leadership. Yet there is still a missing piece in the literature. To date no studies have been done of women leaders in evangelical mission organizations where the gender-role expectations may even have been codified into doctrinal standards of how a good Christian woman should behave. These women may have been appointed to leadership roles which required them to use capacities which align more closely with the gender-role expectations for men. Yet according to the evangelical world view, they may be required to fulfill the gender-role expectations for women. In fact there is very little literature at all regarding women's leadership in any type of evangelical non-profit organization.[100] In her 2010 dissertation, Scott conducted what

---

99. Coghlan and Brannick, *Doing Action Research in Your Own Organization*.
100. Scott, "Women Leaders in Protestant, Evangelical Nonprofit Institutions."

may be the first study of the perception of women leaders in evangelical nonprofit organizations. She included publishers, evangelistic groups, philanthropic organizations, discipleship groups, and service groups, but not mission organizations.[101] Although the literature on gender-role stereotypes for women in business is abundant, there is little literature that applies the theory to women leading in non-profits, evangelical institutions, or mission organizations. This study, therefore, sought to combine these three threads of gender-role stereotypes, women leaders, and evangelical mission institutions, to discover how women navigate these issues and what types of constraints they face as they fulfill their responsibilities. By studying them, we may gain a deeper understanding of the strength of gender-role stereotypes within evangelical religion, and the impact of those role expectations on women living and working within that tradition

There is abundant research on women as organizational leaders and a good deal of scholarship has focused on understanding the diminishing numbers of women at higher levels of the hierarchy. The concept of gender-role stereotypes that are embedded in our society offers a cogent explanation for the lack of women leaders near the top of organizations. These stereotypes color our perceptions of women, portraying them as unsuited to lead if they display female characteristics and unfeminine if they display leader characteristics. Thus women are caught in a double bind where they cannot fulfill both sets of expectations and are correspondingly devalued in one way or the other.

For women in evangelical religion, the situation is similar, with the added restriction of stereotypical behaviors being expressly valued rather than covert. For them to lead they must violate not only a stereotype but an espoused theory of what a "good Christian woman" should be. They must also negotiate a patriarchal structure that offers little in the way of support or training for them in their leadership.

The available research on present-day women missionaries is quite thin. Crawford and DeVries comment that "female missionaries have been a neglected population both in the writing of mission history and in empirical studies in the field of mental health."[102] To that I would add that they have been a neglected population in any kind of study, including the study of leadership. Yet as in so many fields, the women are there, diligently doing the work, whether they are noticed or not. My hope in this study was to give voice to some of them, for their own sakes and potentially for

---

101. Scott, "Women Leaders in Protestant, Evangelical Nonprofit Institutions."

102. Crawford and DeVries, "Relationship between Role Perception and Well-Being in Married Female Missionaries," 187.

the organizations that support them. I also wanted to learn more about how women learn to lead, and how they handle the dissonance that may arise when they do.

SUMMARY OF LITERATURE REVIEW

In the literature review I have taken a bird's eye view of the development of feminism, and looked more closely at its insistence that gender is constructed rather than biological. According to feminist thought, gender as a category serves to support male power and privilege, and enables males to control knowledge production to further cement their power.

I also showed that gender essentialist thought is pervasive in society as well as in organizations, and that it affects women in organizations just as much as in the personal and private sphere. While feminism rejects gender essentialist thought, society continues to be structured and create structures that reinforce essentialist beliefs, leading to essentialist-seeming practices.

In evangelical religion, gender essentialism is openly embraced as true and valid. Because biology is thought to be determined by God, gender roles are also assumed to be divinely ordained. They are then used to determine what women should do, and the fact that religious roles correspond almost completely to social roles is never considered.

5

Methodology

THE PURPOSE OF THIS study was to understand how women lead and make meaning of their leadership in evangelical mission organizations.
    The research questions for this study were:

1. How have these women become leaders and learned to lead?

2. What if any forms of resistance or subversive behavior do they use in order to lead in a patriarchal culture?

3. How do they and the organizations they work in account for their leadership?

In this chapter I will describe the design and methodology of this study, including my epistemological and theoretical frameworks, the sample selection, data collection and analysis plan, validity and reliability issues, and limitations of the study.

DESIGN OF THE STUDY

This was a qualitative study rooted in a constructivist epistemology. It was situated in a critical feminist framework, and intended to produce emancipatory knowledge for both the women I investigated and the organizations in which they worked.

Epistemology

I approached this study with an epistemological framework of constructivism. An epistemology describes "the nature of knowledge or how you know what you know."[1] Epistemology is a fundamental issue in scholarship, since it determines what we can know, how we study it, and whether such knowledge is legitimate and adequate.[2] According to constructivism "each individual mentally constructs the world of experience through cognitive processes."[3] Further, "constructivism . . . points up the unique experience of each of us."[4] So a constructivist epistemology argues that knowledge is constructed through an individual's experiences.[5]

Constructivism was the best approach for my study because it allowed space for each individual's life events, background, understanding, and personality to contribute in constructing the meaning of any given object, event, or experience; moreover, because meaning is constructed through the interaction of people with their world, different people construct different meanings even from the same event.[6] The literature showed that women experience both organizational leadership and evangelical religion differently than men do; constructivism allowed me to investigate each woman's meanings, and considers them true and valid for her.[7] A constructivist framework also allowed me to work together with the participants to understand their experiences and how they make meaning of them.

Women leaders also live and work in a social and cultural system which affects their meaning-making. Social constructionism argues that meaning and culture are both constructed by the members of the society and continually construct those members according to the existing system. Everyone is "born into a world of meaning" which was built by those before us and operates on a more or less consensual basis.[8] Social constructionism also "emphasizes the hold our culture has on us: it shapes the way in which we see things (even the way in which we feel things!) and gives us a quite definite view of the world."[9] The cultural context in which my participants worked creates an entirely different kind of space for women than it does for men. That space is also both like and unlike the space businesses create for women executives. My participants enter

1. Glesne, *Becoming Qualitative Researchers*, 6.

2. Glesne, *Becoming Qualitative Researchers*.

3. Young and Collin, "Introduction."

4. Crotty, *Foundations of Social Research*, 58.

5. Bierema, "Feminist Approach to HRD Research"; Crotty, *Foundations of Social Research*; Merriam, *Qualitative Research in Practice*.

6. Crotty, *Foundations of Social Research*.

7. Crotty, *Foundations of Social Research*.

8. Crotty, *Foundations of Social Research*, 54. Murphy, *Constructivism*.

9. Crotty, *Foundations of Social Research*, 58.

into and further construct, or possibly deconstruct, the existing context, hegemony, and culture, all the while making their own personal meaning of what it is to be a woman executive in such a job. In order to best understand how they do so, I also had to consider their context.

Theoretical Perspective

Constructivism and social constructionism laid a good foundation to understand my participants' experiences. Alone, however, they were not enough to understand the entire story. I also needed to draw on critical theory to further elucidate their stories.

Critical theory. Critical theory is particularly suspicious of the socially constructed meanings of society, since it finds that those meanings are frequently structured to maintain existing hegemonies.[10] My participants' access to and ability to function well in leadership roles had to do with power structures in the organizations. Using critical theory we were able together to question those structures, because critical theory makes existing power structures visible so that they can be challenged and potentially changed for the better of individuals and societies.[11] Yet it also involved risk because by questioning the powers that be, questioners may perhaps place themselves in a position of real or perceived antagonism to those powers. Still, basing the study in critical theory may have helped the participants move towards an activist, transformative stance, and away from an attitude of defeatism. It may have encouraged them to believe that the world can be changed, rather than being entirely beyond their control.[12]

Feminist thought. Within critical theory, this study was further situated in post-structural feminist thought. Feminism specifically addresses issues of power, knowledge, and hegemony as they are created and reinforced through patriarchal social structures that adversely affect women. Patriarchy is firmly grounded in the construction of gender, which in turn determines power, knowledge, and voice and the relative positions of men and women. Patriarchy helped explain the experiences of the women in the study, and the relatively low numbers of women leaders in these organizations.

10. Crotty, *Foundations of Social Research.*

11. Brookfield, *Power of Critical Theory*; Merriam and Caffarella, *Learning in Adulthood.*

12. Freire, *Pedagogy of the Oppressed.*

According to feminism, gender is constructed and serves to maintain males in a position of privilege and power in relation to females.[13] Since gender construction defines masculine as whatever is different from and superior to whatever is feminine, hierarchy is inseparable from the essentialist gender construct.[14] Males can then use that power to determine what is considered knowable, creating knowledge to support their privileged position.[15] Concentrating power and knowledge in male hands has the effect of making women's voices, women's perspectives, and women's ways of making meaning almost disappear.[16] Thus feminist scholars speak of women "coming to voice" or learning to speak for themselves from their own perspectives as part of their emancipation.[17] Often this involves recognizing the social and familial structures that disadvantage women, such as unpaid work and work that primarily supports men, and gaining the confidence to speak those truths aloud.[18]

In this study I was particularly interested in exploring how organizational structures and perspectives may be male-dominated and constructed to favor of men. I was also interested in exploring how women's work, even as organizational leaders, might be constructed as primarily supporting men's work in a two-person career model, rather than leading in their own right. I hoped to learn to what degree the women were aware of this, what strategies they used to function in such an environment, and what happened if they chose to challenge the hegemonic view. Finally, from a critical stance, I was also interested in bringing change, not simply understanding the present circumstances. This goal of change is a hallmark of all forms of critical scholarship.[19]

13. Andersen and Collins, *Race, Class & Gender*; Sheppard, "Women Managers' Perceptions of Gender and Organizational Life"; Maher, "Twisted Privileges."

14. Gilligan, "Woman's Place in Man's Life Cycle"; Marshall, *Women Managers*; Zinn et al., "Sex and Gender through the Prism of Difference."

15. Brookfield, *Power of Critical Theory*.

16. Zinn et al., "Sex and Gender through the Prism of Difference."

17. Gallagher, "Everyday Classroom as Problematic"; Johnson-Bailey and Cervero, "Power Dynamics in Teaching and Learning Practices"; Misawa, "Queer Race Pedagogy for Educators in Higher Education."

18. Andersen and Hysock, *Thinking about Women*.

19. Crotty, *Foundations of Social Research*.

Methodology

In choosing a research methodology, the main consideration is what will best serve the research purpose and best answer the research questions.[20] Since I was "interested in understanding how people interpret their experiences, how they construct their worlds, and what meaning they attribute to their experiences," the best way to do that was to interview women in positions of leadership in evangelical mission organizations.[21] Both the underlying constructivist epistemology and the characteristics of qualitative research made it the most suitable method for my study.

Characteristics of basic qualitative research. Qualitative research has four fundamental characteristics that supported my study in important ways: a focus on meaning, an understanding that the researcher is the primary instrument, an inductive approach, and a rich description of the findings.[22] First, a qualitative study intends to understand meaning as people construct it in interaction with their environment and their experience. Women who have accepted a leadership role in an evangelical mission organization quite likely have spent some time, whether they think of it in those terms or not, constructing meaning for their presence in a job that is supposedly not open to women. They were the ones who could explain how they understand their presence in that role and the meaning they make of not conforming to expectations of female submission.

Second, the idea that the researcher is the instrument also had implications for this study.[23] Since qualitative research depends heavily on a conversation between the researcher and the participant, I as the researcher became central to the process, including how data were collected and understood.[24] My history of work in the same field meant I could be both insider and outsider simultaneously, and on several different identity scales.[25] For example, the participants seemed to perceive me as an "indigenous insider," or a member of the community who wholly identifies with it.[26] Some of them asked me about my history and status as part

---

20. Crotty, *Foundations of Social Research*; Griffin and Phoenix, "Relationship between Qualitative and Quantitative Research"; Gringeri et al., "What Makes It Feminist?"

21. Merriam, *Qualitative Research*, 5; Nielsen, *Feminist Research Methods*.

22. Merriam, *Qualitative Research*.

23. Henwood and Pidgeon, "Remaking the Link."

24. deMarrais and Lapan, *Foundations for Research*.

25. Naples, "Outsider Phenomenon."

26. Acker, "In/out/Side."

of establishing this understanding before the interview started. However, "the boundaries between the two positions are not all that clearly delineated" meaning that their perceptions of my status did not necessarily align with my own perceptions.[27] I considered myself more of an "indigenous outsider" since I am no longer intimately involved with a mission organization.[28] The distinction is still not accurate, however, since my husband is an insider and therefore I am too, by proxy and by virtue of the two-person career model. The complexity involved in determining my status meant that I "experience[d] moments of being both insider and outsider" during the course of the interviews.[29] There was some immediate sense of connection, yet education and ideology also made me something of an outsider. On balance, my history of work in the same field appeared to cause participants to identify me as an insider and appeared to help create rapport as we co-constructed knowledge of their role.[30]

Third, the inductive nature of qualitative research suited this study. An inductive study starts by gathering information to understand what is happening, rather than starting with a hypothesis.[31] This is particularly useful when little data exist or theory has not been studied with a particular group of participants.[32] In this study the inductive quality was particularly important, because this group of women leaders had not yet been investigated. Studies on women in organizational leadership showed some potential similarities, yet until mission organizations themselves were investigated, we could not know to what degree the existing theory applied to them, and where differences lay.

Finally, qualitative studies offer the opportunity to portray the findings through "rich description."[33] For this study, I hope to have become something of a translator regarding my participants' lives, in order to present my understanding of their world.[34] I hope also to have functioned as a transformer, allowing readers to "identify with the problems, worries, joys, and dreams" of the participants so that these women's stories could begin to be told.[35]

27. Merriam et al., "Power and Positionality," 405.

28. Acker, "In/out/Side."

29. Merriam et al., "Power and Positionality," 416.

30. deMarrais and Lapan, *Foundations for Research*.

31. Merriam, *Qualitative Research*; Merriam, *Qualitative Research in Practice*.

32. Merriam, *Qualitative Research in Practice*.

33. Merriam, *Qualitative Research*; Merriam, *Qualitative Research in Practice*.

34. Glesne, *Becoming Qualitative Researchers*.

35. Glesne, *Becoming Qualitative Researchers*, 175.

Characteristics of feminist research. There are three reasons why feminist research was best suited for my study: because it was done "for" women not "on" them, because gender was at the forefront of this study, and because a goal of this research was to enable possible change in the future. Feminism is anything but monolithic, but these three hallmarks characterize most work that is considered feminist.[36]

First of all, feminist research is done "for" women, not "on" them, meaning that it is undertaken to benefit women and other marginalized groups, not just know something about them.[37] This study took a feminist approach because "feminists conduct research for women. Whether it be by seeking knowledge from and about women . . . or to change women's lives . . . a feminist methodology aims at creating knowledge that is beneficial to women and other minorities."[38] The participants were integral contributors to the research process, in keeping with the ideals of a constructivist view of knowledge.[39] Together they and I could begin to create an understanding of evangelical mission organizations that may benefit other women who lead and work there.

Second, this study is feminist because women, and issues of gender, were at the center. Foregrounding gender is fundamental to feminist research.[40] This study focused on the lived experience of women in positions of leadership in a subculture where gender norms were often strongly endorsed. Gender was crucial to the study because it affects the "structure of reality" for these women, meaning it reached into their very ontology.[41] Ontology is also part of a feminist understanding, as Stanley explains:

> That is, "feminism" is not merely a "perspective," a way of seeing; nor even this plus an epistemology, a way of knowing; it is also an ontology, or a way of being in the world. What is distinctly feminist about a concern with research processes is that this

36. Reinharz, *Feminist Methods in Social Research*; Tong, *Feminist Thought.*

37. Bierema, "Feminist Approach to HRD Research"; Harding, "Rethinking Standpoint Epistemology"; Henwood and Pidgeon, "Remaking the Link"; Hesse-Biber and Yaiser, *Feminist Perspectives on Social Research*; Nielsen, *Feminist Research Methods*; Stanley, *Feminist Praxis*; Westkott, "Feminist Criticism of the Social Sciences."

38. Hesse-Biber and Yaiser, *Feminist Perspectives on Social Research.*

39. Crotty, *Foundations of Social Research*; Griffin and Phoenix, "Relationship between Qualitative and Quantitative research"; Gringeri et al., "What Makes It Feminist?"

40. Cook and Fonow, "Knowledge and Women's Interests"; Sandlin, "Structure and Subjectivity"; Creese and Frisby, "Unpacking Relationships in Feminist Community Research"; deMarrais and Lapan, *Foundations for Research.*

41. Crotty, *Foundations of Social Research*, 10.

constitutes an invitation to explore the conditions and circumstances of feminist ontology.[42]

For feminists, ontology considers how the nature of existence and the
structure of reality in an androcentric world have come to regard women
(as well as other groups) as "other."[43] Then scholars can focus on creating
knowledge about women and their world on women's own terms, recognizing that the condition of "other" has often left that knowledge "hidden
from mainstream society."[44] Hidden knowledge lacks power, so making that
knowledge known is one way of moving women towards social and organizational parity.[45] This study intended to bring to light women leaders' work
in an androcentric world, offering them more voice and perhaps greater
power in the future in their organizations.

This potential for change reflects the third quality of feminist research
that applied to this study.[46] Working for change is part of the meaning of
feminist research as knowledge "for" women. As Stanley puts it, "succinct-
ly the point is to change the world, not only to study it."[47] Women make up
the majority of the workforce in most evangelical mission organizations,
yet are remarkably scarce in positions of leadership; this situation needs to
change. This study sought to place women, who have often been invisible
and silent in existing, androcentric research into mission organizations, in
the center. Focusing on them and their experiences was one step towards
disrupting and contesting their oppression in a world constructed with
men as the norm.[48]

This study, in keeping with a feminist research ethos, sought to benefit
women, intended to make women leaders' lives and concerns central, and
sought to unbalance the power that has kept women subordinated to men
for so long. These three characteristics are qualities of research that can be
applied in any study or research approach. So what are the differences between basic qualitative research and feminist qualitative research, and why
was the latter preferable for my study?

**Differences between basic qualitative research and feminist qualita-
tive research.** The main difference between basic qualitative research and

42. Stanley, *Feminist Praxis*.
43. Stanley, *Feminist Praxis*.
44. Hesse-Biber and Yaiser, *Feminist Perspectives on Social Research*, 3.
45. Bierema, "Feminist Approach to HRD Research."
46. Glesne, *Becoming Qualitative Researchers*.
47. Stanley, *Feminist Praxis*.
48. Hesse-Biber and Yaiser, *Feminist Perspectives on Social Research*.

feminist qualitative research is its ultimate purpose. Basic qualitative research is interpretive, seeking to understand, while feminist qualitative research is critical, seeking to change. The former "accepts the status quo" while the latter "seeks to bring about change" by paying attention to power inequities in the status quo.[49] Sandlin states that "a critical study using qualitative methods differs from a mainstream qualitative study in that the research questions and data collection set out to make the workings of societal power visible."[50] So feminist qualitative research embraces the same assumptions, characteristics, and approaches of basic qualitative research and carries them one step further to become an instrument of social change. Since I hoped for change, a feminist qualitative approach was preferable.

This study could also have served to support the women, and in that sense have been for them. If they had thought about gender issues but not had freedom to vocalize that, the study could have affirmed those hidden thoughts. Brookfield explains that "when someone else's words illuminate or confirm a privately realized insight, we feel affirmed and recognized. Seeing a personal insight stated as a theoretical proposition makes us more likely to take seriously our own reasoning and judgments."[51] That affirmation could support them and become another step towards change.[52]

Section Summary

To summarize, a feminist, qualitative research study best suited my research purposes for several reasons. The assumptions underlying qualitative research—a constructivist view of knowledge and a focus on understanding how people experience and make meaning of life events—combined with a critical stance and a desire for change, were foundational to this study. The methodological choice of feminist qualitative research was predicated on what I hoped to learn from the women. Westmarland explains that "although a survey may be the best way to discover the prevalence of problems, interviews are needed to fully understand women's experiences and theorise these experiences with a view towards social change."[53]

A good choice of a research problem is one that may reflect gaps in the literature or represent a concept that has not been examined.[54] It may also seek to explain something that is unclear, or consider a discrepancy

49. Crotty, *Foundations of Social Research*, 113.
50. Sandlin, "Structure and Subjectivity," 372.
51. Brookfield, *Power of Critical Theory*, 5–6.
52. Ely et al., "Taking Gender into Account."
53. Westmarland, "Quantitative/Qualitative Debate and Feminist Research," 230.
54. deMarrais and Lapan, *Foundations for Research*.

between "stated and implemented policies or theories."[55] The study that I conducted was well-suited to feminist qualitative research in all of these ways. Prior to the study I did not find any literature on women leaders in mission organizations, indicating a gap. The presence of women in positions of leadership in a worldview that says women should not lead showed a discrepancy between theory and practice, which a qualitative study was well-suited to explore. A feminist approach was ideal because it took the women's accounts of their experiences seriously and involved them in constructing knowledge about their own situation.[56]

PILOT STUDY

For the pilot study I conducted three interviews in the fall of 2010. Each one was approximately seventy-five minutes long, and I recorded and transcribed all three. Two were conducted face to face and one by phone. I analyzed the data using the constant comparative method as well as narrative analysis, and wrote up the preliminary findings for two classes.

From these studies I found that my interview guide worked fairly well. I had known one woman as a colleague for several years, though since we lived and worked in different countries we rarely talked. The other two I met through email shortly before interviewing them. Yet each of them seemed quite open and honest with me, opening up fairly quickly about some of the less pleasant aspects of their leadership journeys. One repeated several times how good it was to be able to talk about all of that with someone, and my former colleague was insistent that this research needed to be done so that organizational practices can improve.

The most challenging part of the process was monitoring my own responses. First, as an insider, I had to be careful not to assume shared meaning, but to probe for clarification as needed. Second, I had to pay attention to navigating my own emotions and reactions to some of the more egregious parts of their stories. As a feminist constructivist, I recognized that my responses were part of creating the shared meaning; yet I also needed to monitor myself so that my emotions did not become more prominent than those of my respondents.

The other significant thing I discovered in the pilot study, which I had suspected before starting, was the respondents' almost desperate need to be sure of confidentiality in my reporting. One respondent prefaced numerous comments with a need for reassurance that I would not tell anyone she said this. Another participant went so far as to temporarily withdraw her

55. Merriam, *Qualitative Research in Practice*.
56. Reinharz, *Feminist Methods in Social Research*.

permission for me to use her data. After thinking it over again, she decided that the need of the study outweighed her personal worries, fortunately, so that I was able to incorporate the data from the pilot study into my final study. But I was keenly aware that she could change her mind yet again. So a critical lesson for me was that maintaining these women's privacy was indispensable to the success of the study.

SAMPLE SELECTION

In selecting the participants for this study, both the context, in terms of the kind of organization in which the woman works, and the woman's personal qualifications were significant. The type of organization was limited to evangelical mission agencies that work cross-culturally with a primary aim of propagating a Christian message through a variety of religious and humanitarian works. The women were staff members with these organizations and had positions of significant responsibility there.

Context

The context of this study was twelve evangelical mission organizations. Evangelical refers to the faith base of the organization, and mission refers to its purpose. Each organization represented in this study has made a conscious decision to place women in leadership in the organization, indicating openness to female leadership. Of the twelve organizations in this study, ten focused on ministry outside North America, and two provided training and support to such organizations. The ten are involved in a variety of ministries, ranging from education to health care to church planting. The organizations' sizes ranged from less than twenty to over 2000 staff; the average size was just over 550 people. The geographic range spanned the entire globe. One organization was part of a denomination, and the remaining eleven were independent. They recruit staff from any Christian, evangelical denomination or independent church.

As mission organizations, they share some characteristics that distinguish them from businesses, churches, and other non-profit organizations. In all but two cases in this study, staff members raise their own funding, known as "support"; this money provides their salary, benefits, and business expenses. A percentage is typically assessed to keep the North American office running. Organizations typically place a very high value on staff's ability to move to a new location, learn the language, acculturate, and embed themselves as part of the local society. Couples are usually hired as a "unit," in keeping with the two-person career structure common in ministry. This means that financially, there is one salary. Traditionally, an organization would hire the husband as an employee, giving him the salary, and the wife would accompany him to the ministry location as a volunteer worker. Lately, some agencies have begun to divide the salary and list the wife as an employee, or to offer that option to the couple.

Practically, this arrangement means that a married woman may or may not have an official work assignment. The issue does not necessarily depend on her status as employee or volunteer; it may depend on how the organization thinks of her in the reporting structure. Very often the husband's skills are considered in placement and the wife is expected to find her own way, meaning she may work outside the organization's formal structure. Mission organizations rarely dismiss staff; most have policies allowing for removal only in cases of grievous misconduct. So women (and men) who are relieved of leadership responsibilities may still be considered staff in good standing with the organization and be expected to find their own new ministry role.

Another unique characteristic of these organizations is that two-thirds of the workforce is female.[57] Significant numbers of single women work for mission agencies, but single men are rare, which accounts for the gender imbalance. Finally, since they are registered as non-profit organizations in the United States, mission organizations are not held to the same legal standards regarding hiring, discrimination, pay, and other regulations that offer a certain amount of protection and recourse to women working in U.S. businesses.

Participants

For this study I interviewed twelve women who lead or have led at the executive level in an evangelical mission organization. I used purposeful sampling, so that those who were most likely to understand the phenomena under investigation were the ones invited to participate.[58] These women were well-suited to "talk about the topic or phenomenon under study" and were sought as participants.[59] Using a criterion-based selection process enabled me to find women who "have the knowledge and

57. Brereton and Bendroth, "Secularization and Gender"; Robert, *American Women in Mission*.

58. Merriam, *Qualitative Research*; Merriam, *Qualitative Research in Practice*; Roulston, *Reflective Interviewing*.

59. deMarrais and Lapan, *Foundations for Research*, 59.

experience about the particular focus of the study" and were therefore able to help answer the research questions.[60]

The specific criteria for study participants were as follows:

- Women who have or have had a middle- or upper-level leadership position in a mission organization. The position could have been present or past; what mattered was that the woman achieved a significant level of responsibility in the organization. Since the organizations varied substantially in size and structure, rather than specify a level on the organizational chart, I sought women who had responsibility and accountability for key organizational outcomes. They may also have been considered part of a two-person leadership position in keeping with the common mission organization approach of a two-person career model.

- Women who came into leadership by "working their way up." They were promoted from within the mission world, not brought in from a non-mission setting. However, several of them changed organizations along the way.

- Women who have had cross-cultural experience. A key characteristic of these agencies is that they work in different cultures around the globe and are affected by various worldviews. Therefore, the women needed to have some experience of cross-cultural work to fully understand the challenges of leading in an international organization.

- Women who have or have had direct reports. An advisory capacity only without direct supervisory responsibility was not considered organizational leadership for this study.

- Women who are or were not leading women or children exclusively, since those two realms are not contested in regards to women's leadership.

These women could best provide answers to my research questions because they have navigated the patriarchal structure of faith-based non-profit organizations in order to use their leadership abilities in the organization itself. Some of them have gained a clear understanding of what is required to succeed as a female leader in this kind of setting, and some demonstrated reflexivity or awareness of their leadership experiences, challenges, and what they have learned about leading in patriarchal institutions.

The twelve women in this study all worked with the type of organization previously described. See Table 3 for a summary of participant

---

60. deMarrais and Lapan, *Foundations for Research*, 59.

demographics. Two of them were salaried and ten raised their own support. Five were CEOs, though of those only one functioned as the top leader who reported to an organizational board. Three others reported to a denominational or organizational level above them, and the fourth shared the role with her husband. Of the remaining seven women, three were HR directors, two were on the executive council, and two were leaders of large geographical regions. Their years of experience in mission work ranged from sixteen to more than thirty years, yet their years in executive leadership ranged from one to five.

Table 3: *Participants' demographic data*

Position	CEO – 5 women
	HR Director – 3 women
	Executive council – 2 women
	Geographical Leader – 2 women
Years of experience in mission work	<20 = 5 women
	21-29 = 5 women
	>30 = 2 women
Years in executive leadership	1-2 = 6 women
	3-4 = 5 women
	5 = 1 woman
Educational level	Associate's degree = 1 woman
	Bachelor's degree = 3 women
	Master's degree = 6 women
	Doctoral degree = 2 women
Organization size	<100 = 4 organizations
	100-600 = 6 organizations
	> 2000 = 2 organizations
Marital status	Married = 9 women, all with children
	Single = 3 women

No one had led at an executive level for more than five years. Everyone had some higher education: one had an Associate's degree, three had Bachelor's degrees, five had Master's degrees, and two had completed doctoral degrees; one had doctoral work in progress. Nine were married and three were single. All of the married women had children. I did not ask about race or age. A few of the women knew each other, making confidentiality in the study more important and more challenging. On more than one occasion during an interview, a participant asked me if I knew so-and-so, further emphasizing that the number of women leaders is few and the world of evangelical missions is small and tightly connected. Therefore, I did not include participant profiles in this study. I have also eliminated or adjusted potentially identifying features such as countries of service, in accordance with an ethic of confidentiality, so that a participant could recognize herself but no one else could, yet the essential information for the study was preserved.[61]

DATA COLLECTION

The primary method of investigation for this study was interviews. I talked with each woman for anywhere from 75 minutes to two hours. In the first round of interviews I focused on discovering how the women achieved their leadership positions, how they learned to lead, and stories of success and failure they have encountered along the way. I also asked them their thoughts on why they were chosen to lead. I followed a semi-structured interview process to ensure that the main points of interest were covered (see Appendix C for the interview protocols), while leaving the women freedom to converse with me, telling their stories and including whatever information seemed significant to them.[62] Immediately after each interview, I made additional notes to myself about how the conversation went, my impressions and reactions, and thoughts for future conversations, whether with the next participant or if I had a second interview with this woman. Given the sensitive nature of the topic—being a leader in a non-women-leader friendly environment—a feminist approach was also very important in the interviews. Reinharz discusses the need to believe the interviewee and to gain her trust, as part of hearing useful information.[63] Since the women I interviewed were to some extent breaking subculture norms and walking a fine line between conformity and disconformity in the process, believing them and gaining their trust were key aspects of the interview process. As a previous insider to the industry, as well, I had a heightened ability to develop rapport with them.[64] I knew some of the language that they used, although I did not take meaning for granted, and I have some understanding of the types of structures within which they operate.

61. Freyd, "Journal Ethics and Impact."

62. Glesne, *Becoming Qualitative Researchers*; Merriam, *Qualitative Research in Practice.*

63. Reinharz, *Feminist Methods in Social Research.*

64. Glesne, *Becoming Qualitative Researchers.*

Once the initial interviews were finished and the preliminary analysis done, I emailed each participant a list of preliminary themes and asked them to send me written feedback. The document I sent can be seen in Appendix D. I also asked them to let me know if they were available for a second interview. Ten of the women sent me written responses. Seven of them made comments directly on the document, three sent me emails detailing their thoughts, and one sent me both. I was also able to conduct a second round of interviews with five of the participants. Of the remaining seven, four were traveling in inaccessible locations, two were dealing with personal crises, and one was simply not available. In total, I received member-check feedback from eleven of the twelve participants.

In the second round of interviews I concentrated on conversing with the women about their responses to the initial themes, probing to see what meaning they made of the combined responses. In particular, I asked them what resonated with them and whether they disagreed with or were unsure about anything. I asked some of them to elaborate on stories they had told me in the first interview, and I asked if they had new ideas or new stories they wanted to share with me.

Participant confidentiality was a particular concern in this study. All participants were assigned pseudonyms and all organization names and other potentially traceable identifiers were removed from the transcripts. Names of others in their stories, such as husbands or supervisors, were either removed or changed. All quotations from the interviews or written feedback have been attributed to the pseudonyms.

Two of the pilot study interviews were conducted face to face and recorded with a digital voice recorder. The rest of the initial interviews, and all the second-round interviews were conducted via phone and the Internet. I established an account with Free Conference Call so that I and the participants called in to the same line. The calls were recorded and I then downloaded the audio files from the internet site to my computer. I also password-protected the files on the internet site. One participant was unable to use the internet to place her call. We used a regular phone line, and I took detailed notes of our conversation. I emailed those notes to her, and she checked them for accuracy and added additional commentary before returning them to me. The study received IRB approval from my institution, and each participant signed a written consent before we talked, and gave verbal consent at the start of each interview.

DATA ANALYSIS

I began the process of data analysis simultaneously with data collection, in an ongoing analytical process. There are several reasons for "begin[ning] your analysis with the first interview."[65] The main reason for conducting both activities at the same time was so that I could make adjustments as needed along the way.[66] This approach allowed me to make decisions about which themes to pursue with the women, helped me develop additional questions, allowed me to gather participants' thoughts about developing ideas, and enabled me to ask them to reflect on the process in the midst of the interviews themselves.[67] Each interview was transcribed as soon as possible after it was conducted. In most cases I was able to transcribe one interview before conducting the next one. Then I began the analysis of the data using constant comparative analysis.

Constant Comparative Analysis

Constant comparative analysis (CCA) was an ideal way to approach this study of women in leadership in evangelical mission organizations, since we know little about them. Using CCA, I started with their accounts of their experiences and, by comparing stories of leadership from different people, endeavored to construct a theoretical framework for understanding that experience. CCA is one of the fundamental steps of the grounded theory approach.[68] Glaser and Strauss developed the method in the 1960s precisely in order to develop theory from the data itself in an inductive fashion, rather than simply fitting the data into existing theory.[69] In this study I worked to develop an understanding of how the participants make meaning of their leadership roles.

The major steps of constant comparative analysis are coding, categorizing, and comparing data segments. First I carefully coded each data segment by idea.[70] As I found similar or related segments, I sometimes re-examined and re-coded previous sections of data; the whole process was iterative and

---

65. Ruona, "Analyzing Qualitative Data," 237.

66. Merriam, *Qualitative Research in Practice.*

67. Ruona, "Analyzing Qualitative Data."

68. Butler-Kisber, *Qualitative Inquiry.*

69. Boeije, "Purposeful Approach to the Constant Comparative Method in the Analysis of Qualitative Interviews"; Charmaz, *Constructing Grounded Theory.*

70. Charmaz, *Constructing Grounded Theory.*

recursive.[71] This was the "coarse-grained" stage of analysis.[72] Once the basic coding was completed, I began to compare similarly coded segments to further refine the categories to better represent the data; this was the "fine-grained" phase. At this stage I worked to group codes into themes. Once the fine-grained codes were clear, I then reassembled the pieces of data into a coherent picture of what seemed to be happening; this was the theory-generating step.[73] Each of the steps blended into the others, and the process was not as logical or sequential as it sounds. The overall purpose was to examine the data itself carefully, to see what is says, hear what it means, and generate theory that clarifies human actions.

CCA is a rigorous process.[74] The method requires lengthy immersion in the data, leading me to great familiarity with it.[75] The careful, continuous comparison and refining of codes required ongoing analysis, leading to well-supported conclusions. By diligently coding the data and then closely comparing data segments with the same code, I believe I arrived at some understanding of the participants' experiences.

CCA was also ideal for this feminist qualitative study because it takes people's accounts seriously, seeing people as agents rather than simply objects manipulated by external events.[76] It also attempts to start with few preconceived notions about what is going on, and instead focuses on the data itself. It offered an opportunity for me to see the data through "fresh" eyes, allowing the data to speak, rather than fitting the data into a previously determined framework. In addition, CCA allowed me to compare different people's accounts of leadership in order to find similarities, helping to develop theories about how these women experience leadership.

One potential drawback to the process was that data elements could be studied in isolation. By separating the strands out from the text, they can be examined individually but "contextual elements are lost" making it easier to miss environmental factors that impact the events being studied.[77] However, since I used computer software (see next section) in the analysis step, this risk was greatly reduced, because data could easily be tracked back to its original location and studied *in situ*. Therefore, for this study with

---

71. Boeije, "Purposeful Approach to the Constant Comparative Method in the Analysis of Qualitative Interviews"; Ruona, "Analyzing Qualitative Data."

72. Butler-Kisber, *Qualitative Inquiry*, 30.

73. Butler-Kisber, *Qualitative Inquiry*, 31.

74. Butler-Kisber, *Qualitative Inquiry*.

75. Butler-Kisber, *Qualitative Inquiry*; Ruona, "Analyzing Qualitative Data."

76. Charmaz, *Constructing Grounded Theory*.

77. Butler-Kisber, *Qualitative Inquiry*, 24.

multiple participants and settings, CCA was the best approach to yield rich data about women leaders' strategies for effectiveness.

The Analysis Process

For the actual process of data analysis, I followed Ruona's four-stage process of data preparation, familiarization, coding, and generating meaning. Data preparation included producing a clean transcript, ensuring confidentiality by substituting pseudonyms for participant names, removing or disguising any potentially identifiable details, establishing a secure storage system, and storing a duplicate of each transcript.[78]

Step two, familiarization with the data, was already occurring during data preparation.[79] I made each transcript myself, which was one way to get to know the data quite well. I also used the comment feature in Word to include initial thoughts that occurred to me during the transcription and re-reading process. For longer, more substantive responses to the data, I kept a research log.

Step three, coding, lies at the heart of the analysis process. Although I initially intended to use Ruona's approach using tables in Word, I had also experimented with Hyper Research in coding the pilot study interviews; in the end I chose to use that program. I converted each clean transcript into plain text and uploaded it to the program.

From there I coded each transcript, using the annotation feature in the program to write memos as I went. The program allowed me to easily group codes into categories, and re-group them as needed. It also allowed for re-coding when that was needed, and enabled me to sort by code, code group, or respondent to analyze any particular data set. The program also generated a code frequency report, allowing me to quickly see which codes were most prominent across all the data.

Once all the transcripts were coded, I then systematically worked through the data, examining every occurrence of each code across all twelve transcripts. In this way I was able to see what each woman said on any given topic, and compare all women's responses on the same topic across the study. At this stage I also kept a running code log, noting who discussed each code, and noting significant sections of each transcript that I thought would be useful in the findings section. This document then served as one basis of the final stage of analysis, writing up the findings.

---

78. Ruona, "Analyzing Qualitative Data."
79. Ruona, "Analyzing Qualitative Data."

Once the four-step process was complete, I began the final stage of analysis, writing up the findings using thick description.[80] Since words paint the picture of the research process and findings, a descriptive piece with support from the interviews serves both to create an interesting report and validate the claims the researcher makes for the data.[81] Here again, a feminist approach was well-suited to the study. In the written findings of the study, I have attended to gender and tried to write for the potential benefit of the interviewees as well as for potential change in the organizations that accept their work while simultaneously devaluing them as women. I cannot cause change, but I have tried to write in such a way that change could come, and I have believed the women's accounts of their leadership journeys, offering them a chance to tell their stories so that others can gain from the shared knowledge.[82] As I discussed earlier, often women's voices have been marginalized or ignored in studies of leadership; this study is one opportunity to "speak out for" women who do their work even in potentially unsupportive environments.[83]

While it would be usual in a study of this sort to include a section that profiles each of the participants, I have not included that information. After wrestling with the benefits of including such profiles for the completeness of the study, versus the risk to my participants of potentially being identified, I concluded that the risks outweigh the benefits. Given the few women I was able to locate who qualified for this study, the repeated requests they made for assurance of confidentiality, and the fact that several of them named other participants during the course of the interviews, it seemed ethical to refrain from offering any description that could lead to their possible identification. The world in which they work is simply too small and too interconnected to assure confidentiality if I gave their profiles.

TRUSTWORTHINESS OF THE STUDY

As a researcher, I want my study to be believed and trusted. For that to happen, I needed to keep in mind that "all research must respond to canons of quality—criteria against which the trustworthiness of the project can be evaluated."[84] There are certain "canons of quality" which are traditionally used with positivist and quantitative studies, including internal

---

80. Merriam, *Qualitative Research in Practice*.

81. Merriam, *Qualitative Research in Practice*; Glesne, *Becoming Qualitative Researchers*.

82. Reinharz, *Feminist Methods in Social Research*.

83. Reinharz, *Feminist Methods in Social Research*, 16.

84. Marshall and Rossman, *Designing Qualitative Research*, 200.

and external validity, and reliability. However, since qualitative research focuses on understanding a phenomenon rather than measuring it, their suitability for qualitative research has been discussed and adjusted somewhat.[85] Qualitative researchers prefer to focus on ensuring that a study shows quality, credibility, and trustworthiness.[86] Although the terminology differs somewhat, the common requirement for a qualitative study is that the research is believable.[87] Widely accepted hallmarks of a believable qualitative study include (a) truthfulness in reporting findings or results, (b) resonance, meaning the ability of another to connect with the findings of the research, and (c) handling researcher bias.[88] Therefore, these three criteria formed my "canons of quality" to assure a trustworthy study. Next I will describe each of these criteria, and then I will discuss the strategies I used to ensure each of them was met.

Truthfulness, Resonance, and Handling Researcher Bias

The first hallmark of a believable qualitative study is that I as the researcher am truthful in reporting findings.[89] Truthfulness in the study is qualitative research's version of internal validity, which assures us that the study actually measures what it claims to measure.[90] It also parallels quantitative measures of reliability, because another researcher could, under similar circumstances, generate similar findings, although qualitative research recognizes that a different researcher at a different time might get somewhat different results, since knowledge is actively constructed during the interview itself.[91]

A second hallmark of a trustworthy study is resonance, meaning the ability of another to resonate with the findings of the research.[92] Butler-Kisber suggests the term "particularizability . . . meaning how a certain study resonates with people in other situations so they are able to find both

85. Butler-Kisber, *Qualitative Inquiry*; Freeman et al., "Standards of Evidence in Qualitative Research."

86. Butler-Kisber, *Qualitative Inquiry*; Freeman et al., "Standards of Evidence in Qualitative Research"; Lewis, "Redefining Qualitative Methods"; Roulston, *Reflective Interviewing*; Ruona, "Analyzing Qualitative Data."

87. Freeman et al., "Standards of Evidence in Qualitative Research."

88. Butler-Kisber, *Qualitative Inquiry*; Freeman et al., "Standards of Evidence in Qualitative Research"; Lewis, "Redefining Qualitative Methods."

89. Lewis, "Redefining Qualitative Methods."

90. Lewis, "Redefining Qualitative Methods."

91. Lewis, "Redefining Qualitative Methods."

92. Butler-Kisber, *Qualitative Inquiry*; Freeman et al., "Standards of Evidence in Qualitative Research"; Lewis, "Redefining Qualitative Methods."

confirmation and/or new understandings of experiences and phenomena."[93] Resonance is actually qualitative research's version of external validity, meaning that the study also applies to other populations or samples.[94] If other women in similar positions see themselves in my findings, then the study has demonstrated resonance. To some degree this is not within my power but will depend on others who read the research and determine for themselves if it applies or resonates with them.[95]

Finally, a third hallmark of a trustworthy study is handling researcher bias, since "every researcher will possess some sort of bias."[96] While accounting for researcher bias is fundamental to any qualitative study, in a critical, feminist framework it is imperative.[97] My own history with evangelical mission organizations and leadership efforts could both help and hinder my study. Since the researcher is the instrument in a qualitative study, my years of experience in this world seemed to help establish rapport and understanding with my participants, and appeared to make it easier for them to explain their experiences to me. Yet my experiences could also color my understanding of their stories and therefore had to be monitored.

The key concept for me in this balancing act of accepting and including—while not being captive to—my own experience was reflexivity. Reflexivity is the idea that the researcher is thoroughly self-aware.[98] It means thinking carefully about one's experiences and how those experiences construct perspectives, biases, and assumptions about the world around one. Beliefs, value systems, personality, and temperament, as well as race, class, gender, socioeconomic status, and more all contribute to the makeup of the researcher and influence how she goes about her work. Reflexivity involves recognizing that the researcher is an inseparable part of the study and the process; I have known this for some time and found that there were multiple ways for me to "write myself in" to the study. Given my shared background and work experience with the women, I needed to engage in ongoing self-awareness and self-monitoring throughout the project, and I strove to develop an ability to use my "self" in a supportive, not detrimental way, to the research process. I was particularly drawn to Riley, Schouten, and Cahill's notion that the self changes over time, meaning that the reflexivity we bring to our research also

---

93. Butler-Kisber, *Qualitative Inquiry*, 15.

94. Lewis, "Redefining Qualitative Methods."

95. Marshall and Rossman, *Designing Qualitative Research*.

96. Lewis, "Redefining Qualitative Methods," 10.

97. Lewis, "Redefining Qualitative Methods"; Butler-Kisber, *Qualitative Inquiry*.

98. Butler-Kisber, *Qualitative Inquiry*; Etherington, *Becoming a Reflexive Researcher*; Finlay, "Negotiating the Swamp."

changes over time.[99] I am certainly not the same person now that I was five or ten years ago working in that field, and I have changed further over the life of the research process.[100] So both keeping track of myself along the way and recognizing that my "self" was changing were useful components of pursuing this and potential future research projects.

Strategies for Achieving Trustworthiness

There are seven strategies I used to ensure the trustworthiness of this study. They were keeping an audit trail, using direct commentary from the interview transcripts to support claims I made, using thick description, including discrepant data, conducting member checks, writing and using a subjectivity statement, and engaging in peer debriefing. As Table 4 shows, each of these strategies supported at least two of the hallmarks of trustworthiness for this study. In the following section I will describe each strategy and explain how it supported the trustworthiness of my study.

The first strategy was to keep a careful record of the work, known as an audit trail, providing a way for others to trace the work I did and check the steps taken.[101] I kept a log detailing the steps of my study, including, for example, how participants were found, notations of communications between us, and notes. This would allow another researcher to check my work. A second aspect of the log was a journal where I kept track of my responses to participants' stories. Journaling and writing memos about the research process and my responses to it helped me monitor my own influence on the study. The journal section of the log served as part of the process of reflexivity for me, allowing me to surface and examine my own bias, and therefore control for it.

Table 4: *Strategies for achieving trustworthiness*

STRATEGY	Truthfulness	Resonance	Handling Bias
Audit Trail	X		X
Direct Commentary	X	X	
Thick Description	X	X	

99. Riley et al., "Exploring the Dynamics of Subjectivity and Power between Researcher and Researched."

100. Kuntz, "Representing Representation."

101. Freeman et al., "Standards of Evidence in Qualitative Research"; Lewis, "Redefining Qualitative Methods"; Ruona, "Analyzing Qualitative Data."

STRATEGY	Truthfulness	Resonance	Handling Bias
Discrepant Data	X	X	X
Member Checks	X	X	X
Subjectivity Statement	X		X
Peer Debriefing	X		X

The next strategy was using direct commentary from participants' interviews to support my claims.[102] By "showing" what participants said rather than simply "telling" what the data mean, I have strengthened the presentation and shown the study's truthfulness.[103] I used direct commentary from participants to show that their accounts built the ideas I have presented. The use of direct commentary should also increase the study's resonance; as other missionary women read what participants said about their work situations, they may identify with the participants and gain understanding of their own situation.

Third, thick description is another way to support the study's truthfulness. Thick description paints a picture for the reader of the respondent and the world they described to me, so that the reader can understand and draw their own conclusions from the research.[104] Good description can help lead the reader to a moment of illumination, as they gain for themselves an understanding of the participants' worlds. It also supports resonance, as a well-described situation may connect on an emotional and intellectual level with the reader and help her see places of similarity between her experience and that of the participants.

Evidence that did not fit the frame—or discrepant data—was also reported and weighed in evaluating the results, not simply ignored.[105] Including discrepant data clearly supports the truthfulness of the study, and also helps control for bias, since I did not simply exclude data that did not fit my developing frame; I included it in my consideration of the findings. Discrepant data may also support resonance, because a qualitative study does not claim to speak for all members of a particular group. While some readers may resonate with the main body of findings, others may find the discrepant data more closely resembles their situation. Several sections of discrepant data were

102. Freeman et al., "Standards of Evidence in Qualitative Research."

103. Butler-Kisber, *Qualitative Inquiry.*

104. Freeman et al., "Standards of Evidence in Qualitative Research"; Lewis, "Redefining Qualitative Methods."

105. Lewis, "Redefining Qualitative Methods."

present in this study, and I carefully included them, discussed the possible significance, and adjusted my conclusions as needed.

Member checks were a particularly important measure of this study's trustworthiness, since they serve to enhance truthfulness, resonance and controlling for bias.[106] Once I had some preliminary analysis and began to see emerging themes, I constructed a document that summarized those ideas. I then sent that document to all the participants, along with a request for a second interview. In this way almost all of the women were able to evaluate what I saw in the data and five of them talked with me a second time to share their perspectives and help me further develop and refine the themes.[107] Thus participants themselves became part of the data analysis, serving to confirm, challenge, and modify the ideas I drew from the data. Member checks are sometimes considered the most important measure of a study's trustworthiness and in this study that was definitely the case.[108]

The sixth strategy I used to enhance trustworthiness in this study was to write and refer back to my own subjectivity statement; it can be read in Appendix A. This strategy enhanced the study's truthfulness because I made explicit my own history and thinking regarding the study. It helped control for bias because as I was analyzing data, I could refer back to my own statement to remember my own experiences and see what impact they might have had on my understanding of my respondents' stories.

A final strategy I used was peer debriefing, where I talked over what I was learning and my responses to it with outsiders not directly involved in my project. I had two peer writing groups who helped me think through the findings and how I presented them. Two family members who were not connected to the study in any way also served as a sounding board and a source of ideas as I worked through the data analysis process. Of course my major professor gave valuable, detailed feedback from her perspective, and my committee, too, was involved in debriefing. Again, this strategy helps support truthfulness because I have discussed the findings and shown how the interviews support my claims and I have gained feedback from both an academic research perspective and from the perspective of those who understand the evangelical faith. It also helped control for bias because others have challenged my interpretations, helping me be sure I did not read my own experiences into the participants' lives. These conversations helped me think critically and further construct knowledge with the help of informed peers.

106. Roulston, *Reflective Interviewing*; Ruona, "Analyzing Qualitative Data."
107. Lewis, "Redefining Qualitative Methods."
108. Lewis, "Redefining Qualitative Methods."

Additional Considerations

According to Roulston the strategies discussed above (e.g., the audit trail, evidence for claims, member checks, considering discrepant data, controlling for researcher bias) come from a post-positivist framework.[109] This is helpful because it shows how the study incorporates concepts of internal validity, external validity, and reliability in its design. However, there are also some underlying assumptions, namely that the researcher can be basically neutral and that the participants can adequately recall and describe past experiences to the researcher. Since I approached this research from a constructivist perspective, I also needed to pay close attention to how the respondent and I conversed, and how we, together, constructed meaning from the women's accounts of leadership. I was not and could not be completely neutral in the interview setting and the constructivist and critical feminist ideologies underlying this study allowed me some latitude to participate with each interviewee in understanding and evaluating her experiences.

DELIMITATIONS, LIMITATIONS, AND ETHICAL CONCERNS

This study was delimited to women who serve or have served at executive leadership levels of evangelical mission organizations with headquarters in North America. The women must have come up through the ranks into leadership, have cross-cultural experience, and not work exclusively with women or children. Women who were not North Americans or who worked only with women and children were not included in this study, nor were men. The focus was on North American cultural models of leadership and of gender; women from other cultural backgrounds may have substantially different experiences and therefore were not included. Women who work exclusively with children or other women are considered to be functioning within the acceptable boundaries of women's sphere in patriarchal organizations, since they do not have direct authority over men. So although women may be excellent leaders in these situations, if they only led women's or children's departments, they were not included in this study because they are not leading contrary to subculture norms. And although men might have valuable perspectives to contribute to a study of women's leadership in patriarchal organizations, the focus of this study is women's experiences of leadership; therefore men were not included.

Another delimitation is that the sample was small due to the low numbers of qualified women available. Further, the results of the study will not be

---

109. Roulston, "Considering Quality in Qualitative Interviewing."

generalizable in the sense that quantitative studies often are.[110] As a qualitative study, this research is interested in painting a picture of a few women's lives, without claiming that all women leaders' lives are similar.

Limitations

As with all studies, this study had some limitations meaning that I simply did the best I could under the circumstances that arose.[111] The most notable limitation I encountered was the ability to schedule a second interview with participants. Due to the travel schedules of some and the personal crises of others, I was only able to conduct five follow-up calls. Despite this limitation, however, I believe the study was worth conducting, especially since I was able to get written feedback from ten of the participants, so that eleven of the twelve participants were represented in the feedback. Two participants interacted with me multiple times through email, adding further thoughts and explanations to the data. Therefore, the study still does contribute to scholarly knowledge about women's self-directed learning and their meaning-making as oppressed leaders—in itself a seeming contradiction.

Another limitation of the study was that all but two interviews were conducted by phone. Interviewing by phone is not well represented in the qualitative research literature and opinions vary regarding its reliability.[112] Some think it may hinder the development of rapport and make for shorter interviews.[113] Some point out that it removes extra data which could be observed from body language and gestures.[114] Others find that those objections are minor, and that the phone interview is particularly useful in exploring sensitive or difficult topics, potentially yielding rich data.[115] It also makes it possible to interview people who are geographically inaccessible to the researcher, which was the impetus behind phone interviews in this study.[116]

110. Crotty, *Foundations of Social Research*.

111. Glesne, *Becoming Qualitative Researchers*; Marshall and Rossman, *Designing Qualitative Research*.

112. Irvine, "Duration, Dominance and Depth in Telephone and Face-to-Face Interviews"; Lechuga, "Exploring Culture from a Distance"; Novick, "Is There a Bias against Telephone Interviews in Qualitative Research?"

113. Irvine et al., "Am I Not Answering Your Questions Properly?"; Irvine, "Duration, Dominance and Depth in Telephone and Face-to-Face Interviews."

114. Lechuga, "Exploring Culture from a Distance"; Novick, "Is There a Bias against Telephone Interviews in Qualitative Research?"

115. Trier-Bieniek, "Framing the Telephone Interview as a Participant-Centered Tool for Qualitative Research."

116. Lechuga, "Exploring Culture from a Distance"; Trier-Bieniek, "Framing the

In this study I encountered three limitations traceable to using the telephone. First, I was not able to observe the race of the participants, and therefore did not include that data in the participant summary. Second, the time zone differences caused an extra layer of challenge in scheduling talks that were convenient for both myself and the participants. Third, in two cases I encountered technological challenges.[117] One, mentioned previously, was with a participant who was unfamiliar with the technology involved in placing a phone call over the internet. The other was a case where my cell phone dropped the call. Fortunately, in that case the participant was the one talking and the internet line continued recording her comments; I was able to call back in and later download the entire recording, including the section that I missed hearing due to the dropped call. Despite the limitations of the phone and of technology, like Trier-Bieniek I found my participants appeared comfortable with the relative anonymity of the telephone interview and willing to share both difficult and uncomfortable stories.[118]

Ethical Concerns

Finally, the study also included some potential ethical issues that I needed to recognize.[119] One was the relationship between myself and the interviewees. My positionality as a white female with many years' experience in the same type of work undoubtedly affected how they saw me. My education and perspective also mattered, since "researchers' theoretical and disciplinary perspectives, life experiences, cultural backgrounds, genders, ages, physical appearances, and other characteristics influence the way in which they attend to and respond to the conversation and construct meaning within that interview."[120] I attended to these things during the course of the interviews, and took particular care to answer any questions the participants had for me regarding the purpose of the study and my own positionality or regarding my background and experiences.[121]

There were other potentially complicating factors as well. Given that "feminism" is an "f-word" for many in the evangelical subculture, I wrestled with how much to disclose about the purpose and design of the

Telephone Interview as a Participant-Centered Tool for Qualitative Research."

117. Trier-Bieniek, "Framing the Telephone Interview as a Participant-Centered Tool for Qualitative Research."

118. Trier-Bieniek, "Framing the Telephone Interview as a Participant-Centered Tool for Qualitative Research."

119. Merriam, *Qualitative Research in Practice.*

120. deMarrais and Lapan, *Foundations for Research,* 55.

121. Westmarland, "Quantitative/Qualitative Debate and Feminist Research."

study.[122] In the pilot interviews, I had not used the word "feminism" but described feminist purposes and all three women were willing to participate. Following that example, I chose not to use the "f-word" word in my interactions with the rest of the participants, lest some of them decline to participate. However, I did refer to "patriarchal" structures and organizations in the consent forms, and none of the women invited refused to participate. I struggled to discern if the choice of vocabulary meant I was still being truthful enough or if I was engaging in deceit.[123] Was that ethical? Reinharz would say "yes" because it built trust.[124]

Another ethical question I wrestled with continually related to how much safety I could offer them.[125] According to an ethic of care I needed to concern myself with how the research might affect the participants.[126] For example, if somehow they were identified in a published study, would they suffer repercussions at work? Would they suffer censure for speaking to a feminist researcher about patriarchal practices that may reflect poorly on some organizations? The low number of women in such positions could make such identification possible. To answer this, I seriously attended to these concerns as the study progressed, and made certain decisions along the way, such as adjusting identifiable data and not including participant profiles.

CHAPTER SUMMARY

In this chapter I have explained my research approach and goals for the study. Working from a constructivist epistemology, I interviewed twelve women who have experience leading at the executive level in evangelical mission organizations. As I interviewed them using a feminist methodology, we together built an understanding of their experiences as leaders and the meaning this experience holds for them. They are the experts about their lived experience; I as the researcher offered an opportunity for them to tell their story and construct meaning of their experiences.

Semi-structured interviews allowed me to cover main topics while allowing the participants to guide the conversation in related directions that were important to them. I analyzed the interviews using constant comparative analysis to see what themes would emerge, and used member

122. Calás and Smircich, "Using the 'F' Word"; Merriam, *Qualitative Research in Practice.*

123. Gringeri et al., "What Makes It Feminist?"

124. Reinharz, *Feminist Methods in Social Research.*

125. Gringeri et al., "What Makes It Feminist?"; Merriam, *Qualitative Research in Practice.*

126. Gringeri et al., "What Makes It Feminist?"

checks to evaluate those themes. By writing my own subjectivity statement, keeping a research journal, and writing memos, I intended to remain constantly aware of my own bias and influence in the research process. Finally, to the extent I was able, I have sought my participants' good as we constructed knowledge together.

LAST THOUGHTS ON CRITICAL THEORY AND CHANGING THE WORLD

Earlier I showed that the main difference between basic qualitative research and feminist qualitative research is the stance: understand a situation versus challenge it. The main limitation of qualitative research is that the findings are not usually considered to be generalizable. That left me with the question of whether a study that is potentially not generalizable was the best method to challenge the status quo. Some feminist researchers have argued that feminist research should be quantitative, in order to communicate to (male, political) power-brokers and gain attention for change.[127] If that is the case, why was this study better suited to feminist qualitative approach? For now I would say that this research is simply a starting point. "Reporting the numbers can be socially empowering, indicating degrees and/or pervasiveness of inequality. Telling the stories of people's experiences can be personally empowering, supporting empathy and feelings of connection. Persuasive arguments in public discourse require both."[128] By validating individual women's experiences this study could potentially gain voice and empathy for the women, and could be a starting point for challenging an unjust system.

127. Reinharz, *Feminist Methods in Social Research*; Sprague and Kobrynowicz, "Feminist Epistemology."

128. Sprague and Kobrynowicz, "Feminist Epistemology," 91.

6

Findings: Acceptance of Gender Roles

THE PURPOSE OF THIS study was to understand how women lead and make meaning of their leadership in evangelical mission organizations. The research questions guiding the study were:

1. How have these women become leaders and learned to lead?

2. What if any forms of resistance or subversive behavior do they use in order to lead in a patriarchal culture?

3. How do they and the organizations they work in account for their leadership?

This chapter and the two following chapters present the findings of the study. They are arranged in three sections, corresponding to the three research questions. The first finding, corresponding to research question one, is that the women to a large extent accept and follow the prescribed gender-role stereotypes. The second finding, corresponding to research question two and presented in chapter 7, is that they are also able to some extent to use or maneuver the gender stereotypes to support their leadership. The third finding, corresponding to research question three, and presented in chapter 8, is that the organizations as well as the women themselves continue to be ambivalent about women's leadership, despite the women's organizational contributions.

The first finding, Acceptance of Gender Roles, includes three main themes: career trajectory shows family comes first; learning to lead is an individual process; leadership practices are strongly communal. This section answers research question one. In this section I discuss ways in which the women showed conformity to the traditional evangelical gender roles prescribed for them. The second finding, Maneuvers with Gender Roles, is presented in chapter 7. It has four main themes: separating from the two-person career; delegated authority matters; appealing to gifting over gender; cautious advocacy only. These themes answer research question two. They show ways in which the women maneuvered the prescribed gender roles or used the requirements to bolster their leadership. The third finding, Persistent Ambivalence, is presented in chapter 8. It has three themes: organizational ambivalence, subordinates' ambivalence, and women's ambivalence. These themes answer research question three. They show that despite having been selected to lead, the organizations and the women continue to express ambivalence about women's leadership.

In the sections that follow, I will present each of the findings with the corresponding themes and subthemes, using the women's own voices from our interviews to define and support the theme itself. Next, I will present the women's thoughts about what the particular theme means. Their commentary comes from statements they made during the course of the interviews as well as from written feedback they sent in response to the summary sheet I sent them as part of the member check process. The summary sheet can be seen in Appendix D. Third, I will present my own additional analysis from a feminist perspective of what else may be happening in the women's situations. An overview of the findings and perspectives can be seen in Table 5. Although presenting the findings and themes in this manner gives them a feeling of discreteness and linearity, the reality is that they are quite interwoven in the women's stories. Thus some of the categories overlap, such as sponsorship and delegated authority. However, to understand each section clearly, I have presented them as if they were entirely separate.

Table 5: *Data display*

Category	Themes	Women's Perspective	Feminist Perspective
Acceptance of Gender Roles	a. Career trajectory: 2-person career dominates & family comes first b. Learning to lead c. Communal leadership practices	Most women take these aspects for granted, considering them right or natural.	Organizational power structures women as men's supporters, not equals.

Category	Themes	Women's Perspective	Feminist Perspective
Maneuvers with Gender Roles	a. Ending the two-person career b. Delegated authority matters c. Appealing to gifting over gender d. Cautious advocacy only	Most women offer explanations for leading that still align with the prescribed gender roles.	Organizational power and discourse create a constrained space in which women may function.
Persistent Ambivalence	a. Organizational ambivalence b. Subordinates' ambivalence c. Women's ambivalence	The women accept responsibility and do not fight or even name discrimination.	The women encounter structural, systemic discrimination.

ACCEPTANCE OF GENDER ROLES

The first category of themes in this study is the way in which the women accepted and even promoted the gender-role prescriptions of evangelical faith. For married women, it typically meant being the primary caregiver for the children and carrying the main responsibility for the home. For single women it was less well defined, but can be seen in work choices that are female gendered (teaching and nursing were two of the single women's original professions) and in strong feelings of personal responsibility for moral and sexual purity in relation to male colleagues.

This aspect of the gender role is presented matter-of-factly, as something the women simply take for granted. Stephanie commented about her support role in the early days, "I think [it was] a very right and typical role for a woman, also because I was raising my children at that time, so naturally I focused on the home." Carol commented that in her organization, "moms who have kids are pretty much on home assignment, so I wasn't involved in the workplace. Home assignment means you just are home taking care of your kids." Nicole, as a single woman, explained her organization's view of married women: "I think the default is more likely, well, they're busy being moms right now; we won't bother them." Melinda, also single, talked about being on a level platform with her male colleagues, adding that "I've had to be very intentional that my actions don't cause the [wives] to have any feelings of jealousy. I just have to be careful." So both the women and the organizations take for granted that women with children will primarily be in the home, focusing on the family, and that single women will uphold moral purity with their male colleagues.

CAREER TRAJECTORY

Looking at the career trajectories of the women in this study shows married women started as part of a two-person career structure and often did family first, leadership second, both chronologically and commitment-wise. Single women were more able to follow an upward path through the organization. The career trajectory of family first, leadership second is one way in which the women accept the gender roles expected of them.

The Two-Person Career Structure Dominates

The women's acceptance of the gender role showed clearly in their career trajectories. All but one of the married women began their work as part of a two-person career structure, in a support role to their husbands. Carol talked about the early years with her husband:

> We were actually with the founder, we got to know him . . . and when we moved [here] . . . we were part of a small group of young mission advocates that met with him and his wife when he was dreaming about this place. So we helped him actually to found this organization.

Chelsea spoke similarly about her early years, when they moved overseas and learned the local language:

> So we joined [the organization] in 1984 and went to [country]. That was the normal language school and all that. [My husband] was team leader in our first city that we lived in for a while, and then we moved to [another city] and he was the field director. But it was all very informal, my participation was informal.

Stephanie also told a similar story:

> We joined [our organization] in 1987 with a view to serving in [country]. My husband is a health professional. And my train- ing is not in a profession, but I did have, I suppose, leanings to just training in missions. . . . So we went to [country] in 1990 after a period of language study in [continent], and began our career in missions with [our organization]. And for the next 13 years that was our focus. . . . Those were necessary years to focus on the children, and my role in missions was, I felt very much and equally passionate about the call, but I recognized that there

was a role of mother that was really important. And so I just did what I could in ministry on the side.

For Ashley the situation was the same:

> My husband and I joined the organization after we were asked to initiate a church plant by a church in [city]. . . . So that was kind of our first start. And we moved to [city] and I had a three week old and a two year old, so I was very much caught up in being a young mom. And then after a certain point I just needed to take a step back because I had to–with my husband getting so involved in that, I felt I needed to take care of the home front more.

Barbara talked about pastoring with her husband before they joined the mission organization, and Kelly had lived overseas with her family for years before returning to the U.S. and being asked to lead in a different organization.

Three of the women worked in organizations that have purposefully promoted the two-person career model for all couples, including leaders. Both Carol and Barbara talked about their organizations' founder (both organizations were founded by the same man) having a very high view of husband-wife leadership teams. "He always had a high value on both husband and wife in leadership roles," Carol said, "so he actually started talking to us about taking a high-level position." Barbara described how that same founder wanted her and her husband to co-lead in Barbara's organization. "He tried to ask my husband and I to be the co-presidents at one point," she said. Neither Carol nor Barbara wound up in that shared role, but for Stephanie a shared role was the only option. According to her organization's practice, husband and wife are put in leadership together, and permitted to work out the details as it suits them and their supervisors. She commented that in practice, "There has been the tendency of thinking of the man as the main leader and the wife his complement . . . . In other words, you want the husband as leader; you get the wife in the package. Or, despite what we've written, what we really mean is he's the director and she's the director's wife." So for these three women, the two-person career model is foundational to the way the organization operates.

Family Comes First

The women's acceptance of the gender-role requirements also meant that they did family first and leadership second, both chronologically and in terms of level of commitment. In some cases they deliberately resisted opportunities to move into more active ministry or leadership roles when their children were at home. Stephanie, in her shared role with her husband, chose how much to be involved:

> Each stage has had something that helped us determine what my role would be. And for me, it has in the early days depended on the time I wanted, and felt I needed to be focused on the children, and what was required. And I again, the more typical pastor's wife or leader's wife who did what she could or did her part.

Chelsea talked about her early years overseas: "I was a mom and at home, just doing the hospitality thing, that sort of thing. I would participate in individual projects that came up, but I didn't actively have a ministry commitment on a regular basis with the team." Later she added:

> I would say that until our kids were grown, I resisted taking on responsibilities that would be too demanding. So it was pretty deliberate on my part. . . . Once we got back here and our kids were grown, then I felt like, well, if there is something that I can contribute, that's okay. So I felt differently about it then.

For her, she actively embraced the two-person career and her primary responsibility for the children.

For Regina, too, it was a deliberate choice:

> I had four kids at home; I wouldn't have had time to be in a top level organizational position. That's perfectly clear to me with the way that I chose to run my family, and so the choices I made with how I wanted to raise my kids made it obvious that would not happen.

Barbara agreed. She said:

> For me it was a deliberate choice. While my first two children were young, I was a minister of education. It was a half-time position at a church, and it was the type of job where I could have them with me most of the time, except for a couple of things. So then when we were pastoring a very small church I home-schooled my kids. So anything I did they did with me.

Then, when her youngest was eight, she began working in the mission organization. That was hard, because "It's hard if you're pulled in two directions to try to give your best in two worlds at the same time."

Kelly, one of only three women in the study who still have children at home, also found it hard:

> It's a real challenge to try to balance the home and family life. . .
> there are some things that just mom can do, and so I feel the
> weight of that . . . .am I in some way neglecting my other role
> as a mother and as a wife, because I'm in this role? I don't think
> that's a question that most men ever ask.

Regina also found it hard, and she had only one child still at home. "There
is no time or availability with children. I struggle with this and my son is
a senior!" And Tabitha, the third woman with children still at home, commented that sometimes her children say, "Mom, get out of work mode! Just
be mom!" when she comes home.

Leading Comes Later

For married women, their engagement in leadership and sometimes even
active ministry may come relatively late in their careers, because they have
focused on raising their children first, or their career progression may be
somewhat inconsistent.

Chelsea's progression illustrated this. She entered top leadership suddenly, later in her life. Her family had been overseas for 23 years and then
returned to North America; she initially took a part-time coordinator role
on their return, but within a very short amount of time she was placed into
an executive position. Carol, too, came to leadership late, after being with
the organization about 30 years. She and her husband first worked in the
North American office, and then moved overseas for many years. When they
returned, the president quickly placed her into a high-level role:

> I went pretty directly into upper leadership after we returned
> home. It was two years after getting here, but I distinctly felt that
> one big reason I was given higher level leadership was because
> the president was planning to make my husband the new direc-
> tor, and he wanted me to have visibility to everyone.

In a very traditional-sounding move, the president actually asked her husband's permission before offering her the leadership position. "So when he
wanted me to take the regional director role, he first went to my husband and
talked it over with him, to find out what he thought." She went on to say that
there are men in her organization who do not want their wives in leadership,
but want them "home making dinner and cleaning house," so she was thank-
ful that her husband supported her taking a leadership role.

Stephanie, too, engaged fully in leadership only later in life. Although
she has been with her organization for 25 years and in shared leadership
roles with her husband for 17 of those years, she also described not fully

engaging in leadership with her husband until her children were grown. "But as the children have grown up, then the choice of how we work it out has to do with gifting, and literally just, let's divide up the load." So it is only in the last three years or so "that now [we] even equally divide up [the] roles." Previously her family responsibilities limited the work she invested in leading with her husband.

Ashley's story showed a slightly different type of career trajectory. While her family was still overseas, she had started in an administrative assistant role and worked her way up into the leadership team for the region and then the organization. But when her family decided to leave their country of service and return to North America, she stopped working for the organization altogether to support her family through the transition. She explained:

> When we moved to the States I felt for a number of reasons I needed to step out of it. I was very consumed with trying to reorient our family here in the States at that point. And we took quite a hit in our financial support, which often happens when missionaries move to the States. So I took a job.

It was several years after that when the president of the organization asked her to join the executive team.

Barbara's progress was also a tad erratic. She began by volunteering from a distance, moved to the location of her organization and started taking on any jobs that needed doing, and at some point the president wanted her and her husband to take over from him together. She did not want that, and several years more went by with her carrying the load of president without having the title. She explained:

> This went on for a year and a half. He died, and still there was no president. Still they even refused to make me interim CEO. And they said, well you can just report to the board chair. . . . It was just a year ago this month when the board had a meeting where I was finally appointed President, but to the last minute it was a question whether they would be willing to have that vote. They didn't have anybody else in mind. So, you know, this gives me lots of confidence, right? [laughs]

For Barbara, doing the work and being recognized as the one doing the work came at completely different stages.

Another form of inconsistent career trajectory happened for three women who now lead in different organizations from the ones where they started. For them, a change in organization was part of the move to upper leadership. Kelly explained that, "I had a lot of different mission-related experience, very diverse, but I had never been an executive of an organization, had not had any executive experience, although I'd had a lot of leadership experience directing ministry, and in ministry roles." Then she was quickly promoted to a top role within two years of joining a new organization. Similarly, Regina had some experience leading projects and teams in her first organization; the experience she brought to her new organization helped move her to the top ranks within a year of her arrival. Holly also had led an organization many years ago, but left and worked in a variety of different capacities for many years before jumping back into executive leadership in her current organization.

And in a reversal of the progression to leadership, Donna recounted how she expected to take a leadership role, and the role vanished. Between the time the organization employed her and the time she was ready to move overseas, she explained:

> The leadership changed, and so my appointment changed as well. It basically no longer existed. And so I was reappointed, without my knowledge, to another department to be on staff in this other department. And so I declined that and actually came—when we finally moved overseas I had no role.

Constrained by the gender-role requirements and the two-person career frame, even though her position no longer existed, she still moved overseas with her family so her husband could begin his ministry. A number of years later she did wind up in an executive leadership role, but years later than she originally expected.

Single Women's Career Trajectory Differs

Because they were not expected to take on family and home-care roles the way married women were, the single women in this study had more straightforward career trajectories. All three started at a relatively low level of responsibility and worked their way up in the organization. Holly said:

> It may be true if a single woman stays within the same organization, that as single woman it is easier to work your way up the ladder. When I was in my first organization, that was true. I could work my way up.

Melinda also found this to be true for her. She also saw other advantages to being single:

> I do think that once a woman is in the door as a single woman, she's often more heard than a wife is heard. . . . a wife is there because they've invited her husband, whereas . . . I'm invited because of me, not because of a role I play.

Nicole, too, saw advantages:

> I've had married colleagues speak of being almost jealous of the fact that I have these opportunities that were never open to them. If anyone was going to be on whatever leadership group it was, it was always the husband that got chosen. So a single woman just had more chance, more opportunity, more doors open.

Stephanie also noted that single women are more available since they are not hampered by family responsibilities, and therefore more often in leadership in her organization, albeit usually at lower levels.

What the Women Think It Means

In reflecting on their career trajectories, the women offered several different explanations for those patterns. Carol and Chelsea thought it might be partially tied to geographic location, perhaps because both of them entered leadership when they returned to the U.S. from an overseas assignment. In their organizations, the executive positions are located at the headquarters, not overseas. Speaking from the viewpoint of the two-person career, Carol commented that "in a marriage, the woman's role is less of a deciding factor in the couple's choice to move on to something else . . . . the woman follows her husband." So if the leadership job is stateside, and the husband decides to return to the U.S., then the woman is more likely to enter leadership at that time. Chelsea, too, assumed that a leadership position would be located in North America and not overseas. She thought women would not be likely to lead in a local setting, but might at the headquarters. She said:

> I just thought it was interesting that for most of us we didn't start at the bottom and work our way up. We might have just kind of been brought in at a more mature time. But it makes sense if we were serving overseas and stuff, because a lot of us wouldn't have had specific leadership positions overseas. That wouldn't have worked real well. . . . If they are people that have come back from overseas, that kind of makes sense.

Barbara thought it was tied to family responsibilities, commenting that "married women have fewer years of actual experience relative to their age than do males, because of putting a priority on child rearing." Donna also thought family responsibilities might be part of the explanation. She responded that "such a sacrifice of time and emotional commitment [to leadership] results in both children and spouses asserting pressure." So for her it was also logical that married women with children would enter leadership later in life when those pressures diminished.

Regina thought it might have to do with visibility and experience. Reflecting on why married women might enter leadership later but at a higher level, she commented, "I can see why, though. It's because all of a sudden people turn around and say, oh, you have all this experience, why isn't anybody using it?" Melinda had a similar idea:

> These gals have been at the table talking but not had any real authority, and then all of a sudden people go, wow, she really does know something. And her husband may already be at a very high position. So to put her in at a much lower position doesn't seem right. And she may have spent many more years just sitting in limbo and then all of a sudden she gets put into a higher position. I've seen that happen, like, three times in our organization.

So for the women, the career trajectory makes sense due to geographical location, familial responsibilities, experience, and visibility.

What a Feminist Perspective Would Add

The prevalence of the two-person career model is a major structural inequity in these organizations. Although both husbands and wives are required to meet the same standards at the time of recruitment, organizations that hire the husband only and require the wife to work alongside him as a volunteer are perpetuating a structure that privileges men over women. The males receive preference for job assignment and location, and the women, as part of a package deal, are expected to find their own way. Papanek showed that the two-person career structure fundamentally constructs women according to the social gender role stereotypes of females as supporters and nurturers, a pattern which is clearly evident in these women's stories.[1] When only the man receives a salary for his work and the woman is required to work for free, and when her work is viewed as part of his organizational contribution rather than something done in her own right, her work has been rendered completely invisible and her voice silenced; she has been effectively merged with her husband.[2]

1. Papanek, "Men, Women, and Work."
2. Andersen and Hysock, *Thinking about Women*; Zinn et al., "Sex and Gender through the Prism of Difference."

The discourse of evangelical religion regarding marriage and motherhood adds to the pressure placed on these women to accept the unequal structure. Popular sayings such as "motherhood is a woman's highest calling" and the idea that women should be "workers at home" raise the stakes surrounding the relationship of motherhood to the level of a divine command: if motherhood and homemaking are a spiritual calling, then a woman who does not make it her priority is also resisting God's plan for her life.[3] The emphasis on men's spiritual responsibility to provide for their families further reinforces gender roles, which assign men to the public sphere of work and women to the private sphere of home.[4] Like the two-person career, these spheres are based on an essentialist view of men and women, which views women as naturally more suited to nurture children and care for the home than work outside it.[5] In this realm, too, the woman's work is rendered invisible because it takes place within the home.[6] In reality, the women's home and family contributions are absolutely necessary for the family to live and for the men to engage in their ministry, yet the women's contributions are treated as if they were both optional and unimportant. Thus women themselves and their contributions are devalued.[7]

Furthermore, both the two-person career and the family-first requirements for women place men in a position of financial superiority over their wives. Because the women are not paid but counted as volunteers, they are constructed as dependents, relying on the men to provide and care for them. Should problems arise, they are less able to act on their own behalf due to their financial dependence on their husbands.[8] Financial dependence, the pressure of motherhood, the two-person career structure: each of these reinforces and reconstructs the gender essentialist system, functioning to strengthen male hegemony and keep women firmly in a secondary role.

To some extent the single women's career trajectories serve as a foil, showing that absent the pressures of husband and family, women can more easily move into leadership. However, the single women contend with a different aspect of the essentialist system, that which keeps men and women strictly separated, for fear of improper sexual relationships. Sexual relationships are permissible only within marriage, and straying from this

3. Gallagher, *Evangelical Identity and Gendered Family Life.*

4. Bendroth, "Last Gasp Patriarchy"; Ingersoll, "Engendered Conflict"; Ross, "Separate Spheres or Shared Dominions?"

5. Gallagher, *Evangelical Identity and Gendered Family Life.*

6. Andersen and Hysock, *Thinking about Women.*

7. Andersen and Hysock, *Thinking about Women.*

8. Levitt and Ware, "Anything with Two Heads Is a Monster."

boundary is one of the few things that would actually lead to dismissal from the ministry. For the single women this requirement translates into them taking personal responsibility to maintain clear sexual boundaries between themselves and their male colleagues. The current discourse surrounding "modesty" and women's responsibility not to be sexually alluring ("tempting") to men is yet another aspect of the evangelical discourse which preferences men over women, because women are held responsible for men's sexual behavior.[9]

Do the women recognize these dynamics? The way the married women talked shows how these expectations are embedded in their thinking. They spoke in plural pronouns—"we"—as they described supporting their husband's work, and in singular pronouns—"I"—as they described caring for the family. Melinda summed up men's thinking about married women with the comment that "wives are kept in a box"—the confining box of motherhood and the two-person career. And Chelsea, in what might be a *lapsus linguae*, commented, "You're dealing with Christian organizations, and I think that for most women that role plays a heavy—heavy is a negative term, I don't mean heavy—it's a big responsibility that I think most of us take pretty seriously." Male organizational power, male financial power, and the discourse of the evangelical faith do indeed exert heavy pressure on women to conform.

LEARNING TO LEAD FROM MEN

Men played a key role in women's entrance to leadership and in learning to do their jobs. The women in this study, whether married or single, whether they moved into high levels of leadership relatively suddenly in mid-life or worked their way up through the organization, were often sponsored by a high-level male who believed in and supported them. For most of them, learning to lead happened after they were already in a leadership role, they learned primarily from men, and were themselves the initiators of their learning.

Male Sponsorship Is Key

Eight of the women were put into leadership or recommended for their leadership positions by a high-level male who sponsored them. Regina told of participating in a series of conference calls, which led her organization's president to contact her and say, "I think you can do more. You surprised me. I didn't expect you to be this way, but you can do more for the organization."

9. Becker, *Leading Women*.

Ashley too started with something small, and when the top regional leader noticed her ability he moved her quickly into a more responsible position. Her comment was similar to Regina's: "I had a couple of strong mentors in that time that were quick to encourage me that you could do more here." Later, it was a new president who came to her to ask her to join the organization's executive team based on her previous work.

For Holly, an old relationship was helpful to her in getting her current position. "I had worked with my current organization in another country years ago, and had stayed in contact. I was friends with the previous executive director and his wife, and they recommended me to the board," she explained. For her, that friendship led to sponsorship from an influential male in the organization.

Nicole was also very aware of the support her sponsor gave her:

> In fact probably a lot of my story there is thanks to him. He's just a man who recognized that I did have leadership abilities and wanted me to be able to use them, and tried to pave the way for that. He challenged me to try to start a ministry, and backed me all the way, and then when it was time for it to be formalized as a new ministry area he made me the leader of it. So I think he was probably very significant in the story. . . . He actually recommended me to the president for this role on the leadership team. The president didn't know me. And he asked me to join the leadership team really based on the recommendation of the other guy.

For Nicole, the sponsorship of a key male leader was central to her journey to leadership. Interestingly, none of the women talked about female sponsors or role models. In fact, some of them specifically mentioned the absence of such women.

Mentored by Men

Once they were in positions of responsibility none of the women received formal training for their roles. Rather, they found their own ways of learning. For eight of them, it was being mentored or helped by someone, almost always a man, and sometimes the one who had the job before her. Melinda, for example, learned to do her job from the man who had it before her. She explained, "Over the years he's really mentored me in many ways."

Carol also learned from the men in her organization. She explained what happened when she first took a position:

I feel like I've even been, to some extent, really discipled by some men in leadership in a certain sense. . . . Some of what I was doing had been overseen by Bob who was right in the next office over. So I was in his office a lot, saying, Bob, what do I do about this? What do I do about that? So that was one thing. I have . . . a couple of other leaders, and especially a couple of guys who have been around for a long time and they just know our history and . . . I was in that group for a while, and then I had to lead that group for a while. So I guess I would say I learned that by watching how it was done. But I think because we were here before for a long time, I know a lot, I know all of the people who have been around for a long time, and most of them are our leaders, and so I know who to go to. I know who my resources are, and I know who's going to know the answer. Sometimes it's my own husband.

The combination of her years with the organization, knowing who knows things, and watching how the men lead has been Carol's way of learning her job. She was also the only woman to mention having had a female mentor, a counselor who had office space in the building.

Like Carol, Stephanie found watching her own husband and reading to be effective ways to learn leadership. "I have learned . . . through reading books that deal with leadership, and in all honesty through watching my husband, because he's very good at that. In a way maybe he's a role model in some of these things." Ashley also found a man to mentor her, though it was not her husband:

I . . . had a mentor in a guy who's actually still in the organization; he was a very key mentor for me. He's a clinical psychologist and a pastor, and he was very important in helping me grow in this role, and a real encouragement, and helped me sift through the different, you know, he's my process point for leadership questions that I had.

Chelsea, like Carol, would go ask questions of her supervisor, who had the job before her, or of others who might know. She said:

The man that is over me, my supervisor, had been in the position several years ago and so he was also really helpful and willing to sit down and talk with me. It was at my instigation when I would go and ask.

Part of what got her interested in the job in the first place was conversations she had while still living overseas, trying to understand how things worked:

> I had an interest that kind of grew as I saw people with various struggles on the field. And I would think about it, and I would try and understand it. I had a friend that was a counselor . . . and he would let me sit down and talk to him and ask him questions. He would help me try and understand different things, you know, just kind of a teacher by nature and I wanted to learn.

She discovered her interest and found someone to help her learn, informally. In her current role that push to learn for herself has continued; she finds reading books helps her learn more about her job. Given the chance, she would "love to learn more . . . [so] I could give more to the organization."

Reading, as well as looking for workshops and other resources to learn what they needed to know, was common. Ashley said she did it that way because she was personally highly motivated to go after what she needs. Barbara said she did a lot of reading and went to external workshops, since "I like to figure things out myself." Chelsea mentioned reading a book on leadership as one way of improving her capacity. Melinda started reading on leadership and took some master's degree courses once she was in her position. Regina said she retooled with an entire doctoral program, and Stephanie reported watching others, reading, and attending workshops on topics that interested her. Tabitha completed her Master's degree and was about to start a PhD program as part of her learning strategy.

Of course there is some difference between learning to lead and learning the specific skills related to a job. Most of the women talked about learning to do their jobs, rather than learning to lead. Donna's organization did have a leadership training program, but she explained, "I didn't go through [it], but I did go through aspects of that training." Her leadership learning was rather piecemeal: "some of it was provided by the organization, but some of it was just self-discovery kinds of leadership training where I actually became very interested in trying to learn how to do what I was doing better." Stephanie said that her organization had leadership training but added that she herself had "no training seminars." Regina was asked to develop some training for her organization. However, five women specifically said that their organization did not provide any leadership training for them.

Another way that most of the women learned was through experience. All but one of the women named this as one of the most effective ways they learned their jobs and leadership. As Carol mentioned, a long history with the organization helped some of them; general experience in mission organizations proved useful for others. Nicole described her process of learning as something that happened while she went along trying to get a project done. "I mean I was really literally figuring out as we went along and just trying to stay one or two steps ahead of where we actually were." Not everyone on her team liked that approach, but finding her own resources and her own plan was her only option:

> For some people, it feels like you're building the airplane as you fly it, very uncomfortable with that, or changing the tire on a moving car, you know, all those kind of analogies, and it's true, to a certain extent, that is what you're doing, because you can't stop the whole forward momentum of things while you do that.

She had a project that needed doing and no instructions on how to do it, so she got going and learned as she went. Barbara described a similar experience with her team as they launched a new project. "We're learning as we go with [it]," she explained.

Learning what not to do through negative experiences was especially helpful for several women. As they reflected on poor experiences, they learned how not to lead in their own positions. Describing a time when her leader did not support her, Chelsea explained what she learned from that experience: "I'm keenly aware of it now and I'm trying to be really aware of what I'm doing to those who are working with me. You know, do I do that?" For Regina, living through a misuse of power in her previous organization was critical for her learning:

> And having seen that from the underside, it helps me when I'm on top, working down, on how to work leadership. So, I mean, it was a very difficult experience coming out of the former organization, I learned a whole lot of what I needed to be effective in this current organization. But again, it's by bad leadership.

So negative experiences served as examples and cautions for some women, showing them how not to lead. Sometimes the learning was more straightforward; the women simply tried something. Nicole explained that she "ended up filling in wherever there were other needs, and kind of learned a multitude of tasks and roles and jobs." Experience, pursuit of information, mentoring, and sponsoring by males were all crucial aspects of how the women learned to do their jobs.

What the Women Think It Means

The women mostly agreed that they learned things on their own and sought out their own ways of learning their jobs. Carol explained:

> I definitely did not have the opportunity to be trained by anyone for this job. I identify with the "learning through experience"

> option [on the feedback sheet]; though I have had advisors . . . .
> I have a group that includes both men and women . . . . . . that
> is an advisory group for working through issues that come up.
> And I have found that the male leaders I work with have been
> pretty willing to mentor me informally. My husband is also a
> help, of course.

Carol was the only participant to mention other women as part of her learning experience.

Melinda found her sponsorship of others to be less effective than male sponsorship. She explained, "I found that it takes men to sponsor women and when I have sponsored both men and women, more often the men I sponsor are more easily received than the women I recommended." She believes that a male sponsor is necessary for a female, since the females she tries to sponsor do not do as well as the males she sponsors.

Two women added comments about the lack of leadership development in their organizations. They did not think it was only women who were not receiving training, but saw that men were also neglected. Regina explained that "one caveat from my experience would be that there was little in the way of leadership training for men either." And Ashley, in regards to women learning to lead on their own, said:

> Yes this is true for me. Although I observe that mission agencies don't do a good job of providing leadership training/development for any staff. Males may be more motivated to go after formal training like graduate degrees because this is expected of them and they are encouraged to do so by peers. Also I would think many women in ministry do not see opportunities for practical application of leadership training so they don't bother with it.

Her comment leads me to consider what feminism might say about women's lack of preparation for leadership and their reliance on males to sponsor them for leadership and to learn leadership.

What a Feminist Perspective Would Add

Organizationally, males are the ones who hold power. Leaders are almost always male, and males serve as the gatekeepers, determining who is sponsored for leadership and who is not. The organization itself is constructed by males, for males, and represents and recreates male power structures.[10]

10. Bierema, "Critiquing Human Resource Development's Dominant Masculine Rationality and Evaluating Its Impact"; Stead and Elliott, *Women's Leadership*.

Furthermore, males serve as the gatekeepers of knowledge. They are the ones with previous leadership experience, from whom the women can learn. They are the ones with access to knowledge and are the ones who determine what can be learned and who can learn it. In short, they have constructed the organizational knowledge and can offer or inhibit access to that knowledge.[11] By choosing which women are granted access they are able to maintain the existing male power and organizational structures that favor men and carefully control the boundaries of women's leadership.

The discourse of evangelical faith also serves to reinforce the idea of male power.[12] First, God is generally conceived of and represented as male.[13] Though theologians point out that God is not gendered, the popular use of male imagery and male pronouns to represent God creates a powerful connection between maleness and godlikeness.[14] Second is a popular idea that since Jesus' 12 disciples were male, males are meant to be the leaders in evangelical ministry. In both these ways evangelical faith reinforces the hierarchy between males and females, placing men in a position of authority and women in a position of submission.[15]

Associating male with God and therefore rulership serves to reinforce gender essentialist ideas. If gender determines leadership and God determines gender, then the connection is predetermined and outside of a woman's choice and is not negotiable.[16] Allowing men to choose one particular woman to lead and promoting her while limiting access for others serves to reinforce male power: women who please men in some way may be selected for leadership. Thus structurally the organization continues to create male power and privilege, and male hegemony continues unchallenged.

COMMUNAL LEADERSHIP PRACTICES

All the women in this study reported using communal behaviors as a substantive part of their leadership. Communal behaviors are those that focus on the relational aspects of leading, sometimes called the "soft" skills. To the degree that the women use these skills, they are showing both good

---

11. Andersen and Hysock, *Thinking about Women*; Andersen and Collins, *Race, Class & Gender.*

12. Becker, *Leading Women.*

13. Pevey et al., "Male God Imagery and Female Submission."

14. Becker, *Leading Women*; Pevey et al., "Male God Imagery and Female Submission."

15. Becker, *Leading Women*; Pevey et al., "Male God Imagery and Female Submission."

16. Gallagher, *Evangelical Identity and Gendered Family Life.*

leadership and acceptance of the gender-role requirements. The women also report using agentic behaviors as part of their leadership practice. These behaviors are used with care and may also be perceived as high-risk. In their interactions with male leaders in their organizations, women are quite likely to adjust to the male environment, and not challenge it.

Relationships

Building relationships with others is a communal skill that ten women used extensively as part of their leadership practices. Melinda found it helped to build relationships with male colleagues and with their wives, especially to prevent suspicion or jealousy on the part of the wives. Interacting socially with them as couples helped: "I see the couple on Sunday, I speak with the wife, I talk with the wife . . . I do my best to keep it on a very social level." Nicole also found relationships with her colleagues to be helpful to her leadership. "We meet together once a week, and so we have become a real team. I really enjoy them all," she commented. Chelsea thought building relationships with males under her helped her earn trust and be able to succeed as a leader. "I've tried to build a lot of relationships with my field leaders and that sort of thing. I try to be very intentional about that."

Regina found that having relationships with her team helped overcome the weirdness some of them felt from having a female leader:

> In some ways I think I have to connect with the guys, build a friendship as well as a work relationship. I'm not into becoming everybody's best friend, but I want to make sure that they know that I value them not just because they come to work and do a job at the office.

One characteristic of good relationships was having an open door and being accessible to team members. Regina commented:

> I always want to be approachable by the people under me. And so I'll be sitting in my office and somebody will wander down the hall and come into my office and say, you know, I have a question. And maybe it's a big thing, and maybe it's—I have this guy who comes down the hall and just tells me a joke! And to me, I like that, because I want to build community in the office.

Tabitha also found that an open door and accessibility were critical:

> My door is always open. Anybody, I don't care what your job is here, you're part of the team and your voice will be heard. I may not be able to do everything you ask or everything you say, but

I will listen and I think each person here feels valued, that no matter whether they're an assistant for somebody or one of my higher-level administrators, whoever they are, they have a voice.

Relationships could also be useful for handling difficult or challenging situations. Regina could allow relationship strength to help solve issues with a difficult team member, by appealing to others who had better relationships with him to run interference for her. "With the [difficult person] I have to kind of go around the corner and talk to people who he trusts, and let them go back to him." Donna also relied on relationships and communication outside of formal meeting times to get her ideas heard and considered:

I had to invest a lot of time in, well first of all, relationships. . . . I need to make sure that they hear my perspective outside the meetings. I feel that is one way that women [work]: to do a lot of negotiating outside what would normally just be considered the normal call times, the normal meeting times, to try to help people understand a given situation.

Both she and Regina learned to use relationships to handle challenging work situations.

Caretaking Behaviors

Other kinds of communal behaviors that the women reported using involved being the caretakers for others' needs. Melinda explained, "I became . . . Aunt Melinda to all these young guys and their wives. . . . I'll go to their home and we just sit and talk and have a great time." Similarly, Barbara described caring for her staff and added, "They think I'm their mother or something. I love working with our [staff]!"

Another form of caretaking was mediating in relationship issues. Carol described doing this:

There have been other times when a couple of very strong people were just totally constantly miscommunicating, and just sitting them down and I felt like I was successful in helping them understand each other, and really talk through what they needed to do to make their relationship work and to be able to work with one another. They were two very opposite personalities and just had no capacity to communicate but I helped them . . . make it work.

Melinda talked about two men in her region who were at odds with each other. "I just sensed that really, here had been two ships from the same country, passing in the night, thinking they were enemy ships, shooting at each other, and that needed to stop." For Holly it was mediating between a leader and staff. She described working for a leader who was "not a good people person," so her job, she was told, was to "balance with him. He was visionary and I could be the people person." She functioned "as a buffer" between him and others on staff.

Chelsea, Melinda, Tabitha, and Regina all described being a good listener as an important part of their leadership skills. Making sure there was open communication with staff was important to Stephanie, Tabitha, and Regina. Stephanie explained, "A large part of my role is communicator to all our members." Several women worked to make people feel welcomed and valued as well as heard. Holly commented that what others valued about her leadership was "that I pulled people together, made them feel like they belong, are welcomed, valued, and included." Kelly was particularly interested in staff development. "I got into that [leadership] role and began to realize how passionate I was about staff development."

Team building was critical to several of the women, and placing relationships ahead of tasks happened as well, though it could also produce internal stress for the women. Tabitha explained, "We had a very serious situation with one of my team members and instantly the administrator hat goes out the door and the pastor hat goes on. It's just what happens . . . . And they're in conflict sometimes."

Ashley told a story of being placed in a position where she had to choose between being relational with another woman and attending to the task requirement of her job:

> I was in a strategic planning meeting [and] I was the only woman there, so that was already something, but I was pretty used to that. We're meeting all day, and in the evening there was a social. Everyone was invited over to my boss's home. And his wife put on a meal for everybody. And all the guys then said, okay, let's go sit around the fire pit and smoke cigars. . . . And the first thing to happen was the woman, my boss's wife, says to me, well I don't like sitting outside with those guys, so why don't you sit inside with me? So my first dilemma was do I go out there where the actual networking kind of conversation and such is just as important as the meeting I attended all day, it's going to happen around that fire. Or do I support her? Because she obviously expected I would, being the only other woman. And it was difficult, I was like, I don't know what to do. I actually don't like sitting around the fire smoking, so I don't really want to be out

there. But I also knew that those conversations are the ones that
are really mission-critical; I knew that.

In the end she stayed inside with her boss's wife, but she added that she later
regretted her choice:

> I stayed inside . . . and later I regretted it. . . . I wanted to connect
> with her. And I also felt empathy for her. Here she had prepared
> a whole meal for everybody, and all this work, and they were
> all going to abandon her inside while she was there. Not very
> hospitable! I felt like I needed to connect with her.

For Ashley, like Tabitha, the communal requirement to care for people was
the more important value in this difficult situation.

Success Is Defined Communally

Another indication of the strength of communal behaviors is how success
is frequently described in communal terms. When asked to describe a time
when they felt really successful as a leader, the women told stories of establishing or developing functional ministries by supporting or developing
others. Chelsea's story involved helping a couple find a setting for ministry where they could flourish. Regina's involved coaching one of her team
members to become more effective in his role:

> I go into his office almost every day that I'm there, and I say,
> how are you doing, how are things going today? Is there any-
> thing I can help you with? And we're in meetings, sometimes
> I'll prep him for meetings, and sometimes I'll debrief him from
> meetings.

Melinda's success story involved a couple in her area who had significant
performance issues, to the point that they were about to be asked to leave
the ministry by the leader above her. As she got to know them and built
trust with them, she discovered an underlying relational conflict with that
leader which, when solved, allowed the couple to become one of the most
effective couples in her region:

> I just saw them as two major ships passing in the night, and they
> were shooting at each other, not realizing that they were on the
> same team. And so I said to the team member, you know what
> my goal is for this next year between you and your wife and I?
> is that we learn to trust each other. That's my goal for this first
> whole year. So we started talking about [that]. . . . Well, now this

couple, after almost four years under my leadership, is now one of our bright and shining stars in so many ways.

Ashley's story showed the blending of the two aspects: not only did she establish a functional department, she did it by recruiting and building a team who work well together in accomplishing the department's goals. Before she started they did not even have a staff directory, but now they do:

> When I came into this role . . . I was given kind of a carte blanche to say, okay, this whole system is a shambles. You need to please rebuild it. . . . And I just took on the challenge to do that. And so now two years later, I recruited a team . . . empowered all those people and I centralized all the information and now I feel—I look back and I'm proud of that, of where we're at.

Holly's story also involved rescuing a failing ministry; part of the problem was serious conflict among the team members, so the solution involved both building relationships and achieving goals. For the women, then, part of the definition of functional ministry was that people had security, relationships, trust, and the freedom to work well.

Working Harder Than the Men

Another aspect of success that the women mentioned was working harder than the men around them. Six of the women named this as part of their success. Carol commented that, "Sometimes I feel like, as a woman, you almost have to work harder than maybe a guy does." Barbara was more explicit:

> In my own situation I feel like all these years I've worked here, I've worked a lot harder than most of the men I know. . . . If I'm going to get any recognition, I'm going to have to work harder, and I've noticed that the men don't work as hard as I do, and yet they seem to get respect and they're thought highly of and all.

And Melinda added, "I do believe we often have to work much harder (more intentionally) than our male counterparts to be known as good leaders and receive trust."

Agentic Behaviors Are Risky

The women also reported using agentic behaviors as part of their leadership practices. In fact, establishing departments, ministries, and policies, and straightening out neglected areas in the organization were common themes, as we have already seen in some of the narratives. Holly, Tabitha, and Regina were tasked with cleaning up messy situations; Nicole, Ashley, Donna, and Carol established a new department or ministry that the organization needed; Barbara and Kelly were expected to consolidate and establish a ministry on the heels of a visionary founder. These were task-oriented assignments that the women received.

Interestingly, several of the women perceived these assignments or the use of agentic behaviors as being high-risk. Yet they were willing to take on these challenges for the organization's good, showing their willingness to place others' needs ahead of their own. Kelly and Barbara both discussed the risk involved in trying to transition a ministry from the visionary founder's approach to a more established, functional work. Kelly commented, "The organization was essentially set up to be a platform for the founder . . . so to transition him out and someone in who could actually chart the course for the organization without him is a pretty risky thing." Barbara explained her situation:

> You know, you've got the founder stage, and the chaos and we're going to have to codify things. And I'm helping this happen: here's our regulations, here's our policy governance, in order to operate smoothly and grow and not have always chaos and have everybody give up.

She went on to describe the tension she felt between maintaining the original vision and creating an environment where people can work well, and struggled with feeling that she might not be succeeding.

Tabitha described a risky agentic move she made while still considered an interim in her job:

> When I was still the interim, I fired one of my regional leaders, because I felt like he was harming the team that he was in charge of. . . . I thought, as the interim, for me to do that was just crazy! I was in the role about 4 months, and I thought, I could lose my job over this. This might be the end. But I thought, I will not allow him to continue harming the team.

She engaged in highly agentic behavior, which was motivated by communal reasons. For that reason she was willing to take the risk.

Carol also engaged in an agentic process which she perceived as risky but believed was for the organization's good. One of the project leaders had made what she and some others considered to be a mistaken decision. So she began to push for a policy change, so that such decisions would go through a central approval process in the future. She commented:

> I know some of the individual men were entirely in favor of what I was proposing. But since there was resistance from [the project group] about this, and somehow the whole group of leaders did not seem to resonate with my proposal, there was risk involved with insisting on a decision about this. Those who agreed with me did not stick their neck out to take a stand on what we needed to do, but I did.

Because of her strong conviction that a policy change would protect the organization in future, she was willing to risk pushing for a decision.

Both Holly and Regina also received risky assignments, where they were expected to fix or rescue something that was not functional. For Holly, it was to take a camp on the verge of failing because of conflict among the staff, and turn it around into a functional ministry. For Regina, it was to take responsibility for her organization's most problematic geographical area, and turn it into a functional one:

> The president told the board, I mean, he asked me first, but he kind of told the board, the biggest organizational problem we have is in [continent]. That's why I need Regina to be the leader of [continent], because that's the most crucial organizational issue we have right now. So that's how I got there.

Sometimes the move to leadership in and of itself is risky for a woman. Tabitha described choosing to accept a leadership role:

> I knew if I did this as an interim, there was a risk that I could lose everything. They could say, well, we don't want to keep you on full-time, and by that time be too late to go back to my other position; they would have replaced me by then. So it was kind of risky, but I decided to take the risk. So I did it.

And during the course of the study one of the participants, Nicole, lost her leadership role and found herself with no place in the organization. Five years ago she left her overseas assignment to come back to the U.S. and take on an executive role. She wrote, "Things are in chaos for me . . . almost immediately after I talked with you, our board of directors replaced our president [and] his leadership team was also immediately disbanded leaving me without a 'landing place' in the organization." Like Tabitha, going back to the old role was no longer an option, but the organization left her to find her own way in establishing a new role.

Adjusting to a Male Context

In some cases, women deliberately chose to adjust to the male environment, rather than challenge it. As the first high level woman leader in her organization, Chelsea was fairly self-conscious about how she dressed, how she communicated, and how she portrayed herself and her authority. "It is a change for the mission so I do try and be very careful and aware and intentional about how I approach things." She was aware that she was being scrutinized and was therefore deliberate about choices, including clothes:

> I really tried to think through how I would even present myself, in what I would say and even what I would wear. . . . We're now quite a bit more casual in the office, but I find I need to be a step above that. . . I don't dress down as much as others do. So I'm just a little more cautious, if I go out shopping or something; does this look professional enough?

The scrutiny affects her both inside and outside the office.

Melinda also paid close attention to how she communicated and how she took up her authority:

> I do know that there are some other leaders within our organization who are still not perfectly comfortable with a female at my level of leadership. Most of them are gracious and kind and nice, but you don't see them seeking out my input, or seeking out my thoughts, and so I've just learned . . . even the greatest advice if it's not requested becomes criticism. So I try to be careful. There's one in particular who just told me one time, I don't even ask my wife those questions. I said, why not? He goes, she's a woman. I was, like, okay. And I know with him, I'm not necessarily walking on eggshells, but I'm more careful.

She also has encountered men in the U.S. offices who do not accept her authority. So she has learned to use the organization's core values statements to express her needs, rather than directly stating her own opinion. She explained that being direct was not particularly helpful:

> But for me it doesn't help to pull out the "L"-flag for leadership. It's better for me to present a well-thought-through reason for my decision, as opposed to saying I'm making this because I can make this decision, because of who I am.

Nicole has also learned to adjust her communication styles to suit the men's preferences. What she perceived as an engaging conversation they saw as being interrupted:

I want it to be more of a conversation, to be both involved, and they have commented more than once that it feels to them like I'm interrupting them, and I should wait until they're finished and then I can talk. And I wait for the teacher to call on me before I can say anything, instead of just being spontaneous and natural.

She also tried to sound unemotional when she spoke:

So I have to be very conscious about kind of withholding my impulse to jump in and let them finish their thought, think through what they're saying, and then try to respond a lot more measured and try to not have it sound so emotional. But if I'm kind of upset or frustrated about something if I can say it in a very calm voice, they will listen to me a lot better than if I say it in an emotional tone.

Melinda agreed with eliminating emotion:

I have learned that in our organization, if I speak with a gentle tone, if I've pre-thought out things and share it logically and clearly, my same passion can come through and be respected and appreciated. . . . I think as a woman in leadership . . . I have to more carefully choose my words and choose my tone of voice, more so than a man might have to do.

For Regina the challenge has been to adjust to what she described as her organization's indirect method of communication. "In my current job it's difficult because of the direct-indirect interface. Sometimes I'm going forward and I'm thinking, I'm not getting any support from the organization, or from my boss." She was able to talk the issue through with her boss and discovered that he did support her. But she continued to be careful about her communication with others in the organization.

What the Women Think It Means

For the most part, the women seem to value the communal behaviors that they use. After describing how she used the core values to support her position rather than appealing to her positional authority, Melinda commented, "So it makes it a little harder, but I think it's the better thing to do." Ashley said that she could have challenged the men about going to the fire pit to talk, but she did not. She simply stayed with her hostess, because of her empathy for the woman, although she did recognize the difficulty. "I thought, this is the kind of stuff that trips women up when they're leading," she concluded. Tabitha discussed a difficult situation where her supervisor wanted her to be task-oriented in firing someone, but she kept using her communal behavior. He told her, "You tell this guy what he needs to hear, and you get out of there and don't have anything more to do with him. And I was like, uh, no, I'm not doing that!" The women clearly see the value of the communal practices they bring to leadership.

They also accept making adjustments as a necessary part of being a woman in leadership in a man's world. For example, Carol commented:

> I know that I have learned, over the years, to influence men pretty carefully. You can't come across with too much feeling, or take too long to say something, or fail to use hard facts when stating a case. That's ultimately a good discipline, but I do know, too, that men can shut down when a woman is simply too "feminine" in her perspective on things.

Several of the women saw that they brought additional value to the organization. Barbara's opinion was that "women have to work harder to prove themselves, so the organization gets a bargain with a woman leader!" She went on to explain that because women work significantly harder than men, in the end they also contribute far more to the organization than men do. Melinda found that her communal skills filled a need that the male leaders in her organization might not be able to meet. She wrote:

> I do believe that there are many things that I'm able to do much better than my male counterparts because I'm a "nurturing woman." I have found that several of the leaders under me respond to me much better than they did my male predecessor. I also often get requests for advice/counsel from other leaders (all male) when it comes to what they call "soft issues" which to them are the most difficult.

Donna, too, thought she took her responsibilities to the organization's members more seriously than her male counterparts:

> For me, my perception was that I was in that role to have a positive impact by engaging with those we were leading, whether they were in my line of supervision or someone else's. My perception, maybe right or wrong, was that I engaged with those outside our leadership circle significantly more than my male counterparts. I also felt that my male counterparts did not fully understand the personal impact of our decisions.

Carol thought being female made it easier for her to make a risky move. She wrote:

> I think that sometimes I can get away with taking certain less popular positions BECAUSE I am a woman. A man might not be willing to stick his neck out about something, because of how the other guys might think of him. But as a woman, I almost have nothing to lose.

Both Regina and Holly thought they received the risky assignment precisely because they were women. Holly was very clear:

> Women sometimes get handed risky roles because if they fail or get sabotaged, they can be blamed. That camp I was in was risky because of high levels of tension in the board and among the staff. Later they told me they gave it to me because they figured it was ready to die, and since I was young and inexperienced, then they could blame me if it died. And they couldn't believe I brought it back to life!

The organizational leaders expected the camp to fail, and would have preferred the failure to happen under a woman's leadership. Regina struggled with similar feelings. Naming it the glass cliff, she wrote:

> In my most cynical moments I, at times, feel like this is me. If I fail the only one who really pays the consequences is me. They have given me a task that numerous males seem to have failed at. And, personally, that makes me feel like I will die before I call it quits here.

So for most of the women, focusing on the added benefit their communal skills brought to the organization was encouraging to them. They saw the benefit they bring and embrace what they are able to offer, even though they recognize it may come at a price.

What a Feminist Perspective Would Add

Patriarchal organizational structures function to construct the women's leadership practices in accordance with the requirements of the gender role stereotypes. Thus women are allowed to use communal practices, because these practices align with the gender role expectations of females, but they are not as easily permitted to use agentic practices which belong to the male gender stereotype. Only the female as "constructed under patriarchy" is welcomed because in continuing to perform the female role she is mimicking the home setting in the workplace.[17] Communal behaviors are those assigned to her by the role requirements and are the ones looked

17. Calás and Smircich, "Dangerous Liaisons," 74.

upon favorably by the organization, whereas agentic behaviors are not allotted to her and receive disapprobation. Despite the fact that leadership roles frequently require the use of agentic behaviors, the woman is caught in the double-bind where not using them makes her a poor leader but using them goes against the ideal of a good Christian woman.[18]

The stories women told of "glass cliff" situations, where "their leadership appointments are made in problematic organizational circumstances and hence are more precarious" are particularly troubling.[19] Several of them were given leadership of troubled or failing ministries or departments, and tasked with rescue operations. If they failed, the organization would appear justified in rejecting women as incompetent leaders, but if they succeeded, the organization gained the benefit of their work without any obligation to change their beliefs or behaviors accordingly. The women can easily be blamed for failure, but may not be rewarded for success.[20]

The discourse of the faith further works to construct women as communal beings. Talk of women as "princesses" who long to be rescued and of men as "heroes" looking for adventure in popular works such as *Wild at Heart* by John Eldredge, for example, reinforce the idea that women are primarily relational and men primarily active.[21] In this narrative, it is the male gaze that determines women's behavior: women may change the way they dress, speak, and act in order to gain male approval and be "worthy" of "rescue" by a male "hero."

Thus the structures and practices of the organization as well as the discourse surrounding women in the evangelical faith pressures them to conform to the communal role and discourages them from engaging in agentic behaviors, lest they lose male approval. The gender essentialist approach is reinforced and strengthened every time a woman is rewarded or feels successful in using communal behaviors. It is also reinforced when she tries agentic behaviors and encounters disapproval which pushes her back into the approved role.

CHAPTER SUMMARY

The women in this study show signs of accepting the gender-role expectations placed on them. All but one of the married women began as part of a two-person career structure, supporting their husband's work and taking primary responsibility for the home and children. The single women

18. Eagly, "Female Leadership Advantage and Disadvantage."
19. Ryan and Haslam, "Glass Cliff," 86.
20. Ryan and Haslam, "Glass Cliff."
21. Eldredge, *Wild at Heart.*

worked initially in female-gendered jobs, and were highly conscious of their responsibility to maintain purity in their relationships with men. The women gained access to leadership roles primarily through the sponsorship of an influential male in the organization. Their mentors, advisors, and role models for leadership were almost exclusively men. Thus men are the gatekeepers to leadership positions as well as the primary source of leadership knowledge and skills.

Finally, the women in this study use many communal leadership practices. They build relationships, care for their team members, focus on good communication, and use relational networks to get things done. They also use agentic practices, but carefully, when they are sure it is best for the system, and buttressing them with communal behaviors. A number of them took on assignments that were personally risky but potentially highly beneficial for their organizations, showing they place others' needs ahead of their own. And many have learned to adjust the way they lead to the predominantly male environment. In all of these practices, they show themselves accepting of and aligning with the gender-role requirements for women to be communal, nurturing, care for others ahead of themselves, and accept rather than challenge male authority.

A feminist perspective on these practices and behaviors shows how they have been designed to support and reinforce male power and privilege. The combination of gender essentialist beliefs and patriarchal organizational structures places enormous pressure on the women to accept and conform to gendered expectations, and they do. Since the culture will only allow certain approaches to leadership, the women have learned to make the most of those approaches. However, they also appear willing to maneuver around the gender role requirements to a small degree. In the next chapter I will look at some of the ways they resist gendered expectations.

7

Findings: Maneuvers with Gender Roles

IN THE PREVIOUS CHAPTER, Acceptance of Gender Roles, I presented the data to answer research question one. In this chapter I present the second finding, Maneuvers with Gender Roles, which answers research question two, What if any forms of resistance or subversive behavior do women use in order to lead in a patriarchal culture? Although to an extent the women show conformity to the gender-role requirements of their faith, they also are able to use or maneuver around those gender-roles for their own purposes, while not actually subverting them. One of the ways in which they challenge the roles is evident in the way married women separated their role and, therefore, their identity from their husband. Another is their reliance on delegated authority to assure themselves and others of the rightness of their leadership positions. Being gifted for and passionate about her role serves as another reason for women to lead; in a sense, gifting supersedes gender for them. Finally, the women use cautious advocacy to support their leadership. In this chapter I examine ways in which the women maneuvered in the prescribed gender roles or used the requirements to bolster their leadership.

ENDING THE TWO-PERSON CAREER

In the previous chapter we saw that eight of the nine married women began their ministry as part of a two-person career structure. Initially they were the primary caretakers for the family, and were in a support role to their husband's ministry. Only Tabitha, who was ordained as a pastor in her denomination, did not report beginning her career that way. As they made the shift into leadership, all but one separated from their husband's ministry in order to accept a position. For all of them, this change happened

after a time of focusing primarily on the children; though the exact stage
varied somewhat no one entered leadership with preschool-aged children,
and some only began leading as empty nesters. Yet to the extent that the
women separated from their husband's ministry and engaged in their own
independent role, they were resisting the gender role that constructs them
as their husband's helper.

This separation worked in different ways for different women. For
Kelly it happened by working with a different organization where her husband was never involved. Her family had been overseas for many years and
returned to the U.S., where she began working with a different group. She
explained about her new ministry, "My husband has no relationship to my
role and has never worked for the same organization."

For Ashley the whole shift was more intentional:

> You know, it was an interesting dynamic—this happens a lot
> in missions. I was working with my husband. My husband's a
> very strong leader, and he served . . . on many of these occa-
> sions we served together on the leadership team. So kind of
> learning to differentiate myself from him. And he's one of those
> strong voices. That was kind of interesting, navigating that in
> our relationship.

Then, after a period of stepping away from ministry altogether, she came
back into a different leadership role. She commented:

> When I came back in to any kind of responsibility, I came back
> in a completely different door. So from that point on, my lead-
> ership has been completely in the operations sphere, and my
> husband has been in . . . church planting.

For Chelsea, changes in her husband's workload made it possible for
her to separate from him and take on her own leadership responsibility:

> And so for my husband, he was traveling a lot. So that made it
> important to me that I be there to be the stability factor, and that
> I be there when he got home. He always needed to talk about
> what had happened or whatever. So for me that was a factor that
> I didn't even think about taking on any regular day to day sort
> of responsibilities. I would do special projects. But I wouldn't do
> regular day to day responsibilities, until our kids were gone and
> our lifestyle was somewhat changed in terms of, you know, my
> husband doesn't travel quite as much. He still travels, but not as
> much as he did then.

She was still considering him first, but in assessing that his need for her had become less crucial, she decided to make the shift into independent ministry. Barbara too cited her husband's good as militating against a shared role: "I just didn't think it was a good fit for him." When Carol and her husband returned from their overseas work, the president quickly put her into an executive-level position. She thought it was preparation for moving them as a couple into another position, and when they decided not to accept that appointment, she worried she would lose her role. "I remember wondering at the time if he would remove me from the leadership role, once I declined the director role, but he was clear that I was to stay in that role." Since her organization is one of the three that places a very high value on husband-wife teams, her worries seemed well-founded. But she was allowed to continue separately, in her own leadership role.

The notable exception to separating from her husband in order to lead was Stephanie. Her organization's practice is that husbands and wives are appointed to leadership together. They between them then decide who will do what. She was comfortable with that structure and doubted she would continue as a leader alone, if her husband were no longer there. "Honestly I would probably say I just wanted to go home and be with my grandchildren, and let somebody else do it."

What the Women Think It Means

Ashley thought it had to do with different kinds of skills and abilities. She explained that they started out working in church planting together, but that her husband has visionary skills and she has administrative ones. So when she returned to ministry, it was in a different part of the organization. She also thought shared roles were hard on a marriage. If they had kept working together, she said:

> We would have had to do a whole lot more negotiating about how we were going to co-lead a project, and what that looked like, how we would preserve a marriage in the middle of actually trying to lead together where we might disagree, and have to be in a leadership place. I think that's probably pretty difficult. I don't know of many couples that do that successfully.

Barbara also thought it could be hard on a marriage to share a role. She said that the president "tried to ask my husband and I to be the co-presidents at one point. I flatly refused; it would have destroyed our marriage; I knew that it would and I said no." A very interesting perspective on the effect of separating her role from that of her husband came from Carol.

For her it was important that her role not be higher than her husband's; she worried about that:

> There've been times that I've worried that they're putting me in a higher position than my husband, and I won't do that. I'd feel really uncomfortable with that. I won't. I have a hard time with that. That just would be really awkward for us, for me. Not that my husband seeks to claim position at all—he's a really humble guy. But that would just be really awkward for me.

She was pretty emphatic that for her preserving the gender hierarchy was important, but that she was willing to lead separately as long as she was lower in the organizational hierarchy.

What a Feminist Perspective Would Add

The prevalence of the two-person career structure in mission organizations means that even though a woman may separate from her husband and engage in work of her own, there is no organizational obligation to then recognize her work or change her status from that of volunteer to that of employee. The choice of whether to offer the woman employee status lies entirely within the organization's power, and they can continue to benefit from her work without ever formally acknowledging her contributions.[1] This is yet another way of maintaining the woman's work as invisible and her voice as silent.[2]

The gender hierarchy taught by evangelical gender roles shows clearly in the way the women talk about separating their role from their husband's role. When they explain that their husband's position is higher on the organizational chart than theirs, they show how they have been constructed as their husband's subordinate. When they explain that separating their role from his is better for him, or better for the marriage, they show how they have been constructed to fill the communal role which supports the husband's good or that of the marriage above their own. The dominant discourse regarding marriage in evangelical faith centers around the notion of "headship," meaning that the husband should be the head of the household, the spiritual leader of the family, and frequently the primary earner and final decision-maker as well.[3] This discourse functions to cement male power and privilege in the family, and in the case of mission organizations that

---

1. Calás and Smircich, "Dangerous Liaisons."
2. Andersen and Hysock, *Thinking about Women*.
3. Gallagher, *Evangelical Identity and Gendered Family Life*.

privilege carries over into the work setting as well.[4] Thus although a woman may appear to have separated from her husband and established an independent identity, both the organization and her husband continue to expect that she will place his needs and the organization's needs above her own, thus once again fulfilling the communal role of caretaker and maintaining the hegemonic structures of organization and family. Male rule and female submission remain unchallenged.[5]

DELEGATED AUTHORITY MATTERS

The concept of delegated authority as being part of a woman's qualifications to lead was a significant feature in each woman's story of how she arrived at her leadership position. It was also a source of comfort and assurance to a number of the women.

Chosen by Men

Barbara, Holly, Kelly, and Tabitha were each chosen by their organization's board to fill the role. Regina, Ashley, Carol, Chelsea, Donna, and Nicole were chosen by their organization's president. And Stephanie and Melinda were voted in by their teams. So each one clearly knew how she got her role and how the authority structure validated her leadership. In almost every case, the authority behind her position was male.

Sometimes the authority was very strong. Carol talked about the change that happened when her organization got a new leader. He wanted to move her to a different leadership role on the team, one that she did not really want, but others thought she could do. "People were saying, Carol, you should be HR director. And I was like, I do not want that role." She made her preferences clear to them, including to the new president. "I did not want to deal with policies and procedures, [it was] just absolutely the last thing I wanted. I said, please, don't anyone ever talk to me about HR. I don't want to do that." However, the new leader decided to change her role anyway:

> So when push came to shove, he didn't ask me [and] when he created his organizational chart, I was in charge of HR. And I didn't fight it. I said okay, if this is where you want me. I mean, that's kind of how we've always felt in this organization, you can kick and scream until the director makes a decision, and then he decides anyway. I trusted him enough to feel like he really

4. Calás and Smircich, "Dangerous Liaisons."
5. Gallagher, "Marginalization of Evangelical Feminism."

thought that was the best decision and I should do it, so I accepted it without complaining.

The authority structure was strong enough in her organization to cause her to accept a leadership role that she did not really want. Yet the authority was delegated to her and she took it up in her new position.

Ashley, Tabitha, and Regina were all in organizations that are intentionally trying to be egalitarian in their policies. Even so, the assurance of holding delegated authority was still important for them. Tabitha explained how she would use that knowledge with someone who questioned her position:

> The leadership of the denomination have affirmed my call, they've affirmed my gifting, and they've hired me at the highest level here, in the position I'm in. The top board of the denomination is who hired me. And so we put them into authority to make these decisions. And they've made a decision and affirmed that I've been called to do this job.

Being Supported in Leadership

For the women, being supported by their superiors in the organization is important. Since they rely on the organizational authority structure to give credence to their leadership, the support of that structure is critical to their well-being. Melinda described how her supervisor supports her:

> Here he is, technically my boss, and he's what, seven years younger than me, so he's not horrendously younger than I am, but he really affirms me. We were talking about this situation that I've been dealing with, and he's like, Melinda, you've done exactly what I think is appropriate. So he's very affirming. He does ask hard questions. So he's not just giving me fluff compliments. . . . So I appreciate that he affirms me, he doesn't request less of me than he does the other guys, the guys in leadership, which I also appreciate.

For her, being supported and being held to the same standard as her male peers gave her confidence in her leadership.

Carol also found her president's support important to her leadership:

> There've been times when he's just said, I'm really glad you're here. And other times when he's just said, how are you doing, really, personally, with this job? You've got a really tough job. So in different ways he gives me verbal affirmation, he recognizes, you

know, he'll say, I want you to do this because I really think you're really good at that. Or he backs me up in the face of these guys who are trying to get their own way, and I'm not letting them have it, and he'll stand with me and say, "Carol's right. You've got to back down. What you're trying to get is not appropriate." So I really appreciate that about him.

She added that they do not always agree, but they can discuss things well.

For Regina being supported and being able to discuss things well with her supervisor was critical, because without it her job is harder to perform. "That's very demotivating for me when I don't feel like I'm supported," she commented. She told the story of a difficult situation where she did not feel supported by her leader. In this case she contacted him about it:

> You just need to know that I don't feel supported here. And he was like, what? I think both of us are able to talk on that level without getting emotion thrown into the conversation. So he could say, well, if this is what you think, I can see why you don't feel supported. And he wrote, this is kind of where I'm coming from at it, and then I could write back and say, okay, I see that. And this is why I didn't understand, and this is why this, and so we worked it out. . . . In the previous organization it was difficult because policies that we had set down and principles that we had set down meant nothing. And then I was basically castigated for standing my ground, and sticking up for things I thought were right, and more helpful.

Feeling his support as they worked through the problem was key to a successful resolution, and was a pleasant change from her previous organization where she experienced a lack of support.

And for Tabitha, having that support, and knowing how to disagree with her boss and still present a united front publicly is an important part of her leadership:

> I said to my overseer who is the head of the denomination, I shut his door and said, look, I totally disagree with you on this. And this is why, and we'll have a conversation, and I'll say, okay, when we walk out of this door I will not oppose you. I will not. If someone asks me in the meeting, Tabitha, do you agree with him on this, I would have to say no, but you will know exactly what I'll say. But I will not hang you in public, or in a meeting, and if I disagree with you you'll know it ahead of time before we ever enter a meeting with other people. . . . And it's always worked.

Not Seeking Leadership

A third aspect of the concept of delegated authority is that the women were not seeking leadership roles for themselves; in a sense, leadership came looking for them. Half of the women made a comment to this effect. Melinda explained how she first got onto the leadership track:

> I was invited to the table because I was single and because they wanted—our organization has quite a few singles so they wanted my input into singles' ministry, or how singles minister. And I think that's how I first got my foot in the door. Not that I was even seeking to get the foot in the door; it just happened.

Stephanie too said that leadership "happened" to her. "Being a leader has been something that's happened, not something that's pursued," she explained.

Chelsea saw her leadership role as a temporary trust given to her by God for a specific purpose:

> I was never looking for a position. That was not a big deal to me. And even now, to me, this is a trust for this period of time, that the Lord has me in this chair to do something . . . but it's not mine, if you understand what I mean. It's for this period of time.

Ashley entered leadership because she was invited, and encouraged by others who saw her ability. She might not otherwise have considered it:

> I wasn't—I've been invited a lot into leadership. I'm not an ambitious person. I think I've learned to see that I could be more ambitious, I could push more to have my voice contribute, and I think that's a little bit one of my experiences as a woman in this role. . . I hadn't seen a lot of models of women in leadership when I first started down this journey. So it never occurred to me to aspire for it, really. So I'm grateful for those people that pushed me a little bit, because I needed it then.

Kelly was completely caught off guard when the board initially approached her about taking on leadership. She asked for six weeks to pray and think about it before she agreed. She was not expecting to enter leadership either, "So the fact that I'm even in this role today is even quite a surprising journey . . . because it's not something that [I] had ever anticipated."

Carol was the most emphatic participant in explaining that she was not looking for a leadership role. "I never, ever, ever thought of myself in any kind of leadership position or wanted to be," she commented. Yet when the director asked her to do it, she complied.

What the Women Think It Means

Chelsea thought the fact that she was not seeking leadership was part of the reason why she was chosen. "I was not looking for a position. . . . Did they see that? I'm sure they saw that and I wasn't angling for any kind of power or position at all."

Kelly thought women are less interested in having a leadership position than they are in achieving something that matters. She reflected:

> I think so often women may step into leadership not so much because . . . "I want to be a leader, I want to demonstrate leadership." It's because they're compelled by something that's important to them, and so they just do it.

Knowing that they have been given leadership by the recognized authority structures in their organizations and that they were not seeking it for themselves gave the women confidence to accept those roles even in settings where women do not normally lead. And knowing that those authorities take them seriously as leaders and can interact with them about organizational topics helps make it possible for them to function in their leadership roles. These kinds of relationships of support and affirmation go a long way towards making the woman more comfortable and better able to exercise her own leadership.

What a Feminist Perspective Would Add

Similarly to the section on learning to lead, where women are sponsored by and learn to lead from men, the concept of delegated authority shows the structural inequality inherent in the women's position. Organizational power resides in the hands of males who construct the organization and use it to reproduce what is favorable to themselves.[6] The men are the ones who decide who will lead in the organization. The idea that women who are not seeking leadership are most likely to be chosen for leadership is a telling comment on the way power is distributed in the organization. If "not seeking to lead" serves as a qualification for choosing a woman to lead, then she has been chosen precisely because she is "humble," knows her "place," and does not pose a threat to the male power structures. A woman who was ambitious and desired leadership would be breaking the gender requirement of submission and service.

Popular evangelical discourse conceives of leaders as "shepherds" who care for the "flock" and as "servant leaders" whose primary goal is the good of

6. Bierema, "Critiquing Human Resource Development's Dominant Masculine Rationality and Evaluating Its Impact"; Stead and Elliott, *Women's Leadership*.

their followers. This vocabulary is also used to describe husbands' rule in the family.[7] Simultaneously, there is much discussion about the need for followers to show humility and submission to authority, which is also vocabulary used to describe wives' role in the family.[8] There is also a prevailing discourse of leaders as being "chosen by God" or "appointed by God" to lead. All of this terminology can easily lead to an acceptance of hierarchical structures and a belief that submission to authority equals obedience to God.[9]

For women, whether they are in the family or at work in a mission organization, they are treated as being under a double or triple layer of authority: that of God, that of their male husbands, and that of male organizational leaders, whereas men may be perceived as only under the authority of God, since they are believed to be designated as organizational leaders by God. Thus the woman is always under a layer of male human authority, but the man may or may not be, depending on his position. As a result, female authority can never be as powerful as male authority; hers has been delegated down at least twice, while his may have been delegated only once.

This limited authority explains why the support of her male supervisor is so critical to these women's organizational practice: without it they lack the appropriate levels of delegated authority and are rendered illegitimate in their leadership. The concept of delegated authority maintains the gender essentialist idea of males as suited for rulership and females as suited for submission intact.[10] Woman's leadership is still constrained and limited to a form that reinforces, rather than challenges, the gender hierarchy.

APPEALING TO GIFTING OVER GENDER

For the women in this study, the concept of gifting is crucial to their leadership. When they talk of gifting, they are referring to their ability, capacity, and competence for a job, as well as their spiritual qualifications; they are working in an area of strength. This, combined with their passion for the work and their ability to offer something unique to the organization, is critical to their acceptance of a leadership role.

Gifting

Virtually all of the women talked about the importance of working in their area of gifting. For some, it is a key reason for them to be in their leadership

---

7. Gallagher, *Evangelical Identity and Gendered Family Life.*
8. Gallagher, *Evangelical Identity and Gendered Family Life.*
9. Gallagher, *Evangelical Identity and Gendered Family Life.*
10. Gallagher, "Marginalization of Evangelical Feminism."

role. Tabitha explained, "I'm here because I was chosen for the gifting that I have, the strengths that I have, and what I bring to the table, the perspective I have." Kelly commented, "I have a clear sense of the scope of my responsibilities and what my strengths are, what I bring to the role." She talked about discovering her own passion for leading: "I got into [my] role and began to realize how passionate I was about staff development and building a team and investing in our leaders and seeing people understand our strengths."

Melinda thought that a combination of her availability as a single woman and her gifts helped her enter leadership:

> I think my availability in many ways as a single woman has been something positive. I'm able to travel, I'm able to do things that other people may not be able to do. I think I do have giftings that are needed for the things that I do, so I think that plays into it as well.

She added that at one point the organization considered her for a different role, but realized that she did not have the gifts for that and so did not move her. This gave her confidence that her leadership role was appropriate for her skills:

> I was definitely not prepared for that position, could not have done that position, so I wasn't chosen for that position. . . . So I do think that I haven't just been encouraged up the ladder just as a token female.

Carol said she accepted her leadership role because she knew she had skills the organization needed:

> I agreed to this job because I bring to it stronger commitment to building teams and relationships, and I am skilled at it. . . . I resonate mostly in my role with the idea of building community. Community building has been something we've lacked in this heady, intellectually oriented, and male organization.

She was aware of her own strengths and how they contributed to her leadership and benefitted the organization.

For Ashley, learning about her own gifts and her ability to contribute helped her feel confident in her leadership:

> We had a couple of guys who worked with the organization on Strength Finders and Meyers-Briggs and the integration of those two, and then did across-the-board assessments of all the leadership in the organization, and how they work together. So that was really helpful because it first of all was a huge affirmation

for me of these are strengths that turn up in you and this is how it plays itself out. And this is why it's important. There's a lot of commentary about [how] you have some unique things to contribute and you need to step into them.

For Regina, using her gifts in a leadership role was a new and enjoyable experience:

It's been a lot of fun for me. You know, even on the bad days I come home and I really have enjoyed it and I think it's because it's the first time in my life I've actually been able to do the things that my personality allows me to do. I mean, if we're talking in Christian terms, it's the first time I've been able to use the gifts that God has given me. If we're talking secular terms, the first time I've been able to use my talents for a job that I have. And I think that's why I enjoy it so much.

Being aware of gifting may also be a strong focus in their leadership of others. Chelsea was really passionate about making sure she was helping others work according to their gifts. "I do realize that having people in a place of their giftedness or strength or whatever is an overall benefit to our organization but also to the people." She described the joy of helping a couple find a better ministry placement when their initial placement proved unsuitable:

So being able to work through that process of helping them re-adjust who is doing what in the organization and what it looked like, and from what part of the world they were going to do it, all that kind of stuff, you know, that's obviously a lot of hard work and a lot of emotion. But sitting with her at breakfast this morning and seeing how she can see now how God has put each of them in the right place and they are getting to work in their area of strength, that was just a very fulfilling thing.

Kelly also agreed that it was very important for people to use their strengths:

I think it's just been through a whole range of a lot of volunteer opportunities that I've had over the years that have really taught me the value of investing and valuing people, and in helping people understand their strengths and find a fit for the role that's best suited to their strengths. I've just seen it in many, many circumstances, what a difference that makes.

Only one woman did not find that this strategy worked for her. Using her gifts was not useful to her leadership in that organization, as we will see in the section on advocacy. In reflecting on what happened, Donna commented:

> I guess probably what got me chosen originally were peer leaders who felt like they could work with me and just had relationships with me. I guess they . . . I don't know that there was anything necessarily in my qualifications, just that there was in my relationships. And also I think just because they needed a female, and so they, you know, needed to have another female, and it always looks good to have a female.

She found herself in a situation where the organization wanted a token female, not a gifted one.

Five of the women also at one point or another talked about doing things simply because they needed to be done, not because they were particularly good at it. Stephanie explained that sometimes she could say no to things that are not her gifting, but not always:

> At the same time there were things I had to do. I needed to grow in administration, learn how to be better organized. I needed to learn administration, because that came with the role. So that was difficult, yeah, still working on it, too. I mean, I'm not an executive type.

She recognized that some skills go with the job and she needed to develop them, but would prefer to work in her area of strength. She went on to say, "And then there are other roles of a leader, which it's wonderful in the spiritual realm, which are my passions and leanings, and so I naturally grow in those areas." Chelsea also knew that sometimes you have to work outside your strengths:

> So I realize that there are many times when, in order to be part of the team or to get the job done, we need to do things that are not necessarily in our area of strength. It's okay. We just need to all chip in and do it and help it get done so we can move forward.

However, only doing what has to be done did not strike the women as good organizational practice. Carol commented that a previous leader in her organization made need-based assignments rather than considering people's strengths. "He didn't ever use people for what they were really best at, but for what he needed them for. And I had a hard time with that." Holly's first organization got a new leader who tried to change her assignment to one for which she felt totally unsuited. "He offered me a fundraising position, which was not my interest. I'm a trainer and educator, but he only offered that." Because she realized that the job was completely unsuitable, she accepted his alternative offer—to leave—and that was the end of her work with that organization. Her story reflects the level of significance women seemed to attach to working in their area of gifting.

Passion

Passion was another word women used to describe their suitability for their leadership role. Kelly talked of being passionate about staff development and Stephanie about her passion for the spiritual aspects of leadership. Nicole, Ashley, and Melinda also talked about being passionate about what they do. Nicole commented that she discovered a "growing passion for partnership" which became one of her responsibilities on the executive team. Ashley thought her organization knew she was "passionately committed to serving staff well." She expanded on the theme:

> For me it's really more than a job, and getting a paycheck. I feel pretty passionate about what I'm trying to do and the people that I'm serving out there, they're my reason for doing it every day. Yeah. And I think that's been acknowledged by the people I work with, that they know that's what's getting me here, what's keeping me here.

Passion was also important for Melinda. "Others in leadership see me as a person who is passionate about what we do," she said. "Most people see me as a competent, fun-loving, person who's passionate about people serving well on the field." For these women, being passionate about their work, caring deeply about what they are doing and those they are working with is another qualification for their leadership role.

Offering Something Unique

One other way that women explained their suitability for their leadership role was that they offer something unique that the organization needs. Carol saw that the "nerdy" organization needed her people skills; Ashley's Strength Finders and MBTI assessments assured her that she had something unique to offer the organization; Kelly knew her passion for developing people would help the organization transition to a sustainable ministry; Tabitha saw that her commitment to unity and her team-building focus would benefit her organization.

Regina talked about her ability to make decisions as something her organization badly needed:

> One of the issues in this current organization is that people have a hard time making decisions . . . they have great ideas, but enacting them is more difficult. That's not really a problem for me. So I think that when I go ahead and make decisions, people, at least from the top, like the fact that someone's actually moving things forward.

If the women have a skill that the organization needs, then this also supports their presence in leadership.

What the Women Think It Means

The women think that working in their area of gifting is critical to their leadership. They also, perhaps because they find it so personally valuable, are strongly interested in making sure others in their organization or on their teams are working in their areas of strength. Kelly sees gifting as a more important leadership consideration than gender. She wrote, "I am a strong advocate for strengths-based leadership, and while I would like to be working with more women, I am more concerned with having people (male or female) who have the needed gifting than gender."

Tabitha placed a high value on including people with diverse gifts to be on her team. "I'm known as a collaborative leader, one who loves to pull people in to a situation, diverse people, people with different giftings, or different ideas, or different insights, and different experiences that can together help us make a good decision." This plus working in her own gifting has contributed to her success:

> I figure you work in your gifting, if you have to work harder, fine, if you have to prove yourself more, that's fine, whatever. And that's served me well. I've been able to, obviously, succeed in this system, by working hard and proving myself through the gifting that I have and the strengths that I have, and doing my job, you know?

For Chelsea the concept of working in her gifting has become part of her identity. "I've realized over the last two years that is a really big part of who I am. It's helping people to figure out their right place, and that gives me joy when I see that happen." Nicole agrees, and part of the stress caused by losing her leadership role is her sense that the organization does not seem to need her now. "There have been several 'suggestions', but they feel more like 'things you could do' than places where I am really or specifically needed."

She wanted to be in a place where her gifts and strengths are useful. For the participants, working in their gifting is part of what makes having a leadership role acceptable and if that gifting is no longer needed, then perhaps their leadership is not needed either.

What a Feminist Perspective Would Add

The women's discourse about gifting is interesting. A careful look at what they claim as their "gifting" shows that virtually all of it falls under the rubric of communal behaviors. Skills such as developing staff, building teams and relationships, training, and supporting others are all essentialist behaviors that their faith has taught them are appropriate for women. Noticeably absent are discussions of skills of setting vision, establishing direction, accomplishing tasks, and other agentic behaviors. Interestingly, agentic rather than communal behaviors would be expected of CEOs, and five of the women in this study self-identified at that organizational level. However, the behaviors they describe align more closely with middle-management skills than top organizational levels.[11]

A careful look at how these women CEOs are structured may explain the discrepancy. Of the five women in this category, one shared the role with her husband as part of the two-person career; her discussion showed he was primary and she was secondary. Another woman led the missions department of her denomination, and reported to the denominational leader above her. The third led a ministry that belonged to an umbrella organization, and she reported directly to the president of that umbrella, who had the final say over her work. The fourth led the national office of a mission organization, and reported to the international director of the entire organization. The final CEO led a small organization as an independent leader, with a board to advise her. Thus of the five CEOs, only one truly functioned in the classic CEO role.

The organization may give the woman the title of CEO, but the structures show that in four cases she is actually functioning under the direct authority of another male, be it a supervisor or a husband. This is another example of an organizational practice which gives the appearance of supporting women as leaders while in reality constructing them as subordinate to male power. For them as well as for the other women who were chosen by males for their communal skills, the essentialist system that pushes women towards communal behaviors and men towards agentic ones again remains unchallenged and unchanged by women's presence in leadership.

11. Eagly et al., "Gender and the Effectiveness of Leaders."

CAUTIOUS ADVOCACY

A fourth strategy the women use which is simultaneously good leadership practice and a way to maneuver around the gender-role requirements is to use cautious advocacy. The relational aspect of the communal role makes advocacy for others, especially those who are dependent on her, an acceptable behavior for a woman. As leaders, they can use advocacy to, sometimes, advocate for women and occasionally for themselves. They advocate with caution, however, and usually do so for the good of others in the organization or for what they perceive as the organizational good. Thus they do advocate, but in ways that mostly fit the gender-role requirement.

Being a Mother Bear

This is the most common form of advocacy reported by the women, and most of them are quite happy to do this when they find it appropriate. In the earlier section on agentic behaviors, for example, women reported advocating for and establishing organizational practices that would be beneficial to others. In her role, Ashley also found herself speaking for the members of her organization:

> I think that I can certainly use [my] platform to speak, to represent staff, all of our staff. My role is quite often sort of helping the leadership interpret what kinds of initiatives they want to do and how that impacts staff on the ground. So I'm in the role of saying, well, have you considered how this might go over here, here, and here? And that is for men and women equally.

So she was happy to use her position to represent organization members.

Of all the participants in the study, Donna talked the most about trying to be an advocate for her people:

> One of the departments that I was providing supportive leadership for was struggling with pressure that they were receiving within the organization. And it was problems within the organization that I put a lot of energy into trying to solve for them. So I basically became their advocate. . . . In retrospect, they actually shared that as something that they really valued in my leadership, this specific instance of going to bat for them, being an advocate for them. I would have liked for things to even have turned out better than they did. But those that I was leading really felt that I had done everything that I could and that they had experienced some help along the way.

She saw her advocacy as part of the support she provided for her department, even though it did not necessarily yield the results she wanted. She went on to explain how most of her advocacy had to be done outside of the formal meeting times, in an effort to persuade male leaders to pay attention:

> If I felt like something that I was advocating for wasn't going to be well received if it was just me, that I would actually lobby with these other leaders and either get them to where they supported me when I was going to bring it up, or that they actually brought it up themselves, and in many cases thought it was their own idea and then they brought it up and I was able to influence that way.

She tried to use a combination of relationships and advocacy to support her departments. However, in the end she felt the strategy was not successful, and eventually backfired on her. She explained:

> There were probably more stories that I could share where I did advocate and I was clearly not successful and, yeah, in the end just marginalized—no, not marginalized, stereotyped . . . stereotyped . . . that's what one could expect from me, that they would expect that kind of response.

Once the male leaders perceived her as willing to challenge the power structures on a regular basis, they acted to diminish her agency by converting her independent role back to a shared role with a male.

Melinda also used advocacy in her work with the male leadership team. For her it was more successful than it was for Donna:

> So in our organization I believe I'm known as someone who will speak up for those who don't have voice. At one point I said, you know what, I'm just tired of there being invisible members in our organization. We have all these invisible members; they have so much to give but they're just invisible because of their gender or their status.

She added that she was happy to speak for women or singles, since she represents both, but she would not want to spend all her time doing that. "So I started fighting for the underdogs around the group; it's not just the women or the singles." For her the issue is the invisibility of certain members of the organization, and the men did listen to her somewhat.

Regina also advocated for those who were being overlooked:

> I would say I try and help the people that are invisible in a sense. Just this last week I could see the emails flying around and I could see that one person was getting nailed for something. And

I didn't want it to happen, so I circumvented the situation by sending out an email to everybody.

She followed that example with one where she spoke up for a church member; it was not someone in her organization, but was a similar kind of situation. She also commented that she is comfortable advocating for others. "It's interesting because speaking up for someone else, I don't have a problem doing it. First it was my kids in school, I would say, well I'm the mama bear." And then she told another story about advocating for her team in the same kind of way she would for her children.

Carol, too, used the metaphor of a mother bear to explain her advocacy. "If I see any of the women in my department being treated poorly, partly because someone can get away with it because they're women, I'm a mother bear in defense of my women." Carol's entire department is composed of women, so for her, speaking up for her department means speaking up for women. But this is different from speaking up for the women of the organization in general. Most of the women felt less comfortable with that idea.

Cautiously Advocate for Women

The participants expressed somewhat mixed feelings about the idea of advocating for women in their organization. Some, like Melinda, were willing for it to be part of their advocacy, as long as it was not their entire focus. Most were cautious about when or how they would do so, and one was emphatic that it is not her priority.

Donna was perhaps the most positive towards the idea of advocating for women. She explained:

> I think that I definitely tried to be an advocate for women, both directly and indirectly. Directly, there were occasions where I was just able to pretty much tell, whether it was one other leader to influence a conversation that was going to be happening, or several leaders, to help them understand that their perceptions about their supportiveness of women were not valid perceptions, and I would directly tell them why I didn't think they were supportive and give them examples. So, yes, I did that and then there were also times when I advocated more indirectly for women, or for situations that involved women. But it wasn't necessarily—I mean, it certainly wasn't like something that I did all the time. It was just something I did on occasion and as appropriate.

Regina, too, took into consideration whether advocating for women would be appropriate. She explained:

> I just tended to try not to think along those lines. I don't mind being an advocate for it but I don't push that button if it's not the button that's the problem. I think there are times when you need to speak up about it, but if that's really not the issue, then I don't want to bring it into the conversation.

Nicole tended to speak for women if someone directly asked her; otherwise she was not likely to think about it:

> I don't think they would see me like an advocate, you know. They don't say, oh she's waving the flag, or anything. But I think they think that if they want to know something from that perspective, they can get that from me. But as far as myself, I probably don't take that role as much as I could, or should.

She and Kelly were the only ones to express the idea that perhaps they could serve as more of an advocate for women, yet both were still hesitant about it. Kelly commented:

> I've never really seen myself as a big advocate for women's ministry. Really that's not been my passion. But there was a group that met during the conference and focused on women in ministry. I wouldn't naturally go to that kind of meeting. I would be at other things, because that's not really my passion. But I suddenly, in that context, felt like, wow, I have a responsibility to younger women to be a voice of hope to them, and encouragement, and just to be open and authentic about my journey, and to be a mentor to them. And I think that's kind of a new perspective for me. I would see that in other areas, but not so much because I'm a woman, but because I've had experience or something.

Perhaps it had not occurred to her like it had never occurred to her that she would be in leadership at all. For both Nicole and Kelly, this was something of a new idea, that they could perhaps speak for women, or as Kelly put it, encourage and mentor younger women who want to lead.

Ashley's organization was intentionally trying to be egalitarian in its view of women, and that shift has given her a different perspective from the other women in the study about speaking for women. In reply to whether she would serve as the representative for the women in her organization, she said:

I'd think it's unfair, for one thing. So I wouldn't agree to take that
role. But in some ways, I do feel the need to champion women
who I see have potential and for one reason or another are not
being called out into what they could do. I see my role more to
challenge the women than the men.

And later she added, "I just want to be the champion of good leadership. I
don't want it defined by gender." Tabitha too was very strong in her preference
for leadership to be defined by skill, not gender. First she explained that she
has refused requests to advocate for women in her denomination:

We have an organization within the denomination, I don't even
know what they're called, but I choose not to be a part of them....
And some of the guys have challenged me and said, Tabitha, you
should be a part of that group so you can help, maybe, broaden
their mindset a little bit. But I can't even imagine going to one
of their retreats, or one of their sessions, or whatever, because I
know their agenda and I just don't want to even be associated with
it. And so, maybe I take too strong of a stand. I don't know. But I
really shy away from being a part of those groups.

She went on to explain, "So to stand for women in leadership based on gifting and strength, yes, I'm glad to do that. To stand for women's rights in
leadership particularly in a Christian organization, I just probably wouldn't
do it." For both Ashley and Tabitha, advocating for women as women is not
an option. They are also being consistent in their position that gifting is the
most important qualification for leadership.

Challenge the Women Rather Than Advocate for Them

Similarly to Ashley, Carol also thought encouraging the women would be
a preferable approach. She explained that in her organization, which she
characterized as "male, heady and nerdy" the women may not see the value
of their own contributions. "I've had a heart for our women to be encouraged," she said, so she decided to start with a women's retreat, the first one
ever in her organization. "So it happened last year for the first time. And it's
about to happen again. All the women just absolutely loved it." She thought
it was helpful, because:

I want the women in this organization to have a stronger sense
of their value, and wanting to just affirm the contribution that
they have to make even if it just starts with a contribution they
would make to the women. So I think that's kind of one way
that I've tried to encourage that.... kind of trying to listen for

women that feel like God is speaking to them and empowering them and encouraging them to share that and speak up, at least to the rest of the women.

She worried that part of the challenge for women in her organization may be due to the kind of organization it is:

> For some reason we have a lot of women here who just—I don't know if the kind of men who are drawn here are married to the kinds of women that we have here? But it just seems like a lot of the women here, not all, but a lot of the women here are just very hesitant to get up in front. They just feel very uncomfortable getting up in front of people at all. But I'd like to see some of them, more of them encouraged that they could make more of a contribution.

Stephanie also thought that challenging the women was more important than advocating for them:

> I would want to encourage the women in our organization to really be who God has asked them to be in their various levels. And speaking for women in our organization would mean speaking up for women who feel that even though God has called them to missions, their role is focused on the home and letting that be okay. But also it's speaking for women who want to be out there learning the language, doing more an active role in ministry and enabling them to do that. I think that women in [our organization] have a voice.

So unlike Carol, Stephanie does not think the challenge is in the organization, but lies with the women themselves. Since her organization encourages women to lead with their husbands, then if women are not leading, it is because they are holding themselves back. She explained:

> I would say women don't need someone to speak for them, but the interesting question is, are they, some women holding themselves back? And again, we must be talking about married women, because then they, number one, have an excuse to hold themselves back, and it's like culturally and internally they should hold themselves back. . . . But truly because we have this value of women in leadership and this encouragement, to me it's a question to ask our couples, and ask the women that question, do you hold yourself back? Or are you literally holding back because, by golly, you just don't want to do this? And that's perfectly fine.

Stephanie was concerned with leaving the women complete freedom to engage when and how they choose.

Advocate for Self

Only two participants reported advocating for themselves. In both cases the situations which led them to take that step were long-running and severe. For Regina, it was a problem that had been going on for six months and for Barbara it was an ongoing pattern of negative treatment that had gotten so bad she actually wondered if it was intended to make her resign.

Regina described what happened with her:

> I did advocate for myself at a board meeting at the end of December. I'm having problems with [a team member]. And he and I were at a board meeting . . . and he let loose at me, and said that I had mistreated him, and all kinds of things, and . . . I had my personal notes about the meeting that he talked about so I pulled them up on my computer and I was looking at them. At a certain point inside, it felt like something snapped. It was like, I'm sorry, this has gone too far. And so I pushed back. . . . And that was kind of weird.

When I asked what made her decide to speak up for herself in this one instance, she explained, "I [did] it because I felt that it was so unjust, so much spin on it that you couldn't even recognize the truth anymore." Plus, she added, "I've been working on this problem for six months," so it was past time for a solution.

Barbara's story had similar elements. Her organization's president had repeatedly bypassed her in communicating with her team. This time he made decisions regarding her work and announced them in a public meeting without talking to her first. She had become increasingly frustrated, and finally that event felt like the last straw. Still, standing up for herself was very difficult. She sent him an email asking for a meeting, saying "it was only because [the counselor] prompted me to do that rather than waiting until someday when we might meet together." His answer was, "I don't know why I keep doing that." She had brought to his attention before the problem of bypassing her in pulling in her team members to other projects, without any change. So her confidence was shaken:

> And I thought, then he must mean to be doing that! It was hard not to think that, and so I had to interact and get interaction back from him. It was really disconcerting, and my face was

actually burning, I was thinking, why does he keep doing this?! Does he want me to leave?

In both cases where the women did choose to advocate for themselves, it was only after a protracted situation that they had attempted to resolve through communication and explanations. Interestingly, too, in each instance the final straw was a public event where the woman was mistreated. Regina was in a board meeting with her superiors when her team member went after her, and Barbara was in a public meeting when the president blindsided her by announcing changes to her responsibilities.

What the Women Think It Means

The women were sometimes comfortable advocating for others, less comfortable advocating for women, and not at all likely to advocate for themselves. Barbara's response was, "Wow, that does sound like me! Not wanting to just stand up and say women's rights, or anything. That part about trying to advocate for others and insisting on courteous treatment, yeah." Carol too agreed that advocating for "women's right's" was not a good idea. "When you comment on women advocating for 'women's rights' I feel like this would not get a good hearing. I think I would be perceived as being on a personal bandwagon about women stuff." Regina agreed as well, and went on to wonder why:

> I will advocate for other people up and down the line, but I don't tend to advocate for myself. And yet, I look at men and they're advocating for themselves all the time. Somehow it feels not right for me to advocate for myself, and I'm not sure where that message is coming from. Is it our evangelical subculture that's doing that?

She seemed to think that there might be a gender piece affecting how women use their advocacy.

Finally, Tabitha was quite emphatic:

> I don't say, look, I have rights, or I know I have to work three times as hard to get the same recognition. It's all true, but I do not wave that flag ever. I never play the female card. . . . I just choose not to.

She added, "There were definite evidences there [of inequitable treatment]; I just always chose not to make a big deal about them." So the women do not think that advocating for women would be a good idea or well-received, and they choose not to pursue it. In that sense they are making a calculated decision not to do something that might be detrimental to their leadership effectiveness. They may be right, at least in some cases, as the end of Donna's story showed.

What a Feminist Perspective Would Add

Evangelical discourse has done a great deal to discredit and demonize feminism, stigmatizing feminist women as "selfish," "anti-family," and "anti-children."[12] And at its heart, feminism is about advocacy for women. The women in this study have been thoroughly schooled in the "dangers" of feminism and therefore advocacy for women, as shown by their extreme reluctance to advocate generally for the women in their organizations. Yet the women in their organizations are, structurally speaking, the most disadvantaged group, therefore the ones most in need of advocacy and yet least able to get it. Because of hegemonic assumptions of male rule and female submission as representing God's order, to advocate for women would challenge what is presented as a divine mandate and therefore represent resistance not only to unjust power structures but to God's order.

As a result, most of the women appear to represent Bierema's category of "gender unconsciousness."[13] Some of them are totally embedded in the essentialist belief system and do not question it, while others are aware but deliberately choose not to notice or take action because the risk is perceived as too great. Evangelical faith has taught them that their place is supporting, not challenging, male authority, thus further perpetuating male power at the expense of female agency.

CHAPTER SUMMARY

At the time of this study all but one of the married women were no longer functioning as part of a two-person career structure. They had separated professionally and taken on independent leadership roles in their own right. Every woman in the study was given her leadership role by male authority, and many of the women stated specifically that they were not seeking a leadership role, but were chosen because the organization needed their skills. The theme of gifting was important to the women; each of them placed high value on working primarily in their strengths and on helping others on their team work in their strengths. They were passionate about what they do and many were aware that they offer a

12. Bendroth, "Last Gasp Patriarchy"; Gallagher, *Evangelical Identity and Gendered Family Life*; Litfin, "Evangelical Feminism."

13. Bierema, "Role of Gender Consciousness in Challenging Patriarchy."

specific, unique ability to their organization that the organization badly needs. They were fairly willing to advocate for others in their organizations who were somehow invisible or neglected, but they were less willing to advocate for women generally or for themselves.

Despite the fact that these behaviors appear to mildly resist the gendered construction of females in the patriarchal system, none of them offers any serious challenge to male power. The women are able to function within the system by supporting their husband's good and organizational good above their own, by exercising authority delegated to them by males, by using communal skills that fit the gender-role expectations, and by keeping quiet about injustice towards women. Yet even their conformity to the gender essentialist thinking and patriarchal structures is not enough to gain them full support as organizational leaders, as the next chapter shows.

8

Findings: Persistent Ambivalence

IN CHAPTER 6 I presented the finding called Acceptance of Gender Roles. In chapter 7 I presented the finding called Maneuvers with Gender Roles. In this chapter I present the third finding, Persistent Ambivalence, which has three themes: organizational ambivalence, subordinates' ambivalence, and women's ambivalence. These themes answer research question three: How do the women and the organizations they work in account for their leadership? They show that despite having been selected to lead, the organizations and the women continue to express ambivalence about women's leadership, despite the women's organizational contributions. The theme of ambivalence in one form or another was prominent in virtually every woman's story, and as such forms an important part of the results of this study.

ORGANIZATIONAL AMBIVALENCE

All of the women told stories that represent organizational ambivalence towards their leadership. This ambivalence came in various forms, from quite subtle to quite explicit. Towards the subtle end of the continuum was the recognition that the organizational leadership culture is male, and that it is up to the women to fit in. At the other end of the continuum were one woman's stories of being bullied by her own leaders. Whatever its form, each of these incidents showed that the organization did not fully recognize and support the woman's leadership.

Male Organizational Leadership Culture

The most subtle, and probably the most common kind of resistance to these women's leadership was simply an organizational leadership culture that was frankly male, and where the women were quite aware of not fitting in. If they behaved too differently than the men, they experienced negative consequences and quickly learned to conform. Ashley's colleagues who preferred to conduct business while smoking cigars around the fire pit provide one example. So were the women's stories of adjusting the way they talk or dress in order to be taken seriously. Five of the women specifically referred to leadership as male in their organizations. Barbara called it an "old boy network." Carol noticed that they say things like "Okay, guys," and her response is to think, "I'm not a guy!" Holly referred twice to missions as a "boy's club." And Regina described it clearly when she said, "There was a group of men in leadership and they had a group mentality. They talked with each other even outside of meetings and stuff like that." Ashley named it explicitly:

> The leadership team culture is male-dominated. In fact right now I'm one of two women that are in any senior leadership position in the organization. We have women that are leading churches, but in the leadership team there's only two of us. One is chairperson of the board, so she's not actively in leadership. So I'm the only one. So almost every meeting I go to is all men, and the culture of the room that I walk into, I'm aware of that, is guys talking about guy stuff, things that don't really interest me. It's so hard to quantify, I think that's why it's difficult to address.

For some of the women, as time passed they became more comfortable being included in the men's club. But it still had consequences. Ashley explained:

> I know that label gets put on me—I'm a woman in leadership, and whether it's intentional or not they're looking to see how I'm going to handle myself, which is intimidating, because men don't get that. . . . So I had to forge my own way.

She recognized that the isolation of being the only woman added an extra challenge to leading with her male peers:

> I also think there are stylistic culture things that happen which are much more male-oriented that make it difficult for women to stay in leadership roles because they get tired of the organizational culture. . . . I think a lot of men in leadership are not aware of how much that impacts women.

She did not think all women could make the extra effort, or sustain it indefinitely. Regina too found that it could be isolating to be the only woman. In her first organization, she explained, "Women were isolated in different spheres of the organization that didn't overlap even laterally," so they lacked peer support.

Being the Only Woman Present

Another aspect of male organizational culture that these women noticed was that they were often the only woman present. Eight of the women in this study were the first woman leader at their level in the organization, or the only woman leader at their level. Barbara, Holly, Tabitha, and Kelly, as leaders of their respective organizations, were both the first woman in that role and the only woman on the team. In her organization, Ashley and a woman on the board were the only female leaders, as we saw. When Donna joined the executive leadership team, she became the second woman, but the other soon left, leaving her as the only female. Nicole, Carol, and Melinda were the only women at their level in their respective organizations. Chelsea, like Ashley was one of two because she included the board chair who was female. But she was the first woman to lead at the upper level in her organization. Only Regina had two other women leaders in her area, and they were both under her, not at a peer level. Chelsea explained the effect of being the first or only woman when she commented, "I'm the first woman at this kind of a level. And so I guess I don't know exactly what to expect." These women were navigating new territory. An overwhelmingly male culture, coupled with being the only woman in the room made women in this study uncertain of having the full organizational support for their leadership.

Deference to Host Culture

A different aspect of culture that impacts the women is that of the countries where they and their organizations work. Nine of the women talked about how this did and could impact women's leadership. Since all of the organizations represented in this study work cross-culturally and typically place a high value on learning the local language and culture and fitting in locally, navigating gender-role requirements of the host culture can become central to an organization's policies and practices.

Only Ashley said her organization would refuse to uncritically assimilate to a host culture's rejection of women as leaders; she commented "that's an easy out; it's just giving in," and thought that they would look for a way around the problem. At the other end of the spectrum, Stephanie said that host culture expectations would be the deciding factor for women's participation in her organization. She talked at length about what that meant for her leadership:

But there's also the aspect of relating to the host culture and what a leader might need to do. For instance, the leadership might be in contact with the local church if there is one, or might be in contact with local authorities if that's required. And in that sense the importance would be the sensitivity to the culture, and even the theological view that's there. We're not trying to prove a point, so you simply relate to the culture in the way that the culture understands and accepts and I'd say, for instance when we were in [country], we were both field leaders. But my husband was the one invited to a government meeting, even if they knew we both were leaders, they probably would just invite him anyway. And I continued always to serve the function of the one who served the tea, etcetera, etcetera. And I was fine with that, quite honestly, because I didn't really care to meet with all those men, and talk about things. So I think the key is sensitivity to the culture and the theological views where you are, that still needs to happen.

That event was from the early days in her shared leadership with her husband, before she had begun fully engaging in the leadership role. More recently, at their current executive level, she encountered a similar situation:

We're not trying to prove equality; we're just serving in the function that God has given us and being sensitive to the culture if that's necessary. Let me give you an example of even being at this level of sensitivity to culture and maybe church views and church practice. . . . We went to [country] which is a very, still, male-dominated church culture [and] . . . I sit with my husband in these meetings. So I'm the only woman, all these men. . . . And so I'm sitting there, and that's fine, but of course all the questions are related to him about the mission, and speaking on the mission, and the vision of the mission, and goals for the mission. And either no question is directed to me, or again, in order to bring me into a conversation at a meal time, and so tell us about your children. . . . Inwardly I also had to make my own shift to be culturally sensitive. . . . We're not trying to prove a point, it's not about both of us being directors, we have no problem if my husband is the main one, we just work that out as long as it's understandable, it's the norm. . . . I can be sensitive to the culture, understand where they're coming from, and take my place beside my husband and let them speak to him.

Still, despite all her understanding of the host culture, she found it difficult. "Well, I will be honest here, I was aware of how it felt to me. It felt like being invisible." So although she accepted the requirement to submit to the host culture's views, it was uncomfortable for her.

Ashley had the opposite experience. She talked about working in more egalitarian cultures where women's leadership was better accepted than in the U.S. Holly mentioned male-dominant cultures where women are not accepted as leaders, and Melinda explained that she works in a male-dominated culture where she has gained respect by years of patience and behind the scenes service, and because she is single and therefore not pushed into the "married woman box." Nicole worked in countries that did not resist female leadership and knew what a boon that was for her; Regina did too, and she also works in a country that highly values education so her doctorate gives her additional credibility. Tabitha generally finds herself accepted and respected, but adds that "I just have to be very mindful of the culture I'm stepping into." For the women, the organization's willingness to allow the host culture's standards dictate a woman's leadership also reflects ambivalence about having women leaders. Only one organization showed a willingness to take a principled stand in favor of women leaders.

Interim and Job-Sharing Assignments

Another indication of organizational ambivalence towards women's leadership was shown by the interim assignments some women received, and the job-sharing roles given to others. Six of the women had interim assignments where they were either tested to see if they could handle the job permanently, or expected to fulfill the responsibilities temporarily for someone else who made all the decisions. When Tabitha's superiors first approached her about taking on an executive leadership role, they offered it to her on an interim basis:

> So I interviewed, and was asked to take the position as an interim, for a number of reasons. One, they wondered if I could be the one with whom the buck stops if there's a problem, like can I make a hard decision? I had always worked as part of a staff, and not the senior leader. I was female. How would that work around the world? How would that work at this level in the denomination, because nobody had ever broken that barrier before. I was supposed to have a master's degree and I was about two-thirds through that process, but wasn't quite finished. That was a prerequisite that I hadn't met. There was a whole list of things for why I didn't qualify for the job. Yet they hired me anyway, but as an interim, and said, well, we'll work at this for a year and see how it goes.

She agreed to the condition, but did not like it:

> When they said I had to be the interim for a year I didn't like
> that. I thought, if you believe in me, or if you think I'm quali-
> fied for this job, hire me! You know, but they were feeling not
> real ready to take the big leap, and they didn't know how people
> would react to a female at this level in our denomination.

Melinda filled a leadership role as an interim twice in her organization, before they finally decided to put her in the position. The first time
the male leader was going to be on furlough for six months, they asked
her to be acting leader. She handled it well, so three years later when his
furlough came around, they put her in as acting leader once again. She understood the limitations of that role: "When you're an acting leader you're
basically just trying to keep people alive and nothing happening, seriously,
until the regular leader gets back, you know? You're just kind of treading
water." When he eventually moved on, she was finally given the job; they
now knew she could handle it.

Nicole filled multiple interim roles after she came back to the U.S. to
join the executive team. Although they originally wanted her for a specific
task:

> It quickly became obvious that the realignment of the leader-
> ship team had left some holes in the next layer, the next level
> down. And no one was really able to get on board talking about
> partnerships until that seemingly more foundational piece was
> fixed. So long story short, I wound up spending the next three
> years pulling together the pieces that were needed to make that
> foundation more sustainable, and we found someone else to take
> it and lead it, once we kind of got it up and running. And then
> another big hole came open in the area of mobilization. And so
> once again I was asked to fill that role, and so I've been doing that
> since April of this year. At the moment even, I am temporarily
> also serving as the senior director for three countries, because we
> had someone who died of a heart attack suddenly and things had
> to be shifted on the spur of the moment.

Practically since she joined the executive team, she has been filling in temporarily for various other positions in the organization. This works partly
because the role they originally intended for her was not supervisory:

> It's not in the supervisory chain, so to speak. If you're a mission-
> ary on the field you report to your supervisor who reports to
> the field leader, who reports to the director, you know, it kind

of goes up that way. . . . My role . . . is not directly over any field ministries. So I wasn't supervising field ministry in that role. So I think it was an easier way for people to get used to having a woman on the leadership team, and functioning at that level, and having a voice in what was going on. And yet they weren't directly accountable to me.

Like Tabitha, the organization was unsure about having a woman at the executive level. In Nicole's case they first put her in a job with no direct supervisory responsibility, and then assigned her interim positions that did include supervision, but only on a temporary basis. So she was able to give the organization what it needed without presenting too strong a challenge to the male leadership structure.

Chelsea felt differently about an interim assignment; she actually wanted an interim role. "I mean, in my case I asked for an interim assignment, because I wasn't sure I could do it." For her it was a safe way to try out the role. Holly also took on an executive role as an interim, because she did not feel it was the best fit for her abilities. She said, "I didn't think admin was my gift. So when we [grew], I suggested handing over the reins." For her too, an interim assignment felt more comfortable. And Regina commented that her role was also intended to be temporary. "It's not a long-term position. I'm basically getting in there, trying to clean things up, and then we're going to put somebody else in." She still accepted the assignment.

Another organizational practice that may indicate uncertainty about women's leadership is job-sharing assignments. Often these are with their husbands, as we have already seen. Three women work in organizations where that model is promoted. Such a structure may function to maintain a male as the authority figure while allowing a woman to contribute to the work. Stephanie, for example, commented that although the organization allows for equal sharing between husband and wife, "up to this point, again, most of the wives have been still in the traditional model of doing what she can to help out, and the husband being the main one." So when she herself began to attempt to truly share the role with her husband as a partner, people were surprised:

> After a period of time I realized that I was being a bit different. But . . . our staff was quite happy for it, they just had to begin to also refer to me just as much as to my husband. And they were, again, glad to do that. But still, and I felt okay with this, he had more of the connection with the international level of leadership, and the meetings, and the correspondence and all that.

She kept doing her part of the job, while at the same time accepting others' perspectives. She wrote:

> People understandably assume my husband is the director and I'm the director's wife (which, I am that as well :-)). There's no problem with this, but it is a reality. He and I work closely together and we share the responsibilities, but, in my mind, he is the main one.

Job sharing can also function as part of a non-married pair. When Donna's organization became unhappy with her persistent advocacy, the strategy they used to limit her leadership was to add a male to her region and tell her she was now paired with him in a shared role. She told the story:

> Well, when it first was unfolding I tried to be very proactive and become very open to the changes and see what that might look like. And so I actually flew back to the States to meet this new leader. And then I was told that I would be part of the leadership team with him, but the reality was that I wasn't and so that wasn't true. It was just . . . just talk, and not reality. They gave it to somebody else, but the new leader that was brought in was actually telling me, as well as the leadership telling me, that I was going to be part of the leadership in this whole area. So I was going to be part of the team, and the area was growing so it made sense that there would be more of us. But the reality was–and I questioned it when it was going on because I hadn't been involved in the decision making—the reality was that that was not true, and I was not part of the new leadership team. I wasn't included in any of the meetings, the decisions—I knew nothing about anything that was going on. And so I was excluded; whether intentionally or unintentionally, I was excluded from anything having to do with the leadership of that whole area.

What was presented as a team leadership role was in fact an organizational maneuver to remove her from leading at all.

Adjusting the Woman's Role

Another way organizations indicated ambivalence towards women's leadership showed in adjustments that were made to the woman's role. Nicole, for example, not only had several interim positions, but she was initially given a role with no direct oversight of staff. Chelsea was the first woman in her organization to be given leadership at that level, but before they gave her the job they had moved it down a level on the organizational chart.

She explained, "What had happened was that, maybe three years before I took the position, they had reorganized. So this position had been the vice-presidential position, which gave it a lot more authority and input into the overall direction of the mission."

The adjustment also affected her ability to do her job. Shortly after she started, she realized that one man in her department was simply not doing his job. She commented, "I wasn't totally given the freedom to just handle it as being in my department. I had to deal with those over me." She added, "There were a couple of situations where somebody higher up would reverse something, which makes it very hard if your compatriots know the person higher up can and might reverse whatever you said; that's pretty bad." As a result, some of the organization's members did not take her leadership seriously.

Barbara also struggled with limitations on her ability to handle things in her area. When she talked about the leader who bypassed her to recruit a member of her staff, she commented, "not that I can even tell him yes or no" because although she is CEO of her organization, since it belongs to an umbrella organization, that president can bypass her or overturn any decision she makes.

For Melinda the adjustment was geographical, and was made to accommodate a subordinate who refused to report to a female leader:

> There was a team in [country], and the team leader has very, very strong doctrinal issues about women in leadership. . . And when I was acting leader I actually was over his country. But both times, interestingly enough, he was on home assignment . . . But when it came down to me being his regional leader, he threatened to resign from the mission. And I just said, you know what? For me, this is not worth the fight. And the other leader who had all of [country] said, geographically it makes sense to have him.

So the organization changed her region so he could report to a male leader. Melinda commented that it hurt, but that they have remained friends because he insists it is not personal. "But he keeps saying it's not you. It's not you at all. It would be anyone."

For Holly and Tabitha title was a critical issue. Holly was brought in to support an Executive Director whose people skills were lacking, and was told she would be Director of HR. The man changed her title because "he said no one can be called director but me in this office." Tabitha was originally interviewed for a role that carried the title of "bishop" in her denomination, but found:

> They just weren't ready for a female bishop at the time. But yet a month later they invited me to interview for this role, and in essence it's the same level, same pay, I'm on the same leadership team with all the bishops but it's called executive director.

The difference in title made the difference in her getting the role.

Another adjustment that organizations made with their women leaders had to do with finances. For Tabitha it was the classic situation of paying a woman a lower salary than a man. She knew she was hired "at a very poor rate" but they promised that they would raise her salary when more money became available. Then:

> It came time to hire another pastor and they hired a guy, young, he's about my age, hired a guy who did not have the credentials I had, did not have the education I had, and they hired him full-time earning $25,000 a year more than I was making.

She confronted the leader about it and he replied:

> We had to give him this to get him to come here. . . . He's married and has four kids and his wife doesn't work. And I said, well, I'm married, I have three kids, and I can tell my husband to quit his job! That makes no sense! And then the next guy they brought in, they did the same thing.

Later, when she was ready to move on to the next role, the leader suddenly offered her a big raise to stay. She turned it down and moved on.

Chelsea and Holly were less expensive for their organizations because they had personal financial support that they had raised to fund their mission work, meaning that the organization did not have to pay them a salary. Chelsea explained, "And you know, pragmatically, we were here, so we wouldn't have to be relocated, we had some support to put toward my salary, so the salary wouldn't have to be totally funded by the organization." When Holly's current organization was choosing a director, "it came down to the wire between me and a man, and he wasn't willing to raise his own support, so they gave job to me." Changes in pay, title, and responsibility clearly communicate to the women that the organizations are not fully supportive of their leadership.

Blatant Opposition

Holly encountered not one but two instances of blatant opposition from male leaders above her. In her first organization, the board brought in a new president who learned that she had initially been president, in a temporary role. "He started being very controlling of my work: procedures, policies, and training." Next he offered her a fundraising position, which was not her strength. "I prayed about it," she said, and added:

> I think he wanted to put me in a position where I would fail and then he could fire me. But I knew I wouldn't be comfortable there, and friends counseled me not to accept, so instead I accepted a package to leave.

He still continued trying to control her. She explained, "I was paid out monthly instead of in a lump sum. In order to justify that 'salary' he wanted a weekly listing of my work on a job search." She took a part-time position presenting Vacation Bible School material to churches, partly to network as she looked for a new position, and he did not like that either:

> He found out about that, and emailed and called me, threatening me for working "outside my contract." He said I would need to reveal what they were paying so that amount could be deducted from my monthly salary. It was quite an interesting year with him hovering over my shoulder.

After a year she did start working with a new organization, but before long found herself in another difficult situation. Again, the organization brought in a new leader, not the one who had hired her, and the new leader went after her, using some of the same strategies:

> This guy was controlling . . . kept shrinking my job. He eventually excluded me from my role as HR director, and wanted to move me into promotion, media, etc. . . . . Conditions of my new role were to include no face to face meetings, not being on the organization's email list, and no direct supervision of staff. . . . [He was] increasingly controlling me. He tried to cancel my trips that had [been] approved. He was undermining me. He sabotaged a workshop that I was leading by changing the time it was offered, but not changing the published schedule, so when people showed up for it, it had already happened.

She put up with this for 18 months, and then consulted a counselor. "And talking it all through, I realized I was not the person at fault, and that I had to get out of the environment. It was affecting me psychologically and socially, so I finally gave myself permission to quit." This time it took her quite a bit longer to find another organization. She asked careful questions about their thinking on women, and if they would have women in certain roles. The job she finally took was the one where they chose her over the man because she came with support.

What the Women Think It Means

The women recognized that these events occurred, and even expressed dislike for certain aspects. Regarding trying to fit into a male leadership culture, Carol wrote that "the amount of opposition I face has now decreased. Partly because the worst offenders are no longer in the organization. It does remain, though, that there can still be a boys' club atmosphere at the leadership level, the organizational culture." Ashley added, "Ugh, I hate this, but it's true even in my organization which has a clear egalitarian culture." Kelly commented on the challenge of being the only woman, "I agree! It's hard to be one of the only women in the room (often the case for me!) or at an event." Holly also disliked "attending peer events as the only female leader present." She also thought that some men were "uncomfortable with women leaders at the table," and noted that she had experienced "male jealousy of a female leader's influence within and outside (for the benefit of) the organization."

Their opinions on shared assignments were more mixed. Stephanie, not surprisingly, found it to be an ideal arrangement. At one point she repeated "I was happy" with the shared arrangement with her husband three times as she described it:

> I was probably happy for [him] to be the main one. . . I was always invited to come and expected to be a part of it if I wanted to, but he was the one that they particularly asked him to be on . . . [the] main body of our leaders. I was quite happy for that, again, quite happy for him to be the one who has to handle all of that.

She could choose her own level of involvement, and liked that situation.

Carol, whose organization used to favor it more than they currently do, would like to see a return to that model. She commented to the new director that it would be helpful for the leadership team to involve their wives:

> I don't feel like I'm trying to gain position for myself, because I am already a leader and I do have plenty of influence. It's more a principle or a perspective on the significance being given to women overall. . . . . He tells me that they haven't decided yet what to do with the wives. I can imagine them doing something very traditional like inviting us to have dinner with them, or asking us to pray for them. Those are good things, but I don't know if they plan to intentionally access the strengths and giftings that their wives can bring to their leadership of the organization. I am sad. It's a loss to us. . . . The surprising thing to me is that no one else seems to have even noticed this change.

For her, including wives with their husbands on the leadership team would strengthen the organization, and she was quick to point out that she was not simply self-promoting.

Holly had a similar thought, though her organization has never functioned that way. She explained:

> I'm actually surprised there aren't more couples. Why aren't husbands/wives given team leadership roles? I asked about this at the last meeting, why don't you appoint couples—husband-wife as team leader? But I didn't get an answer.

Barbara and Ashley were less positive towards the idea of job-sharing for married couples, as we saw in the section on breaking the two-person career. They both though it could be hard on a marriage; neither of them wanted to work that way long term.

What a Feminist Perspective Would Add

These are both subtle and quite blatant strategies to undermine women's power and authority even with apparent organizational support for women leaders. An organizational leadership culture that is distinctly male and unchallenged presents a barrier for some women, and makes most aware of their outsider status, and sometimes downright uncomfortable. The organizational power structures are precisely those which critical HRD points out as reproducing familial and societal power structures that favor men.[1] Claiming they need to defer to host culture preferences is another way organizations express hesitancy about women's leadership. If deference to the host culture's views, or even deference to a subordinate's views, override the woman's leadership, then the organization is not fully in support of her leadership. Changing her title or using her skills because she comes cheap is another signal that the organization is less invested in supporting the woman than in benefitting from the work she offers. In each of these cases, the organization is perpetuating the structural inequality that privileges males over females, and in so doing perpetuating patriarchy.[2]

The practice of job-sharing is particularly troubling. Stephanie was strongly favorable towards it, and convinced that if women in shared leadership roles are not leading they have only themselves to blame. However, from a feminist perspective, there are several problems with this approach.

---

1. Bierema, "Critiquing Human Resource Development's Dominant Masculine Rationality and Evaluating Its Impact"; Hanscome and Cervero, "Impact of Gendered Power Relations in HRD"; Riehl and Lee, "Gender, Organization, and Leadership."

2. Acker, "Hierarchies, Jobs, Bodies."

First of all is Stephanie's status. In her narrative, she is always the one who makes adjustments in what she does, based on time, interest, or her children's needs. This is a classic description of the two-person career—she is the support person and her work is organizationally invisible.[3] Furthermore, if everything about the role is voluntary, because she can pick and choose which parts she wants to do and which meetings she wants to attend, with no actual expectations placed on her, then she is actually functioning as a volunteer. Volunteers can pick and choose their level of involvement in a job, task, or assignment, and there are rarely any consequences if they choose a low level of involvement. Organizations cannot really demand anything from volunteers, but only persuade; nor are there typically consequences to the individual, such as firing, if they do not perform. This too is in keeping with the two-person career structure that views women as primarily their husband's supporters.[4]

Another problem with this approach is that it enables the organization to appear to embrace equality while continuing to support the gender hierarchy. By saying that women have the title for doing subordinate work, by not having them participate in the most prominent and public spaces of the organization, and by never having space for a married woman to operate other than paired with her husband, the message is clear that the women are there to support the men.[5] The level and degree of support varies, but the structure is always that women support men.

In multiple ways, then, organizational practices show substantial resistance to women's leadership. Women leaders' power may be circumscribed seemingly at will when the organization so chooses, and for any number of reasons. Women's presence in leadership is intended to give the organization the appearance of embracing diversity, while maintaining hegemonic assumptions of male rule.

SUBORDINATES' AMBIVALENCE

Another source of ambivalence towards women's leadership is the behavior of some of their subordinates and team members. Eight women reported incidents of this nature. Challenges included organization members refusing to follow policies, trying to overturn decisions, publicly correcting the woman, resisting in passive-aggressive ways, being publicly disrespectful, or publicly discrediting the woman, by mass emails, for example. For

3. Andersen and Hysock, *Thinking about Women*; Papanek, "Men, Women, and Work."

4. Papanek, "Men, Women, and Work."

5. Acker, "Hierarchies, Jobs, Bodies"; Brown, "Meetings and Intersections."

several women the method of challenge was to threaten to go over her head if she did not comply with a subordinate's request. While taking a concern up the chain is certainly appropriate organizational practice, in these cases of challenge the subordinate was trying to circumvent or undermine the woman's authority by resisting an organizational policy for which the woman was responsible.

Many of the stories have already been told in themes described previously. Melinda told the story of a subordinate-to-be who threatened to resign if he were told to report to a woman. Barbara told the story of the CEO repeatedly bypassing her to have her team members do tasks for him; the team members went along without informing her of the situation until it had already passed. Chelsea told of a man in her department who passive-aggressively resisted her leadership by simply refusing to do his job; he was publicly disrespectful to her as well. She called it an "in-your-face" kind of thing. Regina talked of being "lambasted" and "smushed" in emails sent to a group of people in her organization.

Carol told the story of a man who publicly corrected her during a devotional meeting. "You'll share something and he'll tell you, that's the wrong interpretation of that. And he did it once to me, I'm sitting there, this was in a meeting, I'm leading." She was leading the meeting and he publicly contradicted her opinion about what something meant to her. In each of these cases the man was resisting the woman's authority.

Sometimes the women were able to solve the issue on their own. When she was first appointed to her leadership role, after the one insistent man had been assigned elsewhere, Melinda still had to deal with doubts from other subordinates. Because she was single, some of the couples suggested she could not support them if they had marriage or family struggles. She told them:

> I think that a married man would have the same issues dealing with a single woman as a single woman dealing with a married man. We assume that a married man can be in leadership, but how does he deal with a single woman and her issues? And I brought that up to them and they're like, we've never thought of it that way.

By reframing the issue and then suggesting a peer-support strategy where team members supported each other, she was able to handle their ambivalence.

Carol told the story of a team leader who wanted to add someone to his team without going through the proper selection and hiring process. She had to call in the president and the top leadership team when he refused to accept her insistence that the hiring process be followed. The top leaders supported her, but later that year, after the new member had been properly hired, the same team leader asked her to give the new hire back pay:

> He wanted us to pay him for work that he did on his own before he was even a member. I mean, these leaders who are asking you to do things that are just, in my opinion, absolutely bizarre. We don't pay people for doing stuff that they did on their own . . . who weren't employed by us at that time.

Carol managed to solve the second challenge on her own, but not all women were as successful.

Chelsea had a particularly difficult experience where her team had, they thought, successfully worked through some issues with a couple in their organization. But the next thing she knew, the couple had gone over her head to her boss and appealed the team's decision, without ever asking for reconsideration or telling her they were appealing. Chelsea's boss, rather than check with her and the team, simply reversed the decision. She commented that it "was a horrible painful time" with the result that her team "all of a sudden . . . had zero authority. It didn't matter what we said from then on. Anything was open to appeal. And so it made it extremely difficult."

Regina spoke of a man "under me who's never going to accept the fact that there's a woman over him, and he keeps pulling power plays on me. He won't accept leadership at all." He routinely went over her head when she asked him to do something in his job description, and "the decision gets postponed, and so basically he's getting what he wants." Happily, her leaders have supported her, but the continued nature of the challenges was wearing.

Nicole's leader has also been supportive of her. She had two men under her who:

> Were always pulling the trump card of, oh, I'm going to go talk to Scott, who's the international director. You know, they didn't want to take my word, or just let me have the final say. They were always going to go talk to him, or pull the, well, Scott said, Scott said, Scott said, line.

When it happened, she would go talk to Scott herself, and he would support her. Still, she said, it "of course made me feel bad and undermined my ability to make anything happen."

For Kelly, too, having her authority questioned feels bad, but has little effect on her ability to function. "That's happened," she commented. "There have been those moments where I've felt like I have been questioned and in terms of what happens, I think the first thing that happens is that I feel threatened." In particular, the founder, who is still part of the organization, has at times questioned her decisions about how to move forward. Since she is now the CEO, for her the results of being questioned mean she must accept her feelings, make the best decision she can, and "be willing to stand behind my decision, even if it means I'm wrong or I might fail, or it may not work out the way I hoped." As the only woman in this study who truly functioned as an independent CEO, being challenged has more to do with managing herself and less to do with being supported by her leaders.

Donna's subordinates expressed ambivalence about her leadership in yet another way. She had advocated strongly on their behalf for some changes in organizational practices that would better support their work. In one case she was trying to "build bridges with the headquarters" to work on a particular issue:

> It had to do with processing short-term team applications. And the [field] side kept telling me "No, it's not going to be possible, they're not capable of doing that." And I said, "Yes, yes, I'm sure that they are" and then over time staffing changed and decisions were made to absolutely prove that [headquarters] were not capable of considering the [field] side.

Her subordinates seem to have had a clearer understanding of organizational politics than she did, and realized that changes were unlikely. But she tried, and the result was that she lost her subordinates' trust.

> People would share that they felt like they couldn't share because they felt like they wouldn't be heard or they felt like they would be at risk. And so it kind of prevented me from fully knowing [what was happening]. And I was even told that now, because I was one of the leaders I couldn't be shared with any more.

Though initially hopeful, her department lost faith in her ability to advocate for them and shut down communication with her as a result.

Ashley and Stephanie were the only participants who said that their leadership had never been challenged. Ashley's organization has a well-designed policy that she helped establish for handling disagreements, and so far it has worked. For Stephanie, it could be that since she shares the role with her husband, she simply is not ever challenged. She did tell several stories of host cultures who did not accept her as a leader, but she did not seem to perceive that as a challenge to her leadership.

What the Women Think It Means

The most common response the women made to these kinds of stories was exemplified by a comment Regina made after describing the man who simply would not accept a female over him and kept pulling power plays. She finished up by saying, "But I don't know if it's because I'm female or if it's just because he's not used to having anybody above him that makes him do something he doesn't want to do." Even in the face of clear resistance from subordinates who, in the authority structure of the organization, should be complying with the woman's leadership and following her authority, the women tend to think the problem is personal rather than gender-based. This belief is the theme of the final section, women's ambivalence about their own leadership.

What a Feminist Perspective Would Add

From a feminist perspective, these men—because in every case except Donna's, where it was an entire department, the person resisting the woman's leadership was male—are resisting the woman's designated authority. They are using various maneuvers to shift the balance of power away from the woman and back to themselves. Organizational culture and practice favor male authority, and some subordinates are willing to use that knowledge to oppose women's power.

The contrast between Carol's and Melinda's stories shows how the power imbalance favors males over females, regardless of their respective locations in the organizational hierarchy. Carol's supervisor decided to place her in a role she expressly said she did not want, yet he told her to do it anyway and she acquiesced. Melinda was placed in a supervisory role over a male who flatly refused to report to a woman, and his refusal was accepted and her territory redrawn to accommodate him. In both cases, the woman was the one whose power and agency were truncated in favor of male power and agency.

The discourse used in these encounters also shows how male power and female power are framed differently in these organizations. The man who did not want to report to a woman claimed to have "strong theological issues" with women in leadership; that is, he appealed to the faith's teachings of male authority and female submission to support his own agency in not reporting to a woman. For the women, however, "submission" is the assigned role, therefore each of them had to accept the male decision regarding their role. For Melinda, it meant accepting both the subordinate's resistance and her supervisor's decision to assign him elsewhere, and for Carol it meant accepting a job she did not want because the male authority figure told her to. For either of them to resist would be called "rebellion" in the discourse of evangelicalism, yet neither of the men was considered rebellious when they failed to accept a woman's authority, whether her own authority to choose a preferred role, or her delegated authority in the organization. Since "submission" is the role designated for women, then resistance is constituted as "rebellion," and since "ruling" is the role designated for men, then resistance to being ruled is constituted as "theological soundness." Thus the organizational power coupled with the discourse reinforces and perpetuates the hegemonic assumptions of male rule.

WOMEN'S AMBIVALENCE

We have already seen in the previous section on advocacy that although the women may be quite willing to advocate for others in their organization, they almost never advocate for themselves. Similarly, as they told stories of being resisted, having their authority questioned or their decisions overturned, or otherwise being challenged in their leadership or authority, many of them added that it was not because they were female, but must somehow be their own responsibility, or have happened unintentionally, or because the men were unaware. The women seemed willing to excuse or accept mistreatment, to think that the issues were personal to them rather than systemic, and preferred to step away rather than stand up for themselves.

Gender Is Not an Issue

Some of the women were pretty sure that gender was not an issue for women's leadership in their organization. Others doubted that gender was part of the reason they faced a particular issue or challenge. For example, Chelsea was the first woman to lead at the executive level in her organization, although the position itself was moved down the organizational hierarchy before she was appointed. The result was that she was not considered a Vice-President even though she and others in the organization thought the responsibility of the job required that level of authority. She explained it like this:

> So it wasn't changed because I'm a woman, because it was changed when the man was in this place. So it was nothing to do with gender. And at times I wish that I had more input. And what I've had to try and do is earn trust, which is better anyway, obviously, than just positional. I don't know that that's gender.

She also believed that some of the men under her felt awkward with having a woman leader, and so she concentrated on her communal approaches:

Part of it is trying to figure out what style of leadership people need, too. I tend to try and give a lot of autonomy, and be more guiding than directing. I think I really try and do that with the men especially because I don't want them to think that I'm their mother.

Another aspect of her communal approach was building relationships with the men under her. She added, "I don't know that that has anything to do with gender. I mean, it might be anybody who came into this position would need to do that. But it could be gender. I don't know." She was reluctant to think that gender impacts her leadership strategies or her effectiveness.

When her boss overturned her decision, she did not attribute that to gender either. "And I don't think in this case—it had nothing to do with the fact that I'm a woman, it just was." Nor did she think being excluded from certain events was gender-related; it was simply a matter of practicality:

And in some contexts it's awkward to just have a woman, where, how do I word this, you know, being sensitive to the context and not wanting a man and a woman alone places, just the practical things of being a different gender than they are affects sometimes what I might be included in.

She has chosen to work within the system partly because she knows the organizational history:

And so I think that if I had come into this position and I didn't realize this is what's happened with the organization and with leadership over the last several years, then I might have attributed things to the fact that I was a woman and I don't think that would be fair. But because context is important and I ask questions about where have we come from, I think that perhaps helps me to be more objective.

Each time Chelsea reflected on the question of her gender impacting her leadership, she was doubtful or ambivalent. The only things she originally thought might be related to gender were things of an essentialist nature such as, "we think and we communicate differently than men do." She also thought that women naturally tend to be more nurturing and men more aggressive:

I think that the piece that God put in us of wanting to nurture and care for our families and the whole idea of [the book] *Wild at Heart* and the men are the hunters and they're going out, they want to care for the family too, but they want to do it by going out and conquering, and the women want to make sure that everybody's safe. And most of us feel better if everybody could be under one roof, please, so we know where they all are and they're all safe, I wonder if some of it is just the male-female temperament.

Even here she was not certain, however, adding, "But that's a huge generalization, so I don't know that I'm right on that."

Stephanie was also pretty certain that gender did not impact women's leadership in her organization. She did not think gender affected who was chosen to lead, because "the understanding is that, in [our organization], those who are elected to leadership, gender isn't an issue." A bit later she added, "Leadership has been based on availability, character, and leadership ability, not on gender." She also did not think women needed anyone to speak for them, and told of attending a conference for women in ministry where she felt out of place:

> A few years ago I went to a conference. It was maybe about five or six years ago. And I attended a workshop at that conference on women in leadership. What I heard from there was the need . . . it was about empowering the women in your organization to be able to have a voice, to be more than just seen as the wives, etcetera, etcetera. And, do you know, I felt out of place there? Because I felt [our organization] already does this. That's not to say we're perfect in it, but I felt, I didn't have something to add to the conversation, because we're already there, imperfectly, and in fact if I went to various fields I might find that I am dead wrong, you know, the more I talk to people. But my feeling is we're already there. So it was interesting. . . . So let me say this, we don't have in [our organization], let's say, someone who is working on this, women's ministry, empowering women, because there's not a felt need for it.

She too believed there was an element of what is "natural" in men's and women's roles, which could be an essentialist explanation for the differences between men and women in her organization. She explained that when her children were small "naturally I focused on the home" which is "a very right and typical role for a woman." As she visited other cultures, she thought it was "natural and understandable and fine with me that people might hear these are the directors but . . . what they process is my husband is the director and I'm his wife." Even in her own culture, she thought that "if you are there with your husband, it's a natural thing . . .that he is seen as the leader." And in her organization there "is an indication of a natural leaning towards asking the man, and the men are the ones who are naturally seen as leading the business sessions, leading a strategy session." For her there were no organizational obstacles for women, only "natural" tendencies for women to keep the home and men to lead.

Other women thought that specific problems they encountered were probably not due to their gender. Barbara commented, "I, most of my life, have not attributed the way people relate to me because of being a woman." Nicole described an issue she had with a tech team not delivering as promised, and commented that "those kinds of things happen to everybody, it's not special for women in leadership." When she described the two men who kept going over her head to appeal to the leader, Scott, she added, "I don't know that it would necessarily have been because I was a woman. It's more just this power play thing." She thought the men assumed Scott would use his power to override her, not realizing that Scott was very much a team player with his executive leaders.

Some women were uncertain about the role gender played in their challenges. In reflecting on her first organization, Regina had difficulty figuring out what was related to gender and what was not. When she described her own lack of training, she added that the men were not getting trained either. And when she described being opposed because she was trying to follow organizational procedures, she was not sure that was based on gender:

> No, I would say in the beginning it could have been, but as time moved on, it wasn't based on gender. No. It might have been easier to pound you because you were female, but the men didn't. . . . The men still got pounded, but maybe not as quickly. Not as quickly or as thoroughly.

Similarly in reflecting on the use of power in that organization, she was not sure gender was the reason:

> I've seen these high-power positions where people have really misused power and put themselves above everybody and they make all the decisions; they can't be questioned. . . . When I look at the high-power issues that I've seen before, those were by men but women could do that just as well.

And in her current organization in dealing with the man who attacked her in the board meeting, she wondered, "How much of that is the power issues and how much of that is female? I don't know."

Tabitha's thinking was similar to Regina's. She commented three times that if someone had a problem with her leadership, it could be for lots of reasons rather than gender:

> Whether it's for that reason [gender] or any other reason that they couldn't stand under my leadership—like had a conflict in values, or a conflict in leadership style, to me that's just one thing in a list of many reasons why two leaders may not get along. There's lots of reasons why someone may choose to not work for me. . . . . It's not a different category to me; it's just one of a number of reasons why leaders may be in conflict and can't work together.

One woman thought that gender actually works to her advantage in the mission world. Kelly explained that she has been asked to write and speak, and believed her gender was at least part of the reason:

> Because I'm a woman, I think it's the only reason, I mean, not the only reason but in the [association], the president. . .asked me this past year to write an article for their magazine. And there were a lot of people he could have asked . . . . But he asked me to write that article. I know it was, because we talked about it . . . he very much wants to promote seeing women step into greater roles of leadership in the mission community, and because I'm a woman in that role, focused on this issue, he specifically asked me.

In our follow-up communication, she added that she has now also been invited to speak at a major conference in the summer. She wrote that the attendees will be mostly men, and added, "I wonder if one of the main reasons they've asked me is because I'm younger than 55 and a woman! Sometimes I feel that being a woman provides me with MORE opportunities, especially in the male-dominated ministry world."

Personal Responsibility

A number of the women took personal responsibility for why things happened the way they did. It could be that their own personality, for example, or their upbringing, was partly to blame for the problem. Or it could be particular to one man or one group of men who behaved a certain way.

Holly struggled under a controlling supervisor for a year and a half. She thought her family background was part of the reason she kept going for so long. "My family background had some abuse, so I have stick-to-it-iveness. Hard times growing up gave me determination." During that time, she explained:

> I just kept trying to please him and blaming myself for the situation. I grew up in a dysfunctional home and had therefore developed some tolerance for abuse, so maybe I had more ability to put up with it. Maybe someone without that background

would tolerate less. I tried to talk with my boss about it and he dismissed me, so it wasn't like I wasn't doing anything; I was try-ing to do something, but I was also blaming myself more than the other person.

It took work with a counselor for her to see that she was not the problem, nor was she going to be able to solve the problem, at which point she finally resigned.

Barbara made numerous comments about thinking that problems she encountered were connected to her personality and background. In describing her struggles to work with a male colleague who "definitely know[s] what he thinks is right" and yet does not follow through on doing things, she described what happened when she talked to him about not fulfilling his responsibilities:

> His excuse, if you want to call it that, for the way he comes across, and he did apologize, is that he is so busy he doesn't keep track of what he's promised or what he intended, or he doesn't have the ability to follow through because he didn't have the people in place.

And then she added, "And part of it's my own personality and experiences. I wouldn't have to react to the way they act, if I were someone different or had learned different behaviors of how to react." She went on to add:

> I acknowledged some of my background even from high school experiences I had with just meekly doing all the work without the recognition because they wanted a man to have the title type of thing. And I said I've just learned these behaviors and so, on the one hand I think, well I have to expect it. On the other hand, I'm thinking, that's not right.

When she talked about the leader who repeatedly bypasses her to use her team, she did think there was a gender component involved. "I don't think he would treat a man that way in a million years! No! I don't think he would. No!" Yet that emphatic statement was immediately followed by the disclaimer, "And maybe it's partly my personality, if I was a more man-like woman, and demanded more—I don't know how I, in my personality, could demand more respect."

Barbara also talked at one point about not getting much recognition for her work:

> In spite of the fact that I have worked that hard, and I feel like I've had some commensurate results, I don't consider myself to

be as knowledgeable or as trained as some of the men . . . but in spite of that, and maybe because of my personality, I don't see the—well . . . I'm hesitant to say I've not gotten the recognition I deserve; that doesn't even sound good. But sometimes I'm surprised that with what I've accomplished, it's not recognized.

And later, on the same theme of not being recognized the way the men are, she explained:

Since I've been here, I've thought, if I'm going to get any recognition, I'm going to have to work harder, and I've noticed that the men don't work as hard as I do. And yet they seem to get respect and whatever it is they're doing, you know, they're thought highly of and all. But it may just be specific to me.

She thought her personality and her background accounted for the lack of respect and lack of recognition she received from her organization and some of her male colleagues.

Nicole thought that perhaps some of the problems she encountered were specific to the men she was working with. After describing how she changed her communication style to suit her male colleagues' preferences, she added, "Maybe it's just this group of guys, though." And when she was describing the challenges of being the only woman in a group with six men, she said, "Some of it is just differences of personality more than men and women."

Two of the women attributed some struggles to lower educational levels than their male colleagues. Ashley explained, "I was working with almost exclusively men at this stage, and they all hold seminary degrees and all that stuff. So I could feel a bit like, who am I to challenge this?" She elaborated, "So I just didn't feel as well read, or as articulate as them, and yeah, that was something that was intimidating for me." Carol also talked of being intimidated by educated men when she told the story of the man who corrected her in a public meeting. "People . . . don't feel safe enough, and the truth is we've got a lot of seminary-trained men in this crowd, and we have some men that aren't afraid to just kind of, I mean they've done it to me." Then she described him telling everyone she was wrong, and added:

I was sitting there and the biggest thing in my mind was, what are all the other women in this room feeling? What they're thinking is, I will never share something that means anything much to me, and a lot of our women don't.

For Regina the benefits of education were mixed. It did not help her in her first organization, but did in her second. Speaking of the first one, she explained, "That did not make any difference in my former organization. It made no difference whatsoever. It was just completely glossed over, didn't mean I knew anything." She thought it was because she is a woman that they did not value the contributions her academic work enabled her to make:

> Even at a doctoral level coursework, people would still not listen. And that to me just seemed so crazy. If a guy had been doing his coursework, it would feel to me like they would have at least acknowledged that somebody was analyzing the organization.

But the second organization is different. "I came to this second organization with a different perspective than people had in the organization, and that was because of my education. Just getting my doctorate, because I had information that they didn't have and they needed." So because of her education, they valued her input.

Some of the women took personal responsibility for things that did not go well, even when those things were structural or organizational problems over which they had little or no control. Donna, for example, was not successful in changing organizational practices on behalf of her departments. She repeated twice, "I clearly wasn't successful." She seemed to think the responsibility to change organizational policy was hers alone. Barbara told of two incidents with an outside consultant who wanted certain things changed in her organization. The changes did not happen, and when the consultant scolded her, her response was to think, "I must be the most horrible leader ever, or something, getting in the way of what should be done or not done. . . . I really failed at my leadership role there." Yet the changes were not hers alone to make.

Carol took personal responsibility for a meeting that did not go well, to the extent of not leading anything else for three months. She had helped the organization plan its second retreat, which seemed to go really well. The following week she led a debriefing session in which people were invited to talk about what the experience meant to them:

> But when I asked that question, except for one or two people, our staff was silent, and I was like, oh, my gosh. I was done. . . . I was pretty flabbergasted that no one had anything. I was just beside myself at the end of that meeting. . . . I guess I had hopes that were really highly disappointed, because I had hoped that there would be more to share, at this group, and I just realized my expectations were way too high. And for some reason people didn't share, so I think I probably I overreacted, and that was a bit of a failure.

She held herself personally responsible for others' failure to talk about the weekend, and considered that she had failed. She also informed the director that she would not lead any more meetings that summer.

Other women took personal responsibility for situations that did not improve. Tabitha told of a conflict in her organization that led to the resignation of someone. She would like to reconcile personally with him, but has not been able to do so:

> To this day I know that there's conflict between he and I, there's conflict between him and us in the leadership team now, and it's very sad when that happens. And it never really resolved well. . . . This leader continues to be extremely angry. You know, sometimes after a time you can try to engage and try to work through those differences at least to bring some peace, you know personal peace, or whatever. But that's been one of the major heartaches in this role so far.

Her unsuccessful attempts at reconciliation continued to sadden her.

Melinda also took personal responsibility for a ministry failure and a broken relationship. She had a situation where someone came to her region to work and was not successful. She poured herself into supporting the couple:

> I was at their home every other day, trying to help them, help them with language, help them with getting things, pray with them. . . . I spent so many hours and so much money just trying to meet their every need.

But despite her efforts to help, the couple attacked her and tried to discredit her. "I was accused of all kinds of misuse, abuse of power, of telling—supposedly I had contacted all his supporters and said things about him. I don't even know all of his supporters! But the list was very long." After less than two years, they returned to the U.S. Yet she continued to struggle with feelings that she could have done better, or could do something even now to help them:

> I can see already, I have mutual friends on Facebook, and I can see already where there's things flaring up again and I just feel, part of me is like, how could I speak into that to kind of help? And then I just had to realize, you've just got to let this go, Melinda.

Ashley took personal responsibility for not being able to get the men to listen to her. There were six loud, confident men on the team, and her:

> I am a fairly soft-spoken person by nature, I'm an introvert . . . I found it hard to even be heard in this room full of strong guys.

> I often would privately speak to the director and say, listen, I don't want to have to fight all this testosterone in the room to say anything. You need to help me. You need to help me because I am just not interested in being that aggressive. I almost had to be aggressive, and that's not who I was—in order to get my viewpoint heard. And I thought that was really difficult for a while. I almost gave up.

She enlisted an ally to help her talk, convinced it was her own responsibility to gain a hearing among the loud, confident men in the room.

Men's Behavior Is Unintentional or They Are Unaware

Quite a few women made comments like this as they described the men's behavior. Chelsea described a male leader making a comment on "our ladies" in the board meeting, which she perceived negatively, but excused. "He didn't mean anything bad, but it just hit me wrong. I thought, you wouldn't say, our guys, if we were both men sitting here." She commented about her boss reversing her team's decision, "I don't think [questioning my authority] was the intent. I think that he just fell into that and didn't realize what he was doing." In another instance where a man was talking over a woman, she commented:

> The guy just talked so much that he didn't think to turn to her and say, hey, what do you think? He could carry on by himself forever. He was just unaware, you know, it wasn't intentional. He was just unaware.

She was unsure what to do in that situation:

> It's hard to know what's the role of the individual that's involved. Especially if it is just a lack of awareness, if it's not an intentional thing, if they're not aware, and you don't make them aware in any way, then, I don't know.

Barbara commented that her organization's founder had no problems with women leaders; in fact he wanted husband-wife leadership teams. But she thought the new director had a different attitude. "I think that [the new director], just without realizing it, does have a problem. . . . I don't think that he intends to discriminate against women." Somehow she thought that he was not in favor of women leaders, yet did not intend to discriminate against them. She went on to say that it is unconscious behavior because "he's been too busy, he acknowledges that all the time. When you're too busy you can't think. You just have to act on whatever comes naturally."

Ashley thought that men might be quite unaware of inconsistency between organizational ideals and their practices. "Do you guys realize there's a disconnect between what you say and what you do? And perhaps for many men there isn't; they don't even see it, they don't understand."

Donna was even stronger in her thoughts about the men's lack of awareness:

> They would actually kind of stop themselves and ask, so are we acknowledging you, or the woman's perspective right now. You know, personally, I think that they were pretty unable to see even with that level of awareness. I just don't think . . . I mean it was my impression that they kind of encouraged themselves by thinking that they were aware and sensitive. But I don't think that they were aware or sensitive, and I don't think—I didn't think they had the capacity to understand much more than what I was challenging them on. You know they would be like, trying to convince themselves. "We really are hearing you, Donna," and they were so convinced of it as they shared it with me that . . . I would, I just let them believe what they wanted to believe. . . . I just didn't think that they, if they really thought that enough to come out and identify themselves in that way, they clearly didn't have any self-awareness in this area.

The women seem to think that the men are not intentional in ignoring or treating women poorly.

Not Advocating for Themselves

Only two women told stories of speaking up for themselves, and the cases were ongoing and public. Several of the women talked specifically of not advocating for themselves when they could have or others wanted them too. When Holly was maneuvered into a position of leaving rather than continuing to work in an unsuitable role, others in the organization wanted to petition for her to be reinstated, but she was unwilling. "People across [the country] were supportive; they wanted to insist that the Board reinstate me . . . . They were going to arrange an international petition throughout the organization, but I did not want to be under him."

Nicole recalled a time when she was unwilling to push for a leadership role for which she was the most qualified of the team, because she knew there were some on the team who were "uncomfortable with a woman having that role. . . So I pulled back and didn't push, and didn't try." The team chose a man to lead, and she wound up doing the work for him behind the scenes. She accepted that arrangement for a while:

But over the course of several years, I grew more and more frustrated with that kind of operation, because I guess I sensed or I saw that I could have led and yet wasn't able to. And I had to always lead through him.

Although that was an unpleasant experience, she added, "I still kind of don't push too hard on what roles I can have or should have."

Tabitha was emphatic in her comments about not advocating for herself:

I don't wave the female flag ever. I don't say, look, I have rights, or I know I have to work three times as hard to get the same recognition. It's all true, but I do not wave that flag ever. I never play the female card.

Later she explained more about her thinking. "I know that there is a difference of how one is treated, at least in this culture, there is a difference. I just choose not to hang a flag on that." She went on to tell about how she was being paid less than men who were hired after her with lower qualifications. Rather than advocate for herself, she found a parable in the Bible to illustrate her acceptance of the situation:

There's a story in the Bible about a guy that's hired at the beginning of the day and he gets a certain wage, and a guy at the end of the day comes and is hired and gets the same wage. And that's not fair, but that's just the way life can go. And I chose, I accepted the wage when I was hired, and that's just the way it was.

Not only does she not advocate for herself, she takes personal responsibility for the unjust situation, because she accepted the low salary.

Kelly told a startling story of not only not advocating for herself, but of actually advocating against herself. She was initially quite reluctant when the board asked her to become the new CEO:

I was completely unprepared for that. And I started telling them all the reasons why they were wrong, and how I was certainly not the right person for that role, and all the reasons why I wasn't interested in taking it.

She left the meeting thinking that was the end, but they continued talking with her about why she was the best choice for the position. She asked for six weeks to consider the offer and in the end did accept. Her reluctance to take on the role for which others thought she was clearly suited is a classic case of women not advocating for themselves.

Walk Away

In addition to not advocating for themselves, six women at one point or another actually resigned or walked away from a situation that was no longer bearable. Regina left her first organization and found another where she could use her gifts, and Holly resigned from a situation where she was being mistreated. Barbara said she "put her foot down and refused to be their lackey" any more after working as the person behind the scenes doing the work for a couple who had the role of president. She told the board that it was unworkable to have "someone who in theory should be in charge, someone else who's doing the work." So she preferred to quit filling that role. Donna also stepped away from her leadership role when it was changed to a job-share that meant she would actually be assistant to the new male leader.

Ashley stepped away from her leadership role when conflict with the leader above her became too great:

> When I returned to the States . . . I really ran into a difference of opinion with the president of the organization. . . . He was the classic founder: a visionary, go get it done kind of person. Don't bother me with the details.

Ashley was supposed to be setting up the HR department, and she said to him, you are:

> Resistant to systems being set up because you think they get in the way of pioneering people, or people doing entrepreneurial kind of work. But I'm concerned that without systems we're not providing adequate protection for our staff. We need to give them some thought. And he and I had a very significant difference of opinion on that. And it got to the point where I was just frustrated enough . . . that was just a big contribution to my resigning.

Unable to do her job or persuade the leader of its importance, she simply walked away.

Carol too told of walking away due to conflict. She was very frustrated with the president's behavior:

> I had had some real issues with [his] way of handling people. . . . He didn't have a high people . . . emotional intelligence quotient stuff. . . . The standard thing that would happen would be that if someone didn't do things the way he liked it he would just start going around them, and making their job quite difficult, and make them kind of miserable until it came to the point that they would want to leave.

This pattern, especially because it also affected her and her husband, made Carol want to leave too. She said that initially "my husband didn't see all the stuff I saw. But we had kind of a turning point where I said, we've got to leave. So I actually begged my husband that we could leave, and so he did." They both walked away and went overseas for a lengthy assignment, coming back years later to re-enter leadership under a new president.

What the Women Think It Means

The women mostly thought that problems they encountered were either not gender-based or were specific to them. As they reviewed the themes and discovered that other women had similar struggles, they were both surprised and encouraged. Ashley said:

> It was interesting to read because . . . you do wonder if your experiences or thoughts about something are anywhere close to anyone else's. So I did find that interesting, to see where things lined up and also to see where my experience has really been very different than the other women.

In reflecting on some of the uncertainties, she commented, "Women in some ways are still struggling with their own conviction about their place in ministry leadership, so there's a reluctance on the part of some women to step into it even if they're being welcomed." In her organization this has been a challenge.

Barbara commented, "It was very helpful to me in the overall sense of realizing, oh I'm not alone! I was surprised at the number of common experiences that you had noted in your interviews." She added, "This one here, being willing to overlook and excuse or accept mistreatment, is really something that I was surprised to see that other people feel the same way." And later she commented, "I thought that was a remarkable convergence of how I either feel or aspire to be known as along with the others you interviewed." For her it was quite remarkable that others have encountered similar struggles and have similar thoughts.

Chelsea was very positive about the themes. "I thought you pulled out the kernels and wrote them down. And as I read it I thought, huh, yeah, that's right, yep, yep, that's right! So that was good." She too agreed that it was encouraging to know she was not alone in her experiences.

Regina also found this section on uncertainties to be thought-provoking:

> I thought it was very interesting the section you had on uncertainties regarding women's leadership and how you categorized them out, from the organization, from organization members,

and from the women. That was really interesting. It was just interesting to me when you diced that out, to see the different categories. And I guess it's one thing to talk about yourself and to say oh, yeah, this seems perfectly normal. But it's another thing to look at a study and say, wait a second, there's nine of us that are all doing the same thing. That's maybe not right.

Still, only two women in the study though these issues might reflect discrimination. Ashley somewhat ironically commented that she was watching the series "Downton Abbey" on public television, adding that it was set over 100 years ago yet she saw parallels between the story line and what she experiences today in mission organizations. She went on to add, "The church is about 50 years behind the times in this area and gets away with forms of gender discrimination that has not been tolerated or even legal for many years in secular settings. Similarly, Regina wrote, "The evangelical church is behind the culture by a significant amount of years. Missions are behind the church by another time lag." She added that she would call it discrimination when a woman was expected to do the work behind a man who had the role, and then quipped, "But she [the woman] probably doesn't." In reflecting on this further, she thought that perhaps a woman can only see what was going on after she has left the situation. She wrote:

> Now that I am out of my previous organization (and I took a class) and I am in a much safer environment I can say that I was discriminated against – and quite strongly at times. Removal from the situation may give that clarity.

She also reflected on the tendency to take personal responsibility for things, commenting, "I am seeing that this is my default and I need to look further for solutions before I open my mouth and take the responsibility."

Holly agreed with the idea that being out of the situation and looking back was the start of understanding for her. She explained:

> While it was going on I didn't label it as bullying. I learned that term in a seminar I went to after I left the role. It was a seminar on conflict and in passing someone gave a definition of bullying as something that is beyond conflict. And I recognized it as what had happened to me. They separated it from conflict in the seminar, because bullying is intentional and can't be changed. So then I did some research, read a book or two, read some blogs, and became convinced that it had been an intentional thing.

Distance and outside resources gave her clarity.

Stephanie had a very strong response to the idea that women do not advocate for themselves. She wrote:

> This is interesting to me – the fact that none of the other women have this interest as well. Someone from a secular perspective might sneer at this conclusion and label us traditionally minded women who are behind the times and willing to let a man rule the roost. Unwilling to stand up for our rights, etc. Instead it is probably (hopefully) that our identity in Christ gives us the security of self and awareness of self that enable us to have "nothing to prove" but our love for Christ and desire to serve in any way He calls us.

What a Feminist Perspective Would Add

Critical HRD argues that organizations may present themselves as neutral when they are, in fact, patriarchal.[6] The organizations in this study are clearly patriarchal in their structures, with gender inequality built into many of the organizational practices. The connection to evangelicalism as a faith basis for the organizations' work increases the alignment with gender essentialist beliefs and behavior patterns. Yet these organizations claim to be gender-neutral, and even favorable towards women leaders, which runs counter to the essentialist views of male rule and female submission. This conflict between what is expressed as true and what is true in practice creates cognitive dissonance for those who try to reconcile the conflicting messages.

One result, which is common in an essentialist belief system, is that the women hold themselves personally responsible for their own inability to fit into the existing social structure.[7] They are unable to name organizational practices as discriminatory and sexist. The discourse of male rule includes the hidden assumption that male rule is also beneficent, despite all evidence to the contrary.[8] If the rule is beneficent and the organization is neutral, then the women's only option is to hold themselves personally responsible for any difficulties they face. A second facet of evangelical discourse places additional pressure on the women to hold themselves personally responsible for organizational issues. There is a persistent popular argument that the first woman, Eve, by eating the forbidden fruit rebelled against Adam's

---

6. Acker, "Hierarchies, Jobs, Bodies"; Ely et al., *Reader in Gender, Work, and Organization*; Sheppard, "Women Managers' Perceptions of Gender and Organizational Life."

7. Scholz, "Psychologischer Essentialismus als relevantes Konzept für die Genderforschung."

8. Levitt and Ware, "Anything with Two Heads Is a Monster."

authority over her, bringing evil into the world.[9] In this thinking, for women to take on authority over men is dangerous and potentially destructive; the women must hold themselves carefully in check lest their agency create more problems than it solves. Finally, the discourse continues to reinforce the belief that men should rule and women should submit.

All of these pressures together—male-gendered organizations, the discourse of patriarchy, and the essentialist belief system—create an environment where the women police themselves, engaging in "self-surveillance" to keep themselves in line with the existing hegemonic structures.[10] They watch themselves, sticking to communal practices and supporting the male authority structures, making sure they do not step out of line by challenging or even naming the injustice they experience. The culture does not allow them to name what is happening, as Regina explained:

> We have no Christian definitions for this. What are the messages I am sending when I say that I have been discriminated against? I mean beyond the facts in the sentence. What am I saying about the organization's care for its people if it allows discrimination? What am I saying about my direct supervisor(s)?

What the women are allowed to name is the faith's requirement for submission and service from women, as Stephanie did in her commentary. In the end she spiritualized the problem, turning a legitimate issue of discrimination into a question of whether women are strong enough in their faith to accept organizational inequality.

CHAPTER SUMMARY

Various kinds of organizational behavior show ambivalence to women leaders, despite the fact that the organizations themselves chose the women for their leadership roles. Organizational leadership culture may be overwhelmingly male, host culture preferences may determine a woman's participation in leadership, interim and job-sharing assignments may limit a woman's influence, adjustments to a woman's role including title and salary discrepancies, or limitations in authority and even blatant opposition indicate that organizations are still fundamentally ambivalent about women leading. Subordinates also show ambivalence towards women's leadership by refusing to report to a woman, publicly discrediting her, or trying to circumvent her authority by appealing to the leader above her. Finally, the women themselves also demonstrate a certain amount of ambivalence

9. Becker, *Leading Women*.

10. Brookfield, *Power of Critical Theory*, 133.

towards their own leadership. They are reluctant to attribute problems they encounter to gender, preferring to think that their personality or capacity is the issue. They believe that men are either unaware or unintentional in their opposition to women. They are very reluctant to advocate for themselves, preferring to walk away from a difficult situation rather than fight. In a multitude of ways, then, despite the actual presence of women in leadership roles, there is ample evidence of continued resistance to female leadership in these evangelical mission organizations.

FINDINGS SUMMARY

In this chapter and the two previous ones, I have presented three main findings from this study of women leaders. First, to a large degree they accept and work within the gender roles prescribed for them. Their career trajectories show that they usually begin ministry as part of a two-person structure and put family first, if they are married. Single women started in typically female-gendered jobs and supportive roles to male colleagues. The women are sponsored by an influential male as part of their journey to leadership, and learn to lead from male mentors and teachers. Their leadership practices rely heavily on the communal behaviors.

The second finding is that the women also to a small degree maneuver within the gender roles for their own benefit. They use their husband's good as a reason to end the two-person career, they accept delegated authority which places them in leadership, they appeal to gifting over gender when it comes to leading, and they engage in cautious advocacy for the less-powerful in their organizations. Each of these strategies, which could be used to subvert male power in a subtle way, is actually insufficient to challenge male organizational hegemony. The women take up their authority only within the allotted space, while assuring the males that they are working for the men's and the organization's well-being.

The third finding is that there is persistent ambivalence towards women's leadership in evangelical mission organizations. The organizations in this study span the range from deliberately egalitarian to traditionally male-run. Still, in every case there are signs of uncertainty regarding women leaders, from organizational leadership cultures that are openly male, all the way to deliberate resistance and bullying from leaders and subordinates. The women themselves express some ambivalence about their own leadership as well, and are reluctant to think that gender plays a role in the challenges they encounter. The structural power in the organization clearly favors males, and leaves women at a serious disadvantage as they try to fulfill their leadership roles.

9

Summary, Conclusions, and Implications

THE PURPOSE OF THIS study was to understand how women lead and make meaning of their leadership in evangelical mission organizations. Three research questions guided this study. First, how have these women become leaders and learned to lead? Second, what if any forms of resistance or subversive behavior do they use in order to lead in a patriarchal culture? Third, how do they and the organizations they work in account for their leadership? In this chapter I give a summary of the study, a discussion of the major conclusions, and some implications for theory, practice, and research. I close with some thoughts for the participants themselves.

SUMMARY OF THE STUDY

This was a qualitative study of twelve women who lead or have led at the executive level in evangelical mission organizations. Qualitative research was the most appropriate method for this study because this population of women leaders has never been studied; qualitative research was best-suited to gain an initial understanding of their experiences of leadership and to extend the existing research on women leaders to a new population sample. The women were purposefully selected for this study, and each participated in a seventy-five minutes to two-hour interview with me. After transcribing and coding those interviews, I did a first round of constant comparative analysis. That enabled me to create a sheet of preliminary findings (see Appendix D) which I emailed to the women with a request for their comments. Ten of them sent written feedback about the preliminary findings sheet, and five of them participated in follow-up interviews with me. So eleven of the participants were represented in member-check feedback. I transcribed and coded the second set of feedback and incorporated that material and the written comments in the second round of data analysis.

The first and second round of analysis resulted in three categories of findings. The first finding, which addressed research question one, was that the women, to a large extent, accept and follow evangelical faith's prescribed gender-roles. The second finding, which addressed research question two, was that they were able, to a small degree, to use or maneuver the gender roles to support their leadership. The third finding, which addressed research question three, was that the organizations as well as the women themselves continue to be quite ambivalent about women's leadership, despite the fact that the organizations selected these women for leadership, and despite the women's clear love for their organizations and dedication to their leadership roles.

CONCLUSIONS AND DISCUSSION

I drew two main conclusions from this study. The first conclusion is that the power of the system's structural inequality and sexist practices that favor men is a self-reinforcing system that reconstructs and recreates itself on a continual basis, which the women cannot successfully resist. The women in this study are mostly products of the evangelical, gender-essentialist worldview. They came to leadership within that system and learned to lead without challenging that system; they mostly view themselves as part of and working within that system. As a result, they are unable to offer any serious resistance to the patriarchy that disadvantages them and the system continues to perpetuate itself.

The second conclusion is that, due to their isolation and token status, the women in this study wind up personalizing the problems they encounter. In order to lead, the women in this study did resist to some degree the gender constructions of their worldview, and in return encountered pressure back towards conformity from the system. Because of their commitment to their faith and their embeddedness in the gender essentialist system, the majority of the women in the study believed that the resistance they encountered to their leadership was personal. They attributed it to their own perceived personal shortcomings, rather than to the oppressive system in which they are located.

Conclusion 1: Perpetuating the Essentialist System

The power of the system's structural inequality and sexist practices is a self-reinforcing system that reconstructs and recreates itself on a continual basis.

The power of gender essentialist beliefs which are claimed to be based on God's design for hierarchical order in the world, and particularly between men and women, coupled with the hierarchical organizational structures which are designed to keep women in a position of support and subordination relative to males is extremely effective.[1]

Social roles represent a divine plan. Connecting socially constructed gender roles to a divine plan for order in the world is a powerfully effective way of ensuring that many women (and men), who wish to be faithful Christians, will accept and promote the roles as true and work hard to live in accordance with those role requirements.[2] Yet the roles that are currently promoted as God's design come straight from Victorian social thought regarding separate spheres for men and women and the cult of domesticity for females.[3] These roles were further reinforced in 1950s and 1960s North American culture with the post-war revival of the doctrine of separate spheres that was used to push women back into the home to create room for returning soldiers to enter the workforce.[4] Despite the fact that these gender roles are clearly products of the last three centuries of Western society, the evangelical church has largely chosen to promote them as a divine plan, reading them back into the texts of the Bible and proclaiming them to be God's plan for humanity.[5]

The women in this study are deeply embedded in the evangelical world system which ties faith to gender. The organizations they work for subscribe to a particular worldview and are heavily engaged in promoting that worldview and their faith through religious and charitable work around the world. Further, personal evangelical faith is the main qualification for staff to work with these organizations. Thus believing and belonging are central themes for the women's lives. That they have earnestly embraced and acted on that faith is seen in the degree to which they reflect it in their leadership.

Married women's careers, for example, showed their embeddedness in the gender roles. They were overwhelmingly committed to family first, in keeping with the evangelical gender-role requirements that construct motherhood and homemaking as a woman's most sacred spiritual calling.[6]

1. Litfin, "Evangelical Feminism."
2. Bendroth, "Last Gasp Patriarchy."
3. Ross, "Separate Spheres or Shared Dominions?"
4. Andersen and Hysock, *Thinking about Women.*
5. Gallagher, "Marginalization of Evangelical Feminism"; Ingersoll, "Engendered Conflict."
6. Dowland, "'Family Values' and the Formation of a Christian Right Agenda"; Gallagher, *Evangelical Identity and Gendered Family Life.*

For some this was chronological: raising their children and supporting their husbands first and entering leadership later. Chelsea explained that she only agreed to take on a leadership role after "our kids were gone and . . . my husband doesn't travel quite as much." For others, they began leading earlier, but continued to struggle with feelings of guilt that they might not be properly prioritizing their children and husbands. Kelly questioned, "Am I in some way neglecting my other role as a mother and as a wife, because I'm in this role?" She added that this is a serious pressure for women, which does not exist for men. In this she is correct: evangelical faith places a huge amount of pressure on women to have children and to view motherhood as the most important aspect of their lives. The fact that eight of the nine married women began their mission careers as part of a two-person career structure also shows how embedded they are in the evangelical gender system. The two-person career closely aligns with evangelical faith's gender role requirements for women to be primarily supportive of husbands and family and continues to construct them as supporters of males rather than independent persons.[7]

The single women, too, are embedded in the essentialist system, as shown by their gendered career choices, frequent support of male leaders as primary actors, and acceptance of personal responsibility for moral purity with their male colleagues. Part of the essentialist system is the strict separation of males and females and maintenance of absolute sexual purity between them. Sexual impropriety is one of the few reasons that would cause an organization to dismiss a staff member. Responsibility for this purity rests heavily on the women. Both Nicole and Melinda described how they were careful to make friends with their male colleagues' wives and to maintain distance with the men, showing how they have internalized the essentialist system's separatist construct of males and females accompanied by female responsibility for male sexual behavior.

In order to enter into leadership and learn to lead, the women in this study had to be selected and trained by males, because males are the ones with organizational decision-making power. This construction is considered so normal that only one woman even noted the absence of female role models. Finally, the women are so embedded in the essentialist system that they are mostly only able to use leadership practices that are communal in nature, in keeping with the assigned gender-role requirements that construct women as nurturing caretakers first and foremost. This is the narrow space provided for women to operate, and the women have mostly internalized the requirement and aligned their leadership

7. Murphy-Geiss, "Married to the Minister"; Papanek, "Men, Women, and Work."

practices to match. In all of these ways the women show themselves to be products of the system, aligning well with the prescribed roles for evangelical women seen in the literature.[8]

Mission agencies are patriarchal organizations. Mission organizations, like so many other organizations and businesses, are clearly constructed in such a way as to reinforce male hegemony and perpetuate patriarchy.[9] Organizational policies are designed by men, with men's work and men's benefit in mind. For example, the two-person career structure is clearly a practice designed to support male privilege and keep women in female-gendered, supportive positions.[10] Women are perceived and treated as existing primarily to support men's work. They are constructed as mothers, as wives, as supporters of men's ministry, and as subordinate to male authority, but not as independent agents capable of ministry and service to God in their own, independent right. If women are chosen by men to lead, they quickly learn that to survive, they must support male power and promote male well-being above all. Actions that would even appear to support women's interests or challenge male power are quickly and decisively castigated, so that women learn that if they wish to remain in their positions, they must support male power at all costs. Women in this study were underpaid, ignored, replaced, challenged, criticized, and even bullied to make sure they knew their place and did not challenge male authority. These forms of intimidation and silencing of dissent are types of coercive power males, and organizations, use to keep women in subordination.[11] Because men hold the power and because the organization is not subject to non-discrimination laws, men can act with impunity.

The women function within this system. Not surprisingly, since the women are so thoroughly schooled in and confined by the essentialist system, most of them accept it as normal, and some even defend it. They have been taught that essentialist thinking about males and females represents God's order, and the women, in their desire to please God, show

---

8. Aune, "Evangelical Christianity and Women's Changing Lives"; Frame and Shehan, "Relationship between Work and Well-Being in Clergywomen"; Gallagher, "Marginalization of Evangelical Feminism"; Gallagher and Smith, "Symbolic Traditionalism and Pragmatic Egalitarianism"; Papanek, "Men, Women, and Work."

9. Bierema, "Critiquing Human Resource Development's Dominant Masculine Rationality and Evaluating Its Impact"; Riehl and Lee, "Gender, Organization, and Leadership"; Sloan and Krone, "Women Managers and Gendered Values"; Stead and Elliott, *Women's Leadership.*

10. Papanek, "Men, Women, and Work."

11. Sloan and Krone, "Women Managers and Gendered Values."

conformity to this line of thinking.[12] A number of them made explicit essentialist comments about what men are like or what women are like. Holly and Kelly, for example, both made comments about women's "more relational" nature as compared to men. Chelsea and Melinda talked about men's and women's different ways of communicating as something innate. Barbara specifically attributed differences to God, saying, "God created us male and female and we have to have good relationships between those two sides." So did Chelsea, when she talked about "that piece God put in us of wanting to nurture and care for our families." Most of them seem to accept that gender essentialist beliefs as expressed through evangelical gender roles are correct and reflect God's plan for humanity. In this too they align with the literature which showed that acceptance of gender roles is a marker of faith in evangelicalism.[13]

Given the power and the narrowness of the gender construction, the women's maneuvers and acts of resistance were both mild and limited in scope, offering no serious threat to the gender hierarchy. This is partly due to the women's isolation, as I discuss in conclusion two, and partly due to the strength with which the gender roles have been impressed upon them. The literature showed that acceptance of gender roles has become deeply embedded in evangelical culture and serves as a way of defining orthodoxy; they can be used as a litmus test for true faith.[14] For some women in the study upholding the gender roles is literally an act of faith, as they embody and act on what they believe. For others, supporting those roles is critical for their inclusion in the faith community and in their organizations. Nevertheless, in doing so they also continue to support male power, which the literature showed is one of the main purposes of gender construction.[15]

For example, most of the married women did eventually separate from the two-person career, which seemed to resist the role requirement. Yet the power of the essentialist system is so strong that in order to break that requirement, they had to appeal to another gender-role requirement to uphold their decision. For instance, Barbara told of the organization's president wanting to put her and her husband in a shared role which she

12. Gallagher, *Evangelical Identity and Gendered Family Life.*

13. Dowland, "'Family Values' and the Formation of a Christian Right Agenda"; Ingersoll, *Evangelical Christian Women.*

14. Gallagher, "Marginalization of Evangelical Feminism"; Gallagher and Smith, "Symbolic Traditionalism and Pragmatic Egalitarianism"; Ingersoll, "Engendered Conflict."

15. Andersen and Hysock, *Thinking about Women*; Andersen and Collins, *Race, Class & Gender*; Maher, "Twisted Privileges"; Sheppard, "Women Managers' Perceptions of Gender and Organizational Life."

did not accept. Her reason was that she had seen her husband "not succeed" before in a similar role and she did not want that to happen again.
By placing his good above her own, she shows that she is still confined by
the gender-role requirements placed on women. Carol talked about her
organization's president wanting her in a separate role, and he talked to her
husband before offering it to her. So she had her husband's approval and
support for the job. She also was quite emphatic about making sure her position in the organization was not higher than her husband's as that would
upset the gender hierarchy. In her narrative, she accepted a leadership role
but only with her husband's approval and at a lower level than his, showing
that she too is still confined by the requirement that males lead. Even Ashley, who worked in a more egalitarian organization, found that one reason
for not embracing a shared role was the good of the marriage. The system
has constructed the women in conformity with the gender requirements
seen in the literature: husbands are the leaders and wives the followers, and
the husband's good takes precedence.[16]

Simply taking a leadership role also appeared to be a way of resisting
the gender-role requirements, since evangelicalism teaches that men are
to lead and women are to follow in church and society as well as in the
home.[17] By accepting a leadership role, then, the women seem to have
subverted another role requirement.[18] However, similarly to breaking the
two-person career model, the system requires that even in accepting leadership they fundamentally still uphold male authority. Therefore Carol,
Chelsea, and Kelly all describe having their husbands' support and approval for their leadership; the system requires that they have this approval. Eight women had male sponsors who put them in leadership, showing
male power to select and promote certain women. In order to function in
the system, the women have to show that male authority undergirds their
selection and/or promotion.

Additionally, although they had leadership roles, many of the women
were forced to accept limitations on their power and authority, and found
they could only exercise that authority in small ways, with limited scope,
and under the ultimate authority of a male superior. Chelsea was not allowed to deal with issues in her department and instead had to defer to the

16. Bendroth, "Last Gasp Patriarchy"; Gallagher and Smith, "Symbolic Traditionalism and Pragmatic Egalitarianism"; Sowinska, "Ambiguous Women."

17. Pevey et al., "Male God Imagery and Female Submission"; Sowinska, "Ambiguous Women."

18. Bendroth, "Last Gasp Patriarchy"; Gallagher, "Marginalization of Evangelical
Feminism"; Gallagher and Smith, "Symbolic Traditionalism and Pragmatic Egalitarianism"; Sowinska, "Ambiguous Women."

males above her. Melinda could not argue with a subordinate who refused to report to her as his supervisor. She commented that "it was not worth it" to fight; the system is constructed to support him as a male over her, regardless of her organizational position. Holly did not fight when she was unjustly dismissed from her job, and Tabitha accepted lower pay without fighting for herself. Melinda, Tabitha, and Holly's "choices" were in fact not free choices, but were constrained by the system which does not offer them the support it does to males.[19] This is part of the invidious nature of an essentialist belief system: the woman's lack of system support is recast as her "choice" to conform to the role requirements.[20] In these ways, although the women had positions of responsibility in the organizations, they were constrained by limitations on that responsibility and had to defer to male authority which is greater than their own.

The women's inability to use their positions of authority to advocate for other women in their organizations also reflects the construction of the gender role requirements. They clearly knew that advocating for women would be, in Carol's words, "not well received." Such advocacy, were it to happen, would be seen as an act of resistance to the gender role requirements, and the women lack the support to be able to take that step. In making the constrained choice not to advocate the women make their own jobs easier: "Women who create the perception that their presence as leaders would not challenge any other aspects of the cultural system face much less difficulty than women who, either intentionally or inadvertently, are controversial on other points as well."[21]

Finally, a few of the women were themselves actively involved in defending the gender role requirements. Stephanie was sure that women in her organization did not need anyone to speak for them; she thought they already have voice and need to be challenged to do more. Yet her organization is inflexible in the two-person career structure, meaning married women are always constructed alongside their husbands. Several other women defended or excused male behavior that was hurtful. Chelsea thought men were not aware of what they did, Barbara thought her leader was too busy to think about his behavior, and Melinda said male resistance was not personal to her. The system invests more power in males than females, and male rule is assumed to be beneficent; therefore the women, in order to survive and maintain their sanity, need to excuse rather than challenge poor male behavior.

19. Crompton and Lyonette, "New Gender Essentialism."
20. Crompton and Lyonette, "New Gender Essentialism."
21. Ingersoll, *Evangelical Christian Women*, 127.

The system is perpetuated. Individual women cannot change the system alone. They lack fundamental access to organizational power and support that would allow them to challenge the gender essentialist system. The potential cost to them of such a challenge is too high, the potential for injunctive pressure is too great, and the likelihood of success is far too small to make resistance reasonable. The structural bias in favor of men is extremely powerful, and it coupled with the argument that gender roles represent a divine plan make the sexist constructions unable to be questioned. In order to work within the existing structure, the women must accept and conform to the gender-role requirements. As a result, they continue to co-construct the system with the men and thus become complicit in its oppression. And so the system is perpetuated, with only token female leaders in place.

For some of the women, the collusion is passive and unintentional. Every time they conform to the male culture's demands that they dress a certain way, communicate a certain way, or adjust their expression of emotions to suit male preferences and male comfort, they are not challenging but reinforcing the system. They do not think of it that way, but it is the effect. For them it is the only way to survive in the system, keep their positions, and maintain their sanity. These women reflect a level of "gender unconsciousness" where they are totally embedded in the system and cannot even see the unjust demands it places on them.[22]

Others perpetuate the system indirectly. For example, when they refuse to say what they believe, as Melinda did when she commented, "whether I agree with that doctrinally is neither here nor there," they perpetuate the system. When Tabitha explained that she knew inequality was present but that she chose not to complain, she perpetuated the system. These kinds of comments represent the category of "conscious unconsciousness" where the women know injustice exists, but they actively choose to ignore it because the costs of challenging the system are too high.[23] Given the overwhelming strength of gender essentialist beliefs exhibited by these organizations, their choice makes good sense for their own self-preservation.

One woman was clearly active in perpetuating the system for others. Stephanie talked at length about the good of the system, how well it works in her organization, and how it could not possibly be harmful to the women. In a case of blaming the victim, she argued that "truly because we have this value of women in leadership [alongside their husbands] and this encouragement, to me it's a question to ask the women, do you hold yourself back?" For her, the only thing that could be hurting women in her organization

22. Bierema, "Role of Gender Consciousness in Challenging Patriarchy."
23. Bierema, "Role of Gender Consciousness in Challenging Patriarchy."

was that they might be holding themselves back. In blaming other women for not taking advantage of what she believes are their opportunities, she is actively perpetuating the system.

Conclusion 2: Personalizing the Problem

The majority of the women in this study seemed completely unaware that there were system-level issues contributing to their struggles. The women thought that their struggles and issues were personal to them, and were traceable to their personality, training, upbringing, or some other personal failing. They were initially utterly unaware that other women in leadership roles in similar types of organizations also dealt with similar issues.

The literature showed that one outcome of essentialist views of gender is that it can lead to women blaming themselves, rather than patriarchal structures, for their difficulties.[24] This was particularly a struggle for clergywomen from conservative religious backgrounds like the women in this study.[25] In fact ten of the women in this study believed their issues were personal to them, and the other two considered that possibility. They seemed completely unaware of system-level issues that were occurring in their own ministries and organizations, and they completely overlooked the way the gender-role system oppressed them as women. As a result they blamed themselves for any issues they encountered. Their lack of awareness could be because they are few in number and isolated from one another, and because they lack a natural avenue for connection with each other.

The women think their struggles are personal to them. They thought their personality, their upbringing, their educational level, or some similar factor was the reason they had trouble with the leadership structures in their organizations. For example, Barbara thought her personality was to blame for the lack of recognition she received for her work. Nicole thought that she had to change her own communication style to suit her particular male colleagues' preferences. Holly thought her upbringing in an abusive family accounted for her ability to persevere in a bullying situation at work. Ashley thought her unequal educational level accounted for the men not hearing her. Donna thought her problems had to do with her attitude and her ability to "separate the job from myself" and "not let it define me." In each case the women thought that the struggles they experienced

24. Bohan, "Regarding Gender"; Crompton and Lyonette, "New Gender Essentialism"; Scholz, "Psychologischer Essentialismus als relevantes Konzept für die Genderforschung."

25. Becker, Leading Women; Zikmund et al., Clergy Women.

with their male colleagues were due to something particular and personal about them. They lack the feminist framework to understand that system issues were the root of their problems. The gender essentialist belief system coupled with the patriarchal organizational structure leaves them no option but to blame themselves.

The belief that the struggles were personal rather than systemic led to fully half of the women in this study walking away at one point or another from ministry or leadership. Four of them also consulted counselors, and one even asked flat out what was wrong with her that was provoking the situation. In their belief that the issues are personal, they resemble the Black women in corporate America studied by Cole and the clergy women studied by Zikmund, Lummis, and Chang who tended to take most of the responsibility on themselves rather than looking at the system or environment to understand their problems.[26] The fact that they prefer to walk away rather than fight shows the overwhelming strength of the system which has constructed them to fit in under, not challenge, male power.

They are unaware that other women have similar struggles. A second illustration of how the women thought that problems were personal to them was their lack of awareness that other women had similar struggles and their surprise at learning they were not alone when they reviewed the initial findings I sent to them for a member-check. Ashley, Barbara, Chelsea, and Regina all responded with comments that it was "interesting" or "surprising" to find out that other women had similar issues. Regina commented, "Wait a second! There's nine of us doing the same thing?" She was the only one to realize that this reflected a pattern of women's behavior and a pattern of organizational behavior towards women in leadership roles, leading her to comment, "Something's not right." The general lack of awareness is likely partly due to the women's unfamiliarity with feminism. The literature showed that evangelicalism has portrayed feminism as the enemy of faith. Further, the women have been trained to be "received knowers," who accept the male voice of authority regarding what is known and can be known, and do not question or seek knowledge on their own apart from approved sources.[27] Male authority has taught them that feminist thought is dangerous and contrary to God's plan for home and family.[28] So the women may be completely uninformed about feminist thought regarding power, privilege, and organizational structures favoring males; this knowledge which could

26. Cole, "Courage under Fire"; Zikmund et al., *Clergy Women*.

27. Belenky et al., *Women's Ways of Knowing*.

28. Litfin, "Evangelical Feminism."

shed light on their struggles and show that the issues are systemic and not personal has been forbidden to them.[29]

The second reason they are unaware that other women struggle is the fact that the women in this study were surrounded by men and male leaders, and have only had male role models, not female ones. Some of them have literally never seen another woman leader in their organization. Their organizations are male-dominated when it comes to leadership, and the literature showed that male-dominated organizations tend to structure women as men's supporters, not independent actors.[30] Thus, their only models for women are as submissive helpers, and their only models for leadership are males. As a result they assume that leadership challenges they encounter are personal to them, since the other leaders in their organizations, who just happen to be males, do not have those struggles.

They are isolated from one another. The third factor that contributes to the women believing the problems are theirs alone is their relative isolation from one another. They may actually not know any other women leaders in mission organizations. In recruiting for the study, I always asked if a woman knew someone else who qualified; most of them did not. Even more telling was their desire to know what I learned from this study. Most of them, even a few women I contacted but who did not qualify to participate, told me they were eager to read the results. In chapter one I discussed the lack of women at the national mission leaders' conference on diversity held in 2010. Only two of the women in this study mentioned having attended those national conferences, and even if more women did attend they would still find only a handful of other women present. And some of the women who do attend are wives, accompanying their husbands as part of the two-person career, but not participating as leaders.

The cumulative effect of being embedded in a gender-essentialist belief system, working in a male-dominated structure, having male teachers, sponsors, and role models, being forbidden to consider feminist thought, and being isolated from other women leaders makes it inevitable that the women believe their struggles are personal to them. The entire system is constructed in such a way as to concentrate privilege in the hands of males and communicate to the woman that it is her fault alone if she cannot make the system work for her.

29. Dowland, "'Family Values' and the Formation of a Christian Right Agenda."
30. Shehan et al., "Feeding the Flock and the Family."

The outliers. Two women in this study worked in organizations that are purposefully egalitarian in their practices. One woman, Ashley, said she was not raised in the church, came to faith as an adult, and was never trained in the gender-essentialist role requirements of evangelicalism. "I was not raised in the church. I became a Christian as an adult, and didn't come with any of that baggage," she explained. She also wondered about other women's commitments to the role: "I know they've been raised in the church, but there's so much other thinking out there on that." Her organization made a deliberate choice some years ago to address the topic directly. Potential new missionaries learn about the organization's support for women in any role and are advised that if they cannot work in that structure, the organization will not be a good fit for them.

Regina, unlike Ashley, was raised in the faith and commented that she was a "latecomer" to women's issues. However, her views shifted, she changed organizations, and she now has better organizational support. The president is very supportive of her personally and of women generally, and the organization has made a deliberate choice to support women in all ministry roles. "In my current organization, we have talked about making sure there's equity, like in leadership. And they've actually listened to that in the new . . . leadership cabinet, it's 33% female." They are also working towards ethnic diversity and age diversity in their leadership.

These two women are also the ones who commented on the degree to which the evangelical church and evangelical mission organizations lag behind society on the topic of women's equality. They appear to be aware of these issues partly because of their education. Both of them talked about the way their studies influenced them, and about the benefits of studying at secular rather than religious institutions. Yet despite supposed organizational support and personal knowledge, they continued to struggle periodically with leading as women in their respective organizations. The problem is that the essentialist belief system and the privilege accorded males is so deeply embedded in the faith as well as in these organizations that change would require more than simply affirming women's value as leaders; it would reach into the fabric of the organizational culture and require radically new ways of thinking about men and women.

IMPLICATIONS FOR THEORY, PRACTICE, AND RESEARCH

This research adds to the literature on women in organizational leadership by examining more closely how patriarchal organizations behave and how women lead in them. In particular, it sought to understand the impact of gender essentialist views of men and women on women's leadership and on organizational practices. This study has implications for both theory and practice, and indicates potential areas for future research.

Implications for Theory

This study has examined the intersection of a gender essentialist belief system with patriarchal organizational structures to discover the effects on women's leadership. Oppression is conceived of as a matrix with various elements such as race, class, and gender, rather than being traced to a single factor.[31] For the women in this study, the intersection of gender and organizational type produce a distinct type of oppressive environment. Therefore, the study adds to our understanding of how the intersection of these two strands of oppression, gender essentialist beliefs and patriarchal structures, affects women who attempt to lead. The results have implications for these types of organizations, and for women's learning and meaning making about their leadership practices.

Implications for organizations. I have looked specifically at women's leadership in strongly male-dominated evangelical organizations which hold to gender essentialist beliefs as part of their faith structure. The literature on gender-role stereotypes as the basis for prescriptive and injunctive norms offers a partial understanding of how the women in these organizations exercise leadership.[32] These women, like their counterparts in secular organizations, use many communal behaviors as part of their leadership in order to maintain a certain level of conformity with the gender-role expectations for females.[33]

INJUNCTIVE PRESSURE. However, the women in this study faced particularly strong pressure from injunctive norms, or the expectations of what women *ought* to do.[34] Injunctive norms imply a moral rightness for certain types of behavior and thus allow for censure of those who do not conform. Thus these women met with opposition from both superiors and subordinates as they took up their leadership roles. The difference between them

31. Andersen and Collins, *Race, Class & Gender*.

32. Carli and Eagly, "Gender and Leadership"; Eagly and Karau, "Role Congruity Theory of Prejudice toward Female Leaders"; Heilman and Eagly, "Gender Stereotypes Are Alive, Well, and Busy Producing Workplace Discrimination."

33. Eagly and Karau, "Role Congruity Theory of Prejudice toward Female Leaders"; Heilman and Okimoto, "Why Are Women Penalized for Success at Male Tasks?"

34. Eagly and Karau, "Role Congruity Theory of Prejudice toward Female Leaders."

and the women in secular organizations represented in the literature seems to be traceable to the way evangelical faith has converted social gender-role stereotypes into a divine standard for human behavior. Connecting the social gender role stereotypes to a divine plan for humanity makes them unable to be questioned or challenged, and justifies the use of sanctions or punishments against those who cross the line.

THE DOUBLE-BIND. Thus in this study, the women were also caught in a double-bind, but the nature of the bind was qualitatively different from that described in the literature on women's leadership in secular organizations. The women in this study were constricted in their leadership and chastised for their leadership behaviors, because in the very act of accepting a leadership position they had already broken the gender-role expectations, thus exposing themselves to censure designed to remind them of their rightful place as subordinates to males. In a system where women are not allowed to lead, a woman who accepts a leadership role is immediately susceptible to pressure from the men around her designed to remind her of her proper place and to remind her that any leadership she does exercise is only done on sufferance, and at the whim of the men around her.

STRUCTURAL HEGEMONY. The structural impediments to women's leadership in these evangelical organizations are currently insurmountable. There is pressure on women to pursue marriage and motherhood as their highest spiritual calling, which leaves them neither time nor energy to pursue leadership. There is an expectation that married women will support their husbands in the two-person career structure: this is an organizational policy established by men with male good and male comfort in mind. It renders women's contributions to the organization's work completely invisible and treats them as valueless. There is an expectation that single women will support men's work, and will accept responsibility for men's sexual behavior, another practice established by men with male comfort in mind. There is an expectation that women who are selected for leadership roles will present themselves in ways that are comfortable to males, adjusting themselves in voice, behavior, and even dress to the demands of the male culture. This pressure also has male good and male comfort in mind, preventing men from having to listen to anything that they prefer not to hear. Only a very few women are selected for leadership positions, meaning that women remain in token status and never achieve enough critical mass to seriously challenge existing structures or practices. Thus women's voices are silenced and women's needs and desires remain hidden.

This is more than a case of a glass ceiling, or a stained-glass ceiling: it represents a system that is fundamentally convinced, at its deepest level, that women are not only unsuited for leadership, but are going against God's plan for women if they accept leadership. Although the organizations demonstrate a desire for women leaders at a superficial level, underneath the belief clearly persists that women should not lead. When they do, men take up their power to remind women of their subordinate place. The result is a system that perpetuates itself cyclically and maintains men in positions of power while undermining women's attempts to lead, or to change or challenge the existing system in any way.

THE COST. The cost for this cycle of male rule reinforced as divine plan, coupled with structures designed for men's good and male rule, is high. Women themselves pay the price, since their needs and desires are fundamentally ignored. Furthermore, women's work and women's contributions to the organizational purpose are completely overlooked. In reality, without the women's work, the organizations would not be able to function. Yet rather than recognize and incorporate the women's contributions to organizational purposes, they are structured as invisible and ignored. The organization loses all the benefit that women's enormous pool of talent, wisdom, knowledge, and effort could offer.

Implications for women's learning and meaning-making. This study also has implications for women's ways of learning leadership and making meaning of their leadership practices. The women in this study moved into leadership because they were selected by men, and they learned to lead from men: men were the organizational gatekeepers. The women's practices reflect either silence, where they simply follow the dictates of authority figures, or received knowledge, where they learn and act upon the knowledge provided by the authority figures, but do not create any independent knowledge of their own.[35]

MEANING-MAKING. The women are only able to make meaning of their leadership that fits within the essentialist and patriarchal ways of thinking present in the organizations. Barbara's comment about her leader treating her poorly because he did not have time to think about what he was doing precisely illustrates the problem. His authoritative voice told her what to think, and the system does not allow her to acknowledge the sexist thinking and sexist practices embedded in the very organizational structure.

35. Belenky et al., *Women's Ways of Knowing.*

Women's understanding of their leadership as being primarily communal is also in line with what gender essentialist beliefs and patriarchal organizational structures allot to them. The meaning women make of these practices is that they are good at them, enjoy them, and that the organization benefits from them, because this is what the authority figures assign them as their contribution. They are unable to consider that the structures of the oppressive system confine them to these types of practices, and use injunctive pressure to push them into these behaviors when they show any tendency to step outside the allotted space.

GENDER UNCONSCIOUSNESS. The women also represent a high degree of gender unconsciousness which is also tied to their status as silent and/or received knowers.[36] The voices of authority in evangelicalism mostly reject feminism outright as antithetical to the faith.[37] Additionally, the women live and work within evangelical organizations, and being highly embedded in the subculture leads to greater suspicion of feminist thought.[38] Thus they are unaware of the structural hegemony that disadvantages them, do not question the system, and make no efforts to change it.[39]

THE RESULT. The result is that women, who are not supported in their leadership by either the gender essentialist constructs or the organizational structures, are oppressed on every side. With neither the tools nor the knowledge to question the system as it currently exists, and with the voices of authority telling them that the constructs and structures are good and right, the women blame themselves for the problems they encounter. Rather than evaluating the system as oppressive, they evaluate themselves as falling short.

Implications for Practice

This research has implications for evangelical mission organizations, as well as for adult education practitioners who work with their women leaders. If organizations want to benefit from the tremendous pool of female talent currently being overlooked, and if women want to offer their skills and abilities to lead in mission organizations, a number of concerns need to be addressed.

36. Belenky et al., *Women's Ways of Knowing*; Bierema, "Role of Gender Consciousness in Challenging Patriarchy."

37. Dowland, "'Family Values' and the Formation of a Christian Right Agenda."

38. Gallagher, "Where Are the Antifeminist Evangelicals?"

39. Bierema, "Role of Gender Consciousness in Challenging Patriarchy."

Implications for organizations. These organizations face two main challenges if they truly want to incorporate women into organizational leadership and fully benefit from what women could offer them. The first, and most obvious, challenge is to make a decision in favor of women's leadership and choose to support it fully. The data collected for this study show an enormous amount of lingering ambivalence regarding women's leadership. These organizations have made a choice to invite women to lead, but they have not followed with an unhesitating commitment to women leaders, leaving a great deal of doubt about whether they truly want women to lead in their organizations. Organizations need to make a firm decision one way or the other, and if they choose in favor of women's leadership then they need to back that decision fully with wholehearted organizational commitment.

The second challenge is likely greater than the first. Having made the choice to have women leaders and to support them unequivocally, the organization will need to take a long, hard look at its practices and its underlying belief structures to see what change needs to occur. Among other things, two-person career structures will need to be re-examined and rethought. Systems for determining job assignments will need to be reevaluated. Choices to support women over men in cases of male insubordination will be necessary. Potential criticism and backlash from others within the evangelical community who disagree will need to be anticipated and deflected. Theological and historical studies showing how the gender roles came to be constructed, and deconstructing them, will be paramount. These are significant changes which will not occur quickly or painlessly. Before embarking on such an undertaking, the organization needs to be absolutely clear that the long-term benefits will greatly outpace the short-term costs.

Implications for adult educators. Women leaders in these organizations as they currently function are in a challenging situation requiring empathy and care. Two participants pointed out that evangelical mission organizations are anywhere from 30-50 years behind society in their views on women. And the views they espouse are tied to doctrine, making challenging them not only a question of changing a mindset, but also of changing a faith paradigm. Therefore, an adult educator who wants to enter that space and offer women an alternative way of viewing and understanding the situation must proceed cautiously. If organizational-level change does not occur, then these women will continue trying to lead in high-challenge, high-risk environments, with little likelihood of success.

Their acquiescence to organizational practices indicates these women are accustomed to heeding the voice of authority but less accustomed to evaluating ideas regarding gender for themselves.[40] They are also likely to be isolated from other women who could offer help and support as they navigate their organizations. Establishing an environment for "connected knowing" to occur, where women leaders could meet together and share stories of their experiences, could prove extremely valuable for their personal sanity, and possibly for their professional development.[41] Such an environment is consistent with principles of feminist pedagogy which encourage the development of voice and visibility for women students, including taking their own experiences seriously.[42] An environment where the women could come to know and trust one another would also offer the framework for them to develop an understanding of structural and religious elements that hamper their attempts to lead. The same theological and historical studies needed in organizations, showing how the gender roles came to be constructed, and deconstructing them, would also be critical.

However, the adult educator must be particularly careful about posing as an absolute expert or functioning as a gatekeeper who dictates what women may or may not learn. Replacing one authoritarian voice with another would not result in real transformation, but simply offer a potential swapping of paradigms. A preferable approach would be to establish the holding environment and create conditions where transformative learning could occur.[43] Adult educators know that transformation is more likely to take place in some environments than others; therefore, our responsibility is to help create that environment.[44] In this case it would include recognizing where the women currently are, offering them a supportive environment, and challenging them to consider thinking differently about their experiences.[45] These women need both the information and the opportunity to re-examine some of their experiences, reflect on what they mean in the light of feminist scholarship, and potentially redefine their own perspectives and beliefs about the meaning of those events.[46] This approach challenges the adult learner while respecting her as an adult, acknowledging her ultimate authority in choosing her own meaning. It is congruent with the "learner empowerment" the women need and could help them begin to shift from

40. Belenky et al., *Women's Ways of Knowing*.

41. Belenky et al., *Women's Ways of Knowing*; Bierema, "Role of Gender Consciousness in Challenging Patriarchy."

42. Maher, "Toward a Richer Theory of Feminist Pedagogy"; Tisdell, "Poststructural Feminist Pedagogies."

43. Cranton, *Understanding and Promoting Transformative Learning*.

44. Daloz, "Mentors."

45. Daloz, "Mentors"; Daloz, "Martha Meets Her Mentor."

46. Cranton, *Understanding and Promoting Transformative Learning*.

silence and received knowledge to connected knowledge.[47] If enough women band together in changing their perspectives and raising their level of awareness to "gender consciousness" they might perhaps together create enough momentum to challenge organizational patriarchy.[48]

Nevertheless, if the organizations are not willing to make the decision and commitments described previously, no amount of working with the women is likely to bring significant improvement to their ability to lead. The organizations as currently structured will continue to inhibit and resist women's leadership, which will likely lead to more women cycling through the system and exiting, blaming themselves for the system's injustice.

Implications for Future Research

This study suggests several avenues for future research. Some research has been done on how women who enter fundamentalist, highly authoritarian religious groups learn to conform to gender expectations.[49] The women in this study, however, for the most part grew up inside the faith, and belonged to organizations that were not fundamentalist in that they were at least notionally open to women's leadership. Still, most of the women and the organizations were characterized by gender essentialist beliefs. However, two women in this study did not subscribe to those beliefs, one because she never held it and one because she changed her mind. One fruitful avenue of study could be to investigate women who join these organizations and do not adopt essentialist beliefs. How do they resist the pressure to conform? Another approach would be to investigate women who undergo a change of thinking on gender roles. How do they make that shift? More generally, what factors enable a woman to resist or shift away from an essentialist view to an egalitarian view of men and women in these contexts? What happens to her and her faith when she makes that shift?

Another question that remains is how adult education can offer feminist scholarship to women in conservative, evangelical religions in a way that allows them to consider it without feeling threatened or rejecting it outright. Belenky, et al.'s description of women who can criticize the system but only in the system's own terms describes these women well.[50] What might help them to develop an ability to safely question the system itself? Cranton's ideas about transformative learning events in adult lives

47. Cranton, *Understanding and Promoting Transformative Learning*, 72. Belenky et al., *Women's Ways of Knowing*.

48. Bierema, "Role of Gender Consciousness in Challenging Patriarchy."

49. Cooley, "Discipling Sisters."

50. Belenky et al., *Women's Ways of Knowing*.

could also provide ways for educators to offer the framework and environment for change to women like these.[51] Studies into the efficacy of such approaches, or studies investigating other approaches to paradigm shifts could be useful to the field of adult education.

Third, studies could investigate how adult education can support women from gender essentialist religious backgrounds in their learning so that the women can learn without finding they must choose between faith and feminism. Although some feminist scholars believe that the two are incompatible, others do not.[52] The connection of adult education and spirituality is well-documented and some of that spirituality has come from the Christian faith tradition.[53] Perhaps there are ways to approach feminist teaching that are still in keeping with women's faith. Bruland suggests five areas where feminist and Christian ethics coincide: the importance of personal experience, a high value on relationships, a distrust of strictly rational approaches to knowledge, a sensitivity to power and control, and a desire for structural justice.[54] Research could be done to discover if these values could serve to bridge the perceived gap between faith and feminism, allowing women to incorporate both into their lives.

Fourth, studies could investigate possibilities for women's career development within these types of organizations. The current structures and practices make it very challenging for women to achieve levels of significant responsibility and authority in the organization. Is there a need even with the essentialist structures to help women develop professionally? Is such development even possible within the gender essentialist construct? Would there be any value in developing more women for leadership roles, given that leadership openings for women are few and far between?

Finally, more research could be done on other factors besides gender essentialism that affect women's leadership views and practices. This study has concentrated on the gender-role prescriptions from society and evangelical religion that impact women's leadership. However, oppression is more adequately conceived as a matrix than a single strand.[55] What other factors impact women's leadership in evangelical mission organizations? Do gender role expectations impact women at other types of organizations within the evangelical faith, such as schools and universities? Some

51. Cranton, *Understanding and Promoting Transformative Learning.*
52. Bruland, "Evangelical and Feminist Ethics."
53. English and Tisdell, "Spirituality and Adult Education."
54. Bruland, "Evangelical and Feminist Ethics."
55. Andersen and Collins, *Race, Class & Gender.*

research has been done into women's leadership in those settings, but there is a need for further studies.[56]

CHAPTER SUMMARY

This was a qualitative study of twelve women leaders in evangelical mission organizations with offices in North America. The findings showed that these women are heavily affected by the gender-role stereotypes prescribed for women and men in evangelical religion. The women have learned to exercise leadership within a narrow space where their authority is often contested. They do the best work they can and accept personal responsibility when things are difficult. Two conclusions were drawn from the findings: (a) first, the power of the system's structural inequality and sexist practices is a self-reinforcing system that reconstructs and perpetuates itself, and (b) the constraints of the system lead the women to personalize the problems they encounter as if they were personally responsible.

Implications for theory and practice were then offered. More research needs to be done to find out how organizations can wholeheartedly embrace women as leaders, and how women can resist the gender-role constructs or learn their way to a new understanding of gender that allows them to maintain their faith.

FINAL THOUGHTS

Being "the first" woman is hard. Being the only woman in an all-male environment is hard. Being a female leader in a male-dominated world is hard. Being isolated is hard.

The women in this study worked in highly gendered, male-leadership-dominated organizations. Sometimes they felt more like representatives of a category than real, individual, human beings.

To them I would like to say, it is not your fault: not your personality, not your training, not your upbringing, not your style, or your skill, or your spirituality. It is not you. Blaming yourself can be devastating.

It is a tradition of male leadership that makes men comfortable and women uncomfortable in leadership roles.

It is a pattern of viewing men as first and women as second.

It is a way of thinking that confines women to a box.

---

56. Dahlvig and Longman, "Women's Leadership Development"; Lafreniere and Longman, "Gendered Realities and Women's Leadership Development"; Longman and Lafreniere, "Moving Beyond the Stained Glass Ceiling."

This study has shown that you work in very challenging conditions. Yet you are working faithfully to fulfill your responsibilities, and doing so with little in the way of support. You've been given few tools to help you, and you've been going it alone.

The time has come for that to change. You need to meet each other, get to know one another, learn from each other. You need to connect and network and mentor and sponsor each other and other women in your organizations. Doing so will benefit each one of you. It will give you strength, encouragement, ideas. It will benefit other women in your organizations. It will benefit other Christian women around the world, in all the many and varied places where you work. It will also move you towards your ministry goals. I leave you with these words, addressed to women in the church and equally applicable for you:

> If [missionary] women can overcome the isolation created by the personalization of their "failures" and gain an understanding that their problems are system-based rather than individual or situational, they may be able to mobilize and make significant new contributions to the churches and their ministries by expanding definitions of . . . ministry *and—literally—taking the church into the world* [emphasis added].[57]

---

57. Zikmund et al., *Clergy Women*, 131.

Appendix A

Subjectivity Statement: My Story

AFTER GRADUATION FROM COLLEGE, I went to work in the world of international faith-based non-profits, where I remained for almost twenty years. My first stint was as a recent college graduate, when I did a two-year term in Austria as a family helper and ministry apprentice. During this time I saw some practices regarding married women that disturbed me: they were not supported in language learning although their family functioning depended on their ability to communicate; they were always responsible for child and house-care, regardless of their abilities or wishes; in general they were not consulted or included in decisions regarding their life or work. I saw several families leave their work because the wife could not function in the society; lack of language skills seemed to be a central issue for them.

My second foray came several years later. I had returned to the US, completed a Master's degree in theology, married, and had two children. Based on my earlier experiences, when my husband and I were looking for an organization, we ruled out quite a few that obviously did not support their women staff, particularly in the area of learning the local language. Despite our efforts, however, we still wound up in a situation that was far from ideal for me. For starters, he was hired and I "volunteered." Once overseas, we discovered that he was responsible to "work" and I was to care for the family, regardless of our training and preferences for parenting and family life. He was given a job description and a supervisor; I was expected to find my own way. He had a budget and expense account; any work I did had to be covered out of our personal income. Any work I did or we did together was credited on his quarterly report, since I was a volunteer. It quickly became obvious that we had embarked on what I later learned is called a "two-person career."[1] I watched this play out in our life and in the lives of our colleagues, and I became increasingly distressed. I also watched the attrition of dedicated and passionate women who could not sustain the unfavorable work conditions, and I was incensed to hear a classic blame-the-victim attitude expressed by male leaders: these women were "not good enough" to sustain the rigors of overseas work.[2] The structures that demanded their labor while refusing any kind of support or recognition for that work were completely ignored.

Still, for more than fifteen years, our family persevered. I found ways to engage as an adult educator. In one country, for example, I led a support group for new mothers and taught an introduction to doctrine course for lay women in leadership in a local church. Later on, living in a different country, I taught at the local seminary and also led church-based leadership courses and mother's support groups. In addition to my local responsibilities, during these years I taught leadership development courses through the organization for staff from locations all across the continent, and led continuing professional skills training specifically for women staff from multiple organizations. I hoped in this way to affect the organization from two sides, by improving women's skills and the visibility of their contributions, while broadening the understanding of leadership to include women and structural considerations. Yet nothing ever seemed to change. The only places where women had significant leadership roles were in areas related to children or other women. Women were actively and successfully engaged in every aspect of the organization's work, yet almost never present at the levels of leadership, strategy, and decision-making.

I watched other women over the years in their efforts to lead, and observed that while a few seemed to succeed, most did not. Whereas there were quite a few men who had been in various leadership roles for twenty years or more, no woman seemed to last very long. Some were removed from their roles after a year or two and others resigned fairly quickly. Some left the organization altogether; others found a different organization that welcomed their talents while their husbands continued in the original work. Given the typical mission organization two-person career structure where a married couple is counted as one employee (the husband) and one volunteer (the wife), married women could easily take their skills elsewhere if their own organization had no space for them. Single women used the strategy of secondment to take their talents elsewhere. Some women who clearly had

1. Papanek, "Men, Women, and Work"; Frame and Shehan, "Relationship between Work and Well-Being in Clergywomen."

2. Block et al., "Race, Poverty, and Disability"; Quigley and Holsinger, "Happy Consciousness."

leadership capacities never had a chance to put those abilities to use. Further, I noticed a kind of pervasive cynicism among the middle-aged and older women, single and married both, a feeling that the organization almost literally didn't know they existed. Early in my career this attitude had baffled me, but over time as I observed the organizational processes and behaviors, it made increasing sense. While women comprised more than two-thirds of the workforce, they were barely visible in the structures, strategies, leadership, or budgets. They were the invisible workforce. And as I met and talked with people from similar organizations I began to realize that this condition prevailed across many organizations of this type.

I myself also tried to move into leadership with only limited success. On three occasions I was turned away from leading anything other than women's work and training. I also asked several times to talk with the executive team regarding women's potential leadership contributions, and was refused every time. One male leader told me to talk with his wife so she could tell him what I thought. Not surprisingly, this gave me a somewhat negative view of the strongly patriarchal structures that favor gender over capacity. My own experience that education and ability were insufficient to overcome gender bias against women as leaders makes this study both personally interesting and personally challenging.

As I entered the study, given my history, I held some assumptions I would like to make explicit. First, I assumed that most of the women I interviewed were working in strongly gendered organizations, meaning that gender stereotypes are both pervasive and unquestioned as a foundation for male–female relationships. Next, since these women accepted a leadership assignment in a realm where women are not supposed to lead, I assumed that they might experience some cognitive dissonance. By asking them to lead, the organization indicated that it did not wholly hold to a prohibition on women's leadership. If the women were steeped in gender essentialist beliefs, it might be difficult for them to see and name sexist practices that underlie organizational practices.[3] Or it might make it difficult for them to reconcile mentally and emotionally their ability to do a job that is notionally barred to them. Third, I assumed that if they accepted a leadership role, then they also had some level of ambition and interest in leading. It seems reasonable to say that if they were personally convinced that women should not lead, or were totally lacking in ambition, then they could have chosen to stay in a non-leader role. Fourth, I assumed that

3. Allison, "Organizational Barriers to Diversity in the Workplace"; Marshall, *Women Managers.*

these women were probably self-directed learners.[4] There is some evidence that, like their for-profit counterparts, non-profits may not provide adequate training to their staff.[5] By possibly coming into leadership from outside the usual channels, meaning that they were not identified early on and groomed for leadership, the women might face an even stronger need to learn how to lead quickly and on their own.

I also came to this study with a few assumptions about the organizations themselves. First, soliciting adequate funding is likely to be a consistent challenge and a limiting factor in what staff members are able to do. On the other hand, the needs the organizations are addressing are always greater than the available resources, both in terms of personnel and funding. This led me to expect that the demands on staff were likely more than they could meet, making it challenging for them to set limits, draw boundaries, or say no even when it is necessary. I also assumed a diffuse work force, with teams potentially spread over wide geographic and cultural distances. Offices and decision-makers might be located far away from those on the ground doing the organization's work. All of these factors—finances, needs, distance, culture, geography—therefore added an additional level of complexity to leadership, which is intensified by being female in a male world.

Having these assumptions and making them explicit runs counter to my early training in both positivism and patriarchal values, which were imbued in me through schooling, society, and evangelical religion. Time, experience, and further education have combined to move me towards a constructivist view of knowledge and to embrace a feminist view of society. While I still hold to traditional Christian beliefs, I have come to see that human understanding, meaning, and significance are individual truths, constructed through a combination of context, personality, training, experience, gender, race, and a multitude of other factors. These personal influences preclude the existence of one absolute reality that is the same for every person. Much of that contextual influence is the pervasiveness of a patriarchal worldview, which invests greater power and importance in males than females, and this worldview is virtually ubiquitous. In much of evangelical religion, it is also considered as doctrine.

Given my early training and my shifting understanding, any attempt to study women's leadership in evangelical mission organizations from a so-called objective perspective made no sense to me. Doctoral study gave me a new way of seeing both myself and the study's participants. Feminist

4. Caffarella, "Self-Directed Learning."

5. Chermack et al., "Critical Uncertainties Confronting Human Resource Development"; Gibelman, "Nonprofit Sector and Gender Discrimination."

thought, critical scholarship, transformative learning, and qualitative research methods combined to show me that my own background could serve as an illumination to my studies, as well as providing additional data to inform both the research and the interpretation of findings. This study sought to explore ways women lead in evangelical mission agencies, through the framework of a feminist understanding that there are obstacles women negotiate to lead in patriarchal institutions. I am far from the only woman who has been affected by the patriarchal structures of mission organizations. My insider understanding of the problem coupled with solid academic study should help bring clarity to women's leadership strategies, and might lead to increased opportunities for women who wish to lead in evangelical mission organizations.

Appendix B

Consent Form

Women Leaders in Evangelical Mission Agencies:
Negotiating Patriarchal Structures

[IRB Number XXXX-XXXXX-X]

I, _____, agree to participate in a research study titled "Women Leaders in Evangelical Mission Agencies: Negotiating Patriarchal Structures" conducted by Leanne M. Dzubinski, a student at the University of Georgia. Contact information is listed below and you may contact her anytime with questions or concerns. My major professor, Dr. Wendy Ruona, will supervise the research project.

Purpose of the Study: I understand the purpose of this research project is to gain understanding about how women in faith-based non-profit mission organizations lead in these institutions. Women with leadership experience will be asked to talk about their experiences.

Procedures: I understand that my participation in this study is voluntary.

I understand that I will be participating in a digitally audio recorded interview lasting 60-90 minutes that will occur by phone if we are geographically distant or in person at a mutually-agreed up location if we are close together. The researcher may request a second interview to seek clarification and expansion of information from our first conversation. If I participate in a second interview, I will have an opportunity to discuss the interpretations of the researcher's analysis. I also understand that I may be contacted by telephone or email after an interview to provide further clarification of data or interpretation of data analysis, or to be asked to participate in more interviews. The purpose of any follow-up interviews will be to further explore my leadership practices, expand on my experiences, and confirm the researcher's understanding of my comments. I also understand that publicly available organizational documents may be used as part of the study. The time frame for my participation will be from 3 to 12 months.

Discomfort/Stresses: The discomforts or stresses that may be faced during this study include possible psychological or spiritual anxiety related to discussing personal matters. If I feel any stress or discomfort, I am free to withhold a response, skip a question, take a break, or stop the interview entirely.

Risks: No risks are expected.

Benefits to me: I understand that the researcher is conducting a study about the leadership practices of women in mostly male settings. Understanding how women lead in these settings may help the researcher and the participant develop an understanding of women's effective leadership practices. There will be no direct benefits or financial compensation for this study. I may benefit from the opportunity to talk as openly and honestly as I wish about obstacles to women and women's leadership that I may have encounter in my organization. This may lead to greater self-understanding, as well as a sense of affirmation that I have encountered obstacles in my leadership journey. I may also benefit from being heard.

Confidentiality: I understand that my individually-identifiable information will be kept confidential and used in a manner that will protect my identity. My name and any traceable identifiers will be removed from transcripts before reporting data or results. I understand that I can choose or will be given a pseudonym and any quotations made from my interviews will be attributed to the pseudonym.

I understand that the interviews will be recorded with a digital voice recorder. The recordings will be preserved on a flash drive in a secure location in the researcher's home. These will be deleted when the study is completed (in at least five years). Transcriptions will be stored in password-protected files. Any printed transcriptions will also be stored in a locked file box in the researcher's home with the flash drive, and only the researcher will have access to these files. They will be kept for up to five years.

I understand that if I agree to share some information by email, there is a limit to the confidentiality that can be guaranteed due to the technology itself. The researcher cannot guarantee confidentiality of email communications but will utilize standard confidentiality procedures (pseudonyms, etc.) when the researcher writes up the final research product.

I understand that data and analysis from this study may be used in the researcher's classes, for publication, and in presentations in seminars and research conferences.

Rights of the Participant: My participation in this study is voluntary. I can refuse to participate or stop taking part at any time without giving any reason, and without penalty or loss of benefits to which I am otherwise entitled. I can ask to have all of the information about me returned to me, removed from the research records, or destroyed.

Further Questions: The researcher will answer any further questions about the research, now or during the course of the project, and can be reached at the contact information listed below.

Sincerely,

Leanne M. Dzubinski

Name of Participant	Signature of Participant	Date

Leanne M. Dzubinski		
Name of Researcher	Signature of Researcher	Date

Leanne M. Dzubinski

Please sign both copies, keep one copy, and return one to the researcher.

Additional questions or concerns about your rights as a research participant should be addressed to: Chairperson, Institutional Review Board, University of Georgia.

APPENDIX C

Interview Protocols

SCRIPT FOR INTERVIEW ONE

So, as you know, today we're going to talk about women in leadership in mission organizations. I'll be asking you about your experiences and recording our conversation. Your participation is completely voluntary and you can stop or not answer a question at any time. Whenever I report my findings you'll be referred to by a pseudonym, and your name and the organization's name won't be made public. There's a bit of risk to you that you may find the conversation uncomfortable at times. You won't be compensated for participating. I will make a transcript of our conversation, and you can let me know later if you want a copy. Is all of this okay with you?

Great! Let's get started.

Interview Questions

The numbered questions are the main ones; potential probes are listed as sub-points of the corresponding question.

1. Tell me about your path in the organization.

   Tell me about your role in this organization and how you got here

   How did you learn to do your job?

   What helps you do your job well?

2. Describe a time when you felt really successful in your job.

   Tell me about something that went really well.

3. Describe a time when it was really difficult to do your job.

   Tell me about a time you thought something was difficult or went badly.

4. What is it like to be a woman in a high-level position in your organization?

   What would you think if you were expected to "speak for" women in your organization?

5. Tell me about interacting with other leaders in the organization?

   Can you tell me about a really successful time working with other leaders?

   What about a time that was challenging?

6. How do other people see you?

7. What happens if someone questions your ability or your authority to do your job?

8. Mission organizations don't tend to have many women in leadership roles. What do you think got you selected for this role?

   What is it about you that made them want you in a leadership position?

9. Is there anything else you would like to share with me?

SCRIPT FOR INTERVIEW TWO

Thank you for agreeing to talk with me again about your experience as a leader in a mission organization. Today I would like to talk about the summary I sent you and see what your thoughts are about what I've found so far. I'd also like to ask you a few clarifying questions about what you told me last time. Like last time, your participation is completely voluntary and you can stop or not answer a question at any time. Whenever I report my findings you'll be referred to by a pseudonym, and your name and the organization's name won't be made public. There's a bit of risk to you that you may find the conversation uncomfortable at times. You won't be compensated for participating. I will record this call and make a transcript of our conversation. You can let me know later if you want a copy. Is all of this okay with you?

Great! Let's get started.

Interview Questions

1. What do you think about the summary sheet I sent you?

   Are there things that particularly caught your attention?

   Are there some things that really rang true for you?

   What about things that didn't seem right or didn't make sense?

2. When we talked the first time, you mentioned _____ (something positive or helpful she discussed). I wonder if you could tell me more about that.

3. When we talked, you also mentioned _____ (something difficult or painful). I wonder if you have any more thoughts on that you'd like to share with me today.

4. We also discussed _____ (here I will look for something that sounded like resistance or justification). I wonder if you could talk more about that.

5. Since we talked the first time, how maybe have your thoughts changed about what it's like to be a woman leader in XYZ mission organization?

Appendix D

Initial Themes From Interviews

December 30, 2012

PARTICIPANT SUMMARY—12 women

Positions: 5 CEOs, 3 HR Directors, 2 executive-team leaders, 2 geographic leaders

Marital status: 9 married, 3 single

Years of missionary work: 15-20 years = 5 women, 20-30 years = 5 women, >30 years = 2 women

Years in leadership position at time of interview (current or final position): 1-3 years = 10 women, 4-5 years = 2 women

Organization size: less than 100 = 4 organizations; 100-600 = 6 organizations; over 2000 = 2 organizations

PRELIMINARY THEMES

I. Career trajectory: There is no clearly defined path to leadership for the women in this study. However, some patterns are discernible:

A. Single women—more or less start with low level leadership positions and work their way up.

B. Married women—some start with low levels of leadership and work their way up, perhaps jumping a level or two along the way; others move directly into upper levels of leadership as their children grow up. There appears to be a close connection between marriage/ motherhood and women's leadership. None of the women in this study had small children and only 2 had school-aged children. The rest have grown children.

C. Sponsorship—a number of women attained their initial or current positions because a male with significant organizational power/influence put them forward for leadership. For 3 it was an organization's founder who influenced their placement in upper leadership; for others it was a high-level male who knew them and recommended them.

D. Time frame—no woman in this study had less than 16 years of experience in mission work. However, most women have been in (or were in) this leadership role for 3 years or less. Only two have had top-level leadership for 4-5 years, and no one for longer than 5 years. **I think this may be significant. What does it mean?**

II. Learning to Lead: Similarly, there is little evidence of organizations providing leadership training or development for these women leaders. So the women in this study found their own ways to learn the job and to learn leadership. Some of the main ways are:

A. Self-directed Learning—asking those who had the job before; finding books, materials, internet resources, workshops, seminars, etc. for herself.

B. Learning through experience—by trial and error; by having a long history with organization.

C. Mentoring—someone (perhaps husband) who is also in leadership and helps along the way.

III. Uncertainties regarding women's leadership: every woman told a story reflecting uncertainty, challenge, or hindrances to her leadership. These stories ranged from severely traumatic to subversive to mild resistance. Every woman encountered something. These are some preliminary categories of resistance:

A. From the organization itself

1. Interim assignments until they are sure she can handle the job.
2. Job-sharing assignments with a male (sometimes husband) may preserve appearance of male leadership, or may place woman in a supporting role.

   3. Some women report that leadership is a men's/boys' club—organizational culture favors male leadership.

   4. Some women had a change of title, status, position, or authority, or were somehow less expensive (financially) than a male.

   5. 4 women had stories of blatant opposition, even from those who originally appointed them to leadership.

B. From organization members

   1. Direct challenges—going over her head, refusing to follow policies or practices, threatening to resign. Sometimes the next level up supported the woman, sometimes not.

   2. Indirect challenges—passive non-compliance, marginalizing, stereotyping.

C. From the women themselves

   1. Unclear if issues are gender-based or something else.

   2. Being willing to overlook, excuse or accept mistreatment—not advocating for self.

   3. Take personal responsibility when things go poorly, not considering organizational practices or structures to be part of the problem or challenge they face.

IV. Leadership Practices—strategies & values

   A. Passion for the work/role

   B. Matching people to roles based on gifts and abilities

   C. Using communal behaviors

   1. Building relationships & teams

   2. Minimizing status differences between self and others

   3. Building a sense of community

   4. Nurturing, caring for, and pastoring those under their leadership

   D. Using agentic behaviors

   1. Being very competent & capable

   2. Being knowledgeable

   3. Being assertive

    4. Finding ways to be heard, including networking outside of meetings

E. Fitting in to the "boys' club"

    1. Paying attention to dress

    2. Paying attention to communication styles

    3. Only cautiously advocating for other women, when appropriate

V. Organizational Practices regarding Women

A. Some organizations and some women represent **traditional views on gender roles**. Women, if married, first support their husbands and raise their children and then move into leadership.

B. Some organizations and women represent **egalitarian views of gender and leadership**. A few organizations are deliberately looking for ways to move more women into leadership and have enlisted the current women leaders to help them.

C. Most organizations appear to fall **somewhere in the middle**, defaulting to traditional views of gender roles but willing to have women leaders if someone sponsors or recommends them, or if the women work their way up the ranks, or gain notice in some way.

VI. Conclusions—PRELIMINARY

1. **Being a person** (i.e., seen and treated as an individual) vs. representing a category seems to be significant for male acceptance of women leaders. Several women commented that this was crucial; some think it's easier for single women than married women to achieve this treatment.

2. **Leading in an area of strength**, that suits a woman's gifting and temperament, seems to help her succeed and feel positive about her leadership role, especially in organizations where women leaders are scarce and the organization's position on women leaders is unclear.

3. **Few women reported serious theological obstacles** in their organizations. (This makes sense because organizations with strong theological views against women's leadership would not be represented in this study.) However, the concern seems to lurk below the surface and occasionally prompted speculation on the part of the women regarding why they hit resistance, or prompted direct opposition to a woman's leadership.

4. **The more significant challenge** to women leading well seems to be a combination of a tradition of male leadership that simply overlooks female talent, and an organizational culture that makes men comfortable and women uncomfortable in leadership roles. It's hard to be the first or only woman in the room.

5. **Several women** in the study reported that other women in their organizations are reluctant to lead, even when asked. This may be due to organizational culture already mentioned, to traditional gender views, to a sense of gifting and call, or some other reason. More study needs to be done on this question.

6. **None of the women** in this study were interested in advocating for themselves or for "women's rights". They see themselves as qualified and gifted and called for the role at this time. When faced with opposition, no one made a fuss. They would rather bend in a situation or rely on upper leadership to support them than escalate conflict. However, they were often willing to advocate for others, to insist on proper and courteous treatment of those in their departments, to push for ministry placements based on gifting and ability rather than gender.

7. **Risk and Consolidation**—Women seem to be tapped for these roles; at least 7 participants reported this kind of situation. The risky position may be taking on a department or ministry that has fallen into disarray; other times it's following on the heels of a visionary founder who didn't establish any kind of order or procedures. **Are women seen as uniquely suited to these roles for some reason? This may also be significant.**

Bibliography

Acker, Joan. "Hierarchies, Jobs, Bodies: A Theory of Gendered Organizations." *Gender & Society* 4.2 (1990) 139–58.

Acker, Sandra. "In/out/Side: Positioning the Researcher in Feminist Qualitative Research." *Resources for Feminist Research* 28.3/4 (2001) 153–72.

Adams, Jimi. "Stained Glass Makes the Ceiling Visible: Organizational Opposition to Women in Congregational Leadership." *Gender & Society* 21.1 (2007) 80–105. https://doi.org/10.1177/0891243206293773.

Allison, M. T. "Organizational Barriers to Diversity in the Workplace." *Journal of Leisure Research* 31.1 (1999) 78–101.

Andersen, Margaret L., and Dana Hysock. *Thinking about Women: Sociological Perspectives on Race and Gender.* 8th ed. Boston, MA: Pearson, 2009.

Andersen, Margaret L., and Patricia Hill Collins, eds. *Race, Class & Gender: An Anthology.* 6th ed. Belmont, CA: Thomson Wadsworth, 2007.

Anderson, Donald L. *Organization Development: The Process of Leading Organizational Change.* 2nd ed. Los Angeles: Sage, 2012.

Armstrong, Evetta Rose. "How Evangelical Black Women Learn to Negotiate Power Relations Based on Race and Gender in Their Ministry Preparation and Practice." PhD diss., Univeristy of Georgia, 2007.

Aune, K. "Evangelical Christianity and Women's Changing Lives." *European Journal of Women's Studies* 15 (2008) 277–94. https://doi.org/10.1177/1350506808091508.

Avolio, Bruce J., et al. "Leadership: Current Theories, Research, and Future Directions." *Annual Review of Psychology* 60 (2009) 421–49.

Barclay, S. "Are Mission Agencies 'Institutionally Sexist'? An Examination of the Possible Factors Preventing Women Reaching Leadership Positions in UK Missions Today." *Global Connections Occasional Paper* 22.1 (2006) i–iv.

Barres, Ben A. "Does Gender Matter?" *Nature* 442.13 (July 13, 2006) 132–36.

Bartol, Kathryn M., and Anthony D. Butterfield. "Sex Effects in Evaluating Leaders." *Journal of Applied Psychology* 61.4 (1976) 446–54.

Bass, Bernard M., and Bruce J. Avolio. "Shatter the Glass Ceiling: Women May Make Better Managers." *Human Resource Management* 33.4 (1994) 549–60.

Bass, Bernard M., et al. "The Transformational and Transactional Leadership of Men and Women." *Applied Psychology* 45.1 (1996) 5–34.

Baumgartner, Mindy S., and David E. Schneider. "Perceptions of Women in Management: A Thematic Analysis of Razing the Glass Ceiling." *Journal of Career Development* 37.2 (2010) 559–76.

Becker, Carol E. *Leading Women: How Church Women Can Avoid Leadership Traps and Negotiate the Gender Maze.* Nashville: Abingdon, 1996.

Belenky, M. F., et al. *Women's Ways of Knowing: The Development of Self, Voice, and Mind.* 10th anniversary ed. New York: Basic, 1997.

Bem, Sandra Lipsitz. "Gender Schema Theory: A Cognitive Account of Sex Typing." *Psychological Review* 88.4 (1981) 354–64.

Bendroth, Margaret Lamberts. "Fundamentalism and Femininity: Points of Encounter between Religious Conservatives and Women, 1919–1935." *Church History* 61.2 (1992) 221–33.

———. *Fundamentalism & Gender, 1875 to the Present.* New Haven, CT: Yale University Press, 1993.

———. "Last Gasp Patriarchy: Women and Men in Conservative American Protestantism." *Muslim World* 91.1–2 (2001) 45–54.

Bierema, Laura L. "Critiquing Human Resource Development's Dominant Masculine Rationality and Evaluating Its Impact." *Human Resource Development Review* 8.1 (2009) 68–96. https://doi.org/10.1177/1534484308330020.

———. "A Feminist Approach to HRD Research." *Human Resource Development Review* 1.2 (2002) 244–68.

———. "A Model of Executive Women's Learning and Development." *Adult Education Quarterly* 49.2 (Winter 1999) 107.

———. "The Role of Gender Consciousness in Challenging Patriarchy." *International Journal of Lifelong Education* 22.1 (2003) 3–12. https://doi.org/10.1080/02601370304825.

Bikos, Lynette H., et al. "First-Year Adaptation of Female, Expatriate Religious and Humanitarian Aid Workers: A Mixed Methods Analysis." *Mental Health, Religion & Culture* 12.7 (2009) 639–61.

Bishop, N. "Book Reviews: Evangelical Feminism." *Feminist Collections* 27.4 (Summer 2006) 1–5.

Blackmore, Jill. "Social Justice and the Study and Practice of Leadership in Education: A Feminist History." *Journal of Educational Administration & History* 38.2 (2006) 185–200. https://doi.org/10.1080/00220620600554876.

Block, Pamela, et al. "Race, Poverty, and Disability: Three Strikes and You're Out! Or Are You?" In *Race, Class, & Gender: An Anthology,* edited by Margaret L. Andersen and Patricia Hill Collins, 426–32. Belmont, CA: Thomson Wadsworth, 2007.

Boeije, Hennie. "A Purposeful Approach to the Constant Comparative Method in the Analysis of Qualitative Interviews." *Quality & Quantity* 36.4 (2002) 391–409.

Bohan, Janis S. "Regarding Gender: Essentialism, Constructionism, and Feminist Psychology." *Psychology of Women Quarterly* 17.1 (1993) 5–22.

Bosker, Bianca. "Fortune 500 List Boasts More Female Ceos Than Ever Before." *The Huffington Post* (May 7, 2012). http://www.huffingtonpost.com/2012/05/07/fortune-500-female-ceos_n_1495734.html.

Bowles, Hannah R., et al. "Social Incentives for Gender Differences in the Propensity to Initiate Negotiations: Sometimes It Does Hurt to Ask." *Organizational Behavior and Human Decision Processes* 103 (2007) 84–103.

Brenner, O. C., et al. "The Relationship between Sex Role Stereotypes and Requisite Management Characteristics Revisited." *Academy of Management Journal* 32.3 (1989) 662–69.

Brereton, Virginia Lieson, and Margaret Lamberts Bendroth. "Secularization and Gender: An Historical Approach to Women and Religion in the Twentieth Century." *Method & Theory in the Study of Religion* 13 (2001) 209–23.

Brizendine, Louann. *The Female Brain.* New York: Broadway, 2006.

Brookfield, S. D. *The Power of Critical Theory: Liberating Adult Learning and Teaching.* San Francisco: Jossey-Bass, 2006.

Brown, Reva Berman. "Meetings and Intersections: Organizational Theory Encounters Feminist Theorising." *Women's Studies International Forum* 18.2 (1995) 197–203. https://doi.org/10.1016/0277-5395(95)80055-t.

Bruland, Esther Byle. "Evangelical and Feminist Ethics: Complex Solidarities." *Journal of Religious Ethics* 17.2 (Fall89 1989) 139.

Burke, W. W. *Organization Change: Theory and Practice.* Thousand Oaks, CA: Sage Publications, 2002.

Butler-Kisber, Lynn. *Qualitative Inquiry: Thematic, Narrative, and Arts-Informed Perspectives.* Los Angeles: Sage, 2010.

Caffarella, Rosemary S. "Self-Directed Learning." In *An Update on Adult Learning Theory*, edited by Sharan B. Merriam, 25–35. San Francisco: Jossey-Bass, 1993.

Calás, Marta B., and Linda Smircich. "Dangerous Liaisons: The 'Feminine-in-Management' Meets 'Globalization.'" *Business Horizons* 36.2 (1993) 71–81.

———. "Using the 'F' Word: Feminist Theories and the Social Consequences of Organizational Research." In *Gendering Organizational Analysis*, edited by Albert J. Mills and Nancy Tancred, 222–34. Newbury Park, CA: Sage, 1992.

———. "Voicing Seduction to Silence Leadership." *Organization Studies* 12.4 (1991) 567–601. https://doi.org/10.1177/017084069101200406.

Callahan, Jamie L. "Gazing into the Crystal Ball: Critical HRD as a Future of Research in the Field." *Human Resource Development International* 10.1 (2007) 77–82. https://doi.org/10.1080/13678860601170344.

Carli, Linda L., and Alice H. Eagly. "Gender and Leadership." In *The Sage Handbook of Leadership*, edited by Alan Bryman et al., 103–17. Los Angeles: Sage, 2011.

———. "Gender, Hierarchy, and Leadership: An Introduction." *Journal of Social Issues* 57.4 (2001) 629.

Catalyst. *The Bottom Line: Connecting Corporate Performance and Gender Diversity.* New York: Catalyst, 2004.

Charmaz, Kathy. *Constructing Grounded Theory: A Practical Guide through Qualitative Analysis.* Los Angeles: Sage, 2006.

Chermack, Thomas J., et al. "Critical Uncertainties Confronting Human Resource Development." *Advances in Developing Human Resources* 5.3 (2003) 257–71. https://doi.org/10.1177/1523422303254628.

Coghlan, David, and Teresa Brannick. *Doing Action Research in Your Own Organization.* 2nd ed. Thousand Oaks, CA: Sage, 2006.

Cole, Deretta R. "Courage under Fire: How Black Women Have Learned to Survive in Corporate America." PhD diss., University of Georgia, 2010.

Cook, Judith A., and Mary Margaret Fonow. "Knowledge and Women's Interests: Issues of Epistemology and Methodology in Feminist Sociological Research." In *Feminist Research Methods: Exemplary Readings in the Social Sciences*, edited by Joyce McCarl Nielsen, 69–93. Boulder: Westview, 1990.

Cooley, LuAnn C. "Discipling Sisters: How Women Learn the Culture of a Conservative Christian Church." PhD diss., University of Georgia, 2006.

Coontz, Stephanie. *The Way We Never Were: American Families and the Nostalgia Trap.* New York: Basic, 1992.

Cranton, P. *Understanding and Promoting Transformative Learning.* San Francisco: Jossey-Bass, 1994.

Crawford, Nancy, and Helen M. DeVries. "Relationship between Role Perception and Well-Being in Married Female Missionaries." *Journal of Psychology and Theology* 33.3 (2005) 187–97.

Creese, Gillian, and Wendy Frisby. "Unpacking Relationships in Feminist Community Research: Crosscutting Themes." In *Feminist Community Research: Case Studies and Methodologies*, edited by Gillian Creese and Wendy Frisby, 1–15. Vancouver, BC: University of British Columbia Press, 2011.

Crompton, Rosemary, and Clare Lyonette. "The New Gender Essentialism—Domestic and Family 'Choices' and Their Relation to Attitudes." *British Journal of Sociology* 56.4 (2005) 601–20. https://doi.org/10.1111/j.1468-4446.2005.00085.x.

Crotty, Michael. *The Foundations of Social Research: Meaning and Perspective in the Research Process.* Thousand Oaks, CA: Sage, 1998.

Dahlvig, Jolyn E., and Karen A. Longman. "Women's Leadership Development: A Study of Defining Moments." *Christian Higher Education* 9.3 (2010) 238–58. https://doi.org/10.1080/15363750903182177.

Daloz, Laurent A. "Martha Meets Her Mentor: The Power of Teaching Relationships." *Change* 19.4 (1987) 35–37.

———. "Mentors: Teachers Who Make a Difference." *Change* 15.6 (1983) 24–27.

DeBerg, Betty A. *Ungodly Women: Gender and the First Wave of American Fundamentalism.* Minneapolis: Fortress, 1990.

deMarrais, Kathleen Bennett, and Stephen D. Lapan. *Foundations for Research: Methods of Inquiry in Education and the Social Sciences.* Mahwah, NJ: Lawrence Erlbaum Associates, 2004.

Denmark, Florence L. "Styles of Leadership." *Psychology of Women Quarterly* 2.2 (1977) 99–113. https://doi.org/10.1111/j.1471-6402.1977.tb00493.x.

Diamond, Marian C. "Male and Female Brains." *New Horizons for Learning* (2003). https://web.archive.org/web/20170504030206/http://education.jhu.edu/PD/newhorizons/Neurosciences/articles/Male%20and%20Female%20Brains//.

Dowland, Seth. "'Family Values' and the Formation of a Christian Right Agenda." *Church History* 78.3 (2009) 606–31. https://doi.org/10.1017/s0009640709990448.

Eagly, Alice H. "Female Leadership Advantage and Disadvantage: Resolving the Contradictions." *Psychology of Women Quarterly* 31.1 (2007) 1–12.

Eagly, Alice H., and Blair T. Johnson. "Gender and Leadership Style: A Meta-Analysis." *Psychological Bulletin* 108.2 (1990) 233–56.

Eagly, Alice H., and Linda L. Carli. "Women and the Labyrinth of Leadership." *Harvard Business Review* 85.9 (2007) 63–71.

Eagly, Alice H., and Mary C. Johannesen-Schmidt. "The Leadership Styles of Women and Men." *Journal of Social Issues* 57.4 (2001) 781–97. https://doi.org/10.1111/0022-4537.00241.

Eagly, Alice H., and Steven J. Karau. "Role Congruity Theory of Prejudice toward Female Leaders." *Psychological Review* 109.3 (2002) 573–98. https://doi.org/10.1037/0033-295x.109.3.573.

Eagly, Alice H., et al. "Gender and the Effectiveness of Leaders: A Meta-Analysis." *Psychological Bulletin* 117.1 (1995) 125–45. https://doi.org/10.1037/0033-2909.117.1.125.

Eenigenburg, Sue, and Robynn Bliss. *Expectations and Burnout: Women Surviving the Great Commission.* Pasadena, CA: William Carey Library, 2010.

Ehrenreich, Barbara, and Deidre English. *For Her Own Good: Two Centuries of the Experts' Advice to Women.* 2nd ed. New York: Anchor, 2005.

Eldredge, John. *Wild at Heart: Discovering the Secret of a Man's Soul.* Nashville: Thomas Nelson, 2001.

Elliott, Carole, and Valerie Stead. "Learning from Leading Women's Experience: Towards a Sociological Understanding." *Leadership* 4.2 (2008) 159–80. https://doi.org/10.1177/1742715008089636.

Ely, Robin J., et al. "Taking Gender into Account: Theory and Design for Women's Leadership Development Programs." *Academy of Management Learning & Education* 10.3 (2011) 474–93.

Ely, Robin J., et al., eds. *Reader in Gender, Work, and Organization.* Malden, MA: Blackwell, 2003.

English, Leona M., and Elizabeth J. Tisdell. "Spirituality and Adult Education." In *Handbook of Adult and Continuing Education,* edited by Carol E. Kasworm et al., 285–93. Los Angeles: Sage, 2010.

Etherington, Kim. *Becoming a Reflexive Researcher: Using Our Selves in Research.* Philadelphia: Jessica Kingsley, 2004.

Evans, Judith. *Feminist Theory Today: An Introduction to Second-Wave Feminism.* Thousand Oaks, CA: Sage, 1995.

Farley, P. C. "Psychological Type Preferences of Female Missionaries from the United Kingdom." *Mental Health, Religion & Culture* 12.7 (2009) 663–69.

Fine, Cordelia. *Delusions of Gender: How Our Minds, Society, and Neurosexism Create Difference.* New York: Norton, 2010.

Finlay, Linda. "Negotiating the Swamp: The Opportunity and Challenge of Reflexivity in Research Practice." *Qualitative Research* 2.2 (2002) 209–30. https://doi.org/10.1177/146879410200200205.

Fitzgerald, T. "'To Unite Their Strength with Ours': Women and Missionary Work in Aotearoa / New Zealand 1827-4/." *The Journal of Pacific History* 39.2 (2004) 147–61.

Fleishman, Edwin A. "The Description of Supervisory Behavior." *Journal of Applied Psychology* 37.1 (1953) 1–6. https://doi.org/10.1037/h0056314.

Fletcher, Joyce K. "The Greatly Exaggerated Demise of Heroic Leadership: Gender, Power, and the Myth of Female Advantage." In *Reader in Gender, Work, and Organization,* edited by Robin J. Ely et al., 204–10. Malden, MA: Blackwell, 2003.

Forsyth, Donelson R., et al. "Biases in Appraisals of Women Leaders." *Group Dynamics: Theory, Research, and Practice* 1.1 (1997) 98–103. https://doi.org/10.1037/1089-2699.1.1.98.

Fox, Melodie J. "Prototype Theory: An Alternative Concept Theory for Categorizing Sex and Gender?" *Knowledge Organization* 38.4 (2011) 328–34.

Frame, Marsha Wiggins, and Constance L. Shehan. "Care for the Caregiver: Clues for the Pastoral Care of Clergywomen." *Pastoral Psychology* 52.5 (2004) 369–80.

———. "The Relationship between Work and Well-Being in Clergywomen: Implications for Career Counseling." *Journal of Employment Counseling* 42 (2005) 10–19.

———. "Work and Well-Being in the Two-Person Career: Relocation Stress and Coping among Clergy Husbands and Wives." *Family Relations* 43.2 (1994) 196. https://doi.org/10.2307/585323.

Freeman, Melissa, et al. "Standards of Evidence in Qualitative Research: An Incitement to Discourse." *Educational Researcher* 36.1 (2007) 25–32.

Freire, Paolo. *Pedagogy of the Oppressed.* 30th anniversary ed. New York: Continuum International, 2006.

Freyd, Jennifer J. "Journal Ethics and Impact." *Journal of Trauma & Dissociation* 10.4 (2009) 377–84. https://doi.org/10.1080/15299730903140499.

Friedan, Betty. *The Feminine Mystique.* 20th anniversary ed. New York: Norton, 2001.

Gallagher, Kathleen. "The Everyday Classroom as Problematic: A Feminist Pedagogy." *Curriculum Inquiry* 30.1 (2000) 71–81.

Gallagher, Sally K. *Evangelical Identity and Gendered Family Life.* New Brunswick, NJ: Rutgers University Press, 2003.

———. "The Marginalization of Evangelical Feminism." *Sociology of Religion* 65.3 (2004) 215–37.

———. "Where Are the Antifeminist Evangelicals? Evangelical Identity, Subcultural Location, and Attitudes toward Feminism." *Gender & Society* 18.4 (2004) 451–72. https://doi.org/10.1177/0891243204266157.

Gallagher, Sally K., and Christian Smith. "Symbolic Traditionalism and Pragmatic Egalitarianism: Contemporary Evangelicals, Families, and Gender." *Gender & Society* 13.2 (1999) 211–33.

Gaunt, Ruth. "Biological Essentialism, Gender Ideologies, and Role Attitudes: What Determines Parents' Involvement in Child Care." *Sex Roles* 55.7/8 (2006) 523–33. https://doi.org/10.1007/s11199-006-9105-0.

Gibelman, Margaret. "The Nonprofit Sector and Gender Discrimination." *Nonprofit Management & Leadership* 10.3 (2000) 251.

Gilligan, Carol. "Woman's Place in Man's Life Cycle." In *Feminism and Methodology,* edited by Sandra Harding, 57–73. Bloomington, IN: Indiana University Press, 1987.

Glesne, Corinne. *Becoming Qualitative Researchers: An Introduction.* 3rd ed. Boston: Pearson, 2006.

Goff, Jeremy. "Playing with the Boys: Why Separate Is Not Equal in Sports." *Marquette Sports Law Review* 21 (2010) 449.

Greenberg, Herbert, and Patrick Sweeney. "Leadership: Qualities That Distinguish Women." *Financial Executive* 21.6 (2005) 32–36.

Gregory, Ann. "Are Women Different and Why Are Women Thought to Be Different? Theoretical and Methodological Perspectives." *Journal of Business Ethics* 9.4/5 (1990) 257–66. http://www.jstor.org/stable/25072034.

Griffin, Christine, and Ann Phoenix. "The Relationship between Qualitative and Quantitative Research: Lessons from Feminist Psychology." *Journal of Community & Applied Social Psychology* 4.4 (Special Issue Oct 94, 1994) 287–98.

Gringeri, Christina E., et al. "What Makes It Feminist? Mapping the Landscape of Feminist Social Work Research." *Affilia* 25.4 (November 1, 2010) 390–405. https://doi.org/10.1177/0886109910384072.

Groothuis, Rebecca Merrill. "'Equal in Being, Unequal in Role': Exploring the Logic of Women's Subordination." In *Discovering Biblical Equality: Complementarity without Hierarchy*, edited by Ronald W. Pierce and Rebecca Merrill Groothuis, 301–33. Downers Grove, IL: InterVarsity, 2005.

———. *Women Caught in the Conflict: The Culture War between Traditionalism and Feminism*. Grand Rapids, MI: Baker, 1994.

Hale, Judith. *The Performance Consultant's Fieldbook: Tools and Techniques for Improving Organizations and People*. 2nd ed. San Francisco: Pfeiffer, 2007.

Hall, M. Elizabeth Lewis, and Nancy S. Duvall. "Married Women in Missions: The Effects of Cross-Cultural and Self Gender-Role Expectations on Well-Being, Stress, and Self-Esteem." *Journal of Psychology and Theology* 31.4 (2003) 303–14.

Hanscome, Lynda, and Ronald M. Cervero. "The Impact of Gendered Power Relations in HRD." *Human Resource Development International* 6.4 (2003) 509–25.

Harding, Sandra. "Rethinking Standpoint Epistemology: What Is 'Strong Objectivity?'" In *Feminist Perspectives on Social Research*, edited by Sharlene Hesse-Biber and Michelle L. Yaiser, 39–64. New York: Oxford University Press, 2004.

Hartmann, Heidi I. "The Family as Locus of Gender, Class, and Political Struggle: The Example of Housework." In *Feminism and Methodology*, edited by Sandra Harding, 109–34. Bloomington, IN: Indiana University Press, 1987.

Haslam, Nick, et al. "Are Essentialist Beliefs Associated with Prejudice?" *British Journal of Social Psychology* 41.1 (2002) 87.

———. "Essentialist Beliefs about Social Categories." *British Journal of Social Psychology* 39.1 (2000) 113–27. https://doi.org/10.1348/014466600164363.

Heilman, Madeline E. "Description and Prescription: How Gender Stereotypes Prevent Women's Ascent up the Organizational Ladder." *Journal of Social Issues* 57.4 (2001) 657–74.

Heilman, Madeline E., and Alice H. Eagly. "Gender Stereotypes Are Alive, Well, and Busy Producing Workplace Discrimination." *Industrial & Organizational Psychology* 1.4 (2008) 393–98. https://doi.org/10.1111/j.1754-9434.2008.00072.x.

Heilman, Madeline E., and Tyler G. Okimoto. "Why Are Women Penalized for Success at Male Tasks? The Implied Communality Deficit." *Journal of Applied Psychology* 92.1 (2007) 81–92. https://doi.org/10.1037/0021-9010.92.1.81.

Helgesen, Sally. "The Female Advantage." In *Reader in Gender, Work, and Organization*, edited by Robin J. Ely et al., 26–33. Malden, MA: Blackwell, 2003.

———. *The Female Advantage: Women's Ways of Leadership*. New York: Doubleday, 1990.

Henwood, Karen, and Nick Pidgeon. "Remaking the Link: Qualitative Research and Feminist Standpoint Theory." *Feminism & Psychology* 5.1 (1995) 7–30.

Hesse-Biber, Sharlene, and Michelle L. Yaiser, eds. *Feminist Perspectives on Social Research*. New York: Oxford University Press, 2004.

Hoyt, Crystal L. "Women and Leadership." In *Leadership Theory and Practice*, edited by Peter G. Northouse, 265–99. Thousand Oaks, CA: Sage, 2007.

Hubbard, M. Gay. *Women: The Misunderstood Majority.* Eugene, OR: Resource, 1992.

Ingersoll, Julie. "Engendered Conflict: Feminism and Traditionalism in Late Twentieth-Century Conservative Protestantism." PhD diss., University of California, 1997.

———. *Evangelical Christian Women: War Stories in the Gender Battles.* New York: New York University Press, 2003.

Irvine, Annie. "Duration, Dominance and Depth in Telephone and Face-to-Face Interviews: A Comparative Exploration." *International Journal of Qualitative Methods* 10.3 (2011) 202–20.

Irvine, Annie, et al. "'Am I Not Answering Your Questions Properly?' Clarification, Adequacy and Responsiveness in Semi-Structured Telephone and Face-to-Face Interviews." *Qualitative Research* 13.1 (2013) 87–106. https://doi.org/10.1177/1468794112439086.

Johanson, John. "Perceptions of Femininity in Leadership: Modern Trend or Classic Component?" *Sex Roles* 58.11/12 (2008) 784–89. https://doi.org/10.1007/s11199-008-9398-2.

Johnson, Larry, et al. "African Americans and the Struggle for Opportunity in Florida Public Higher Education, 1947–1977." *History of Education Quarterly* 47.3 (2007) 328–58.

Johnson-Bailey, Juanita, and Ronald M. Cervero. "Power Dynamics in Teaching and Learning Practices: An Examination of Two Adult Education Classrooms." *International Journal of Lifelong Education* 17.6 (1998) 389–99.

Katz, Daniel, et al. *Productivity, Supervision and Morale among Railroad Workers.* Ann Arbor, MI: University of Michigan, 1951.

Katz, Daniel, et al. *Productivity, Supervision and Morale in an Office Situation.* Ann Arbor, MI: University of Michigan, 1950.

Katz, Phyllis A. "Sex Roles: A Journal of Research." *Sex Roles* 1.1 (1975) 1–2.

Keefe, Joe, and Jacki Zehner. "Saying 'No' to All-Male Corporate Boards." *The Huffington Post* (April 6, 2011). http://www.huffingtonpost.com/joe-keefe/women-workplace_b_845174.html.

Kidd, Sue Monk. *The Dance of the Dissident Daughter: A Woman's Journey from Christian Tradition to the Sacred Feminine.* New York: HarperCollins, 1996.

Kilbourne, Jean. "Still Killing Us Softly: Advertising's Images of Women." Cambridge: Cambridge University Films, 1987.

Koenig, Anne M., et al. "Are Leader Stereotypes Masculine? A Meta-Analysis of Three Research Paradigms." *Psychological Bulletin* 137.4 (2011) 616–42. https://doi.org/10.1037/a0023557.

Kolb, Deborah M., et al. "Making Change: A Framework for Promoting Gender Equity in Organizations." In *Reader in Gender, Work, and Organization*, edited by Robin J. Ely et al., 10–15. Malden, MA: Blackwell, 2003.

Korabik, Karen. "Androgyny and Leadership Style." *Journal of Business Ethics* 9.4/5 (1990) 283–92.

Kouzes, James M., and Barry Z. Posner. *The Leadership Challenge.* 3rd ed. San Francisco: Wiley, 2002.

Kuntz, Aaron M. "Representing Representation." *International Journal of Qualitative Studies in Education (QSE)* 23.4 (2010) 423–33. https://doi.org/10.1080/09518398.2010.492769.

Lafreniere, Shawna L., and Karen A. Longman. "Gendered Realities and Women's Leadership Development: Participant Voices from Faith-Based Higher Education." *Christian Higher Education* 7.5 (2008) 388–404.

Lapovsky, Lucie. "The White House Project Report: Benchmarking Women's Leadership." https://scholar.harvard.edu/files/shaunashames/files/benchmarking_final_report_11.15.09.pdf.

Lechuga, Vicente M. "Exploring Culture from a Distance: The Utility of Telephone Interviews in Qualitative Research." *International Journal of Qualitative Studies in Education* 25.3 (2012) 251–68.

Levitt, H. M., and K. Ware. "'Anything with Two Heads Is a Monster': Religious Leaders' Perspectives on Marital Equality and Domestic Violence." *Violence against Women* 12.12 (2006) 1169–90.

Lewis, John. "Redefining Qualitative Methods: Believability in the Fifth Moment." *International Journal of Qualitative Methods* 8.2 (2009) 1–14.

Lippert-Rasmussen, Kasper. "Gender Constructions: The Politics of Biological Constraints." *Distinktion: Scandinavian Journal of Social Theory* 11.1 (2010) 73–91.

Litfin, A. Duane. "Evangelical Feminism: Why Traditionalists Reject It." *Bibliotheca Sacra* 136.543 (1979) 258–71.

Longman, Karen A., and Shawna L. Lafreniere. "Moving Beyond the Stained Glass Ceiling: Preparing Women for Leadership in Faith-Based Higher Education." *Advances in Developing Human Resources* 14.1 (2012) 45–61. https://doi.org/10.1177/1523422311427429.

Lyness, Karen S., and Madeline E. Heilman. "When Fit Is Fundamental: Performance Evaluations and Promotions of Upper-Level Female and Male Managers." *Journal of Applied Psychology* 91.4 (2006) 777–85. https://doi.org/10.1037/0021-9010.91.4.777.

Maher, Frances A. "Toward a Richer Theory of Feminist Pedagogy: A Comparison of 'Liberation' and 'Gender' Models for Teaching and Learning." *Journal of Education* 169.3 (1987) 91–100.

———. "Twisted Privileges: Terms of Inclusion in Feminist Teaching." *Radical Teacher* 83 (2008) 5–9.

Marshall, Catherine, and Gretchen B. Rossman. *Designing Qualitative Research.* 4th ed. Thousand Oaks, CA: Sage, 2006.

Marshall, Judi. *Women Managers: Travellers in a Male World.* Bath, UK: Wiley, 1984.

Merriam, Sharan B. *Qualitative Research: A Guide to Design and Implementation.* The Jossey-Bass Higher and Adult Education Series. San Francisco: Jossey-Bass, 2009.

Merriam, Sharan B., ed. *Qualitative Research in Practice: Examples for Discussion and Analysis.* The Jossey-Bass Higher and Adult Education Series. San Francisco: Jossey-Bass, 2002.

Merriam, Sharan B., and Rosemary S. Caffarella. *Learning in Adulthood: A Comprehensive Guide.* San Francisco: Jossey-Bass, 1999.

Merriam, Sharan B., et al. "Power and Positionality: Negotiating Insider / Outsider Status within and across Cultures." *International Journal of Lifelong Education* 20.5 (2001) 405–16.

Misawa, Mitsunori. "Queer Race Pedagogy for Educators in Higher Education: Dealing with Power Dynamics and Positionality of Lgbtq Students of Color." *International Journal of Critical Pedagogy* 3.1 (2010) 26–35.

Murphy, Elizabeth. *Constructivism: From Philosophy to Practice.* US Deparment of Education (1997).

Murphy-Geiss, Gail. "Married to the Minister: The Status of the Clergy Spouse as Part of a Two-Person Single Career." *Journal of Family Issues* 32.7 (2011) 932–55.

Naples, Nancy A. "The Outsider Phenomenon." In *Feminist Perspectives on Social Research*, edited by Sharlene Nagy Hesse-Biber and Michelle L. Yaiser, 373–81. New York: Oxford University Press, 2004.

Nielsen, Joyce McCarl, ed. *Feminist Research Methods: Exemplary Readings in the Social Sciences.* Boulder: Westview, 1990.

Northouse, Peter G. *Leadership Theory and Practice.* 4th ed. Thousand Oaks, CA: Sage, 2007.

Novick, G. "Is There a Bias against Telephone Interviews in Qualitative Research?" *Research in Nursing & Health* 31.4 (2008) 391–98.

"No Women at the Table." *Bloomberg Businessweek* (June 23, 2011). https://www.bloomberg.com/news/photo-essays/2011-06-23/where-the-women-arent-public-companies-with-no-women-at-the-top.

O'Connell, Matthew, and Mei-Chuan Kung. "The Cost of Employee Turnover." *Industrial Management* 49.1 (2007) 14–19.

Papanek, Hanna. "Men, Women, and Work: Reflections on the Two-Person Career." *The American Journal of Sociology* 78.4 (1973) 852.

Pavalko, Eliza K., and Glen H. Elder. "Women Behind the Men: Variations in Wives' Support of Husbands' Careers." *Gender & Society* 7.4 (1993) 548–67.

Penney, Sherry H. "Voices of the Future: Leadership for the 21st Century." *Journal of Leadership Studies* 5.3 (2011) 55–62.

Peters, April. "Elements of Successful Mentoring of a Female School Leader." *Leadership and Policy in Schools* 9.1 (2010) 108–29.

Pevey, C., et al. "Male God Imagery and Female Submission: Lessons from a Southern Baptist Ladies' Bible Class." *Qualitative Sociology* 19.2 (1996) 173–94.

Powell, Gary N., et al. "Sex Effects in Evaluations of Transformational and Transactional Leaders." *Academy of Management* (2004) E1–E6. https://doi.org/10.5465/ambpp.2004.13863020.

Quigley, B. Allan, and Ella Holsinger. "'Happy Consciousness': Ideology and Hidden Curricula in Literacy Education." *Adult Education Quarterly* 44.1 (1993) 17–33.

Regan, Helen B., and Gwen H. Brooks. *Out of Women's Experience: Creating Relational Leadership.* Thousand Oaks, CA: Corwin, 1995.

Reinharz, Shulamit. *Feminist Methods in Social Research.* New York: Oxford University Press, 1992.

Riehl, Carolyn, and Valerie E. Lee. "Gender, Organization, and Leadership." In *International Handbook of Educational Leadership and Administration*, edited by Kenneth A. Leithwood et al., 873–912. Dordrecht, The Netherlands: Kluwer Academic, 1996.

Riley, Sarah, et al. "Exploring the Dynamics of Subjectivity and Power between Researcher and Researched." *Forum Qualitative Sozialforschung* 4.2 (2003) 122–36.

Robert, Dana L. *American Women in Mission: A Social History of Their Thought and Practice.* The Modern Mission Era, 1792–1992: An Appraisal. Edited by Wilbert R. Schenk. Macon, GA: Mercer University Press, 1997.

———. "Women in World Mission: Controversies and Challenges from a North American Perspective." *International Review of Mission* 93.3 (2004) 50–61.

Robinson, Dana Gaines, and James C. Robinson. *Performance Consulting: A Practical Guide for Hr and Learning Professionals.* 2nd ed. San Francisco: Berrett-Koehler, 2008.

Rosener, Judy B. "The 'Terrible Truth' about Women on Corporate Boards." *Forbes* (June 7, 2011). http://www.forbes.com/sites/womensmedia/2011/06/07/the-terrible-truth-about-women-on-corporate-boards/.

———. "Ways Women Lead." *Harvard Business Review* 68.6 (1990) 119–25.

Rosik, Christopher H., and Jelena Pandzic. "Marital Satisfaction among Christian Missionaries: A Longitudinal Analysis from Candidacy to Second Furlough." *Journal of Psychology & Christianity* 27.1 (2008) 3–15.

Rosin, Hanna. "The End of Men." *The Atlantic* (July/August 2010). http://www.theatlantic.com/magazine/archive/2010/07/the-end-of-men/8135/.

Ross, Cathy. "Separate Spheres or Shared Dominions?" *Transformation* 23.4 (2006) 228–35.

Roulston, Kathryn. "Considering Quality in Qualitative Interviewing." *Qualitative Research* 10.2 (2010) 199–228.

———. *Reflective Interviewing: A Guide to Theory & Practice.* Thousand Oaks, CA: Sage, 2010.

Rowney, J. I. A., and A. R. Cahoon. "Individual and Organizational Characteristics of Women in Managerial Leadership." *Journal of Business Ethics* 9.4/5 (1990) 293–316. http://www.jstor.org/stable/25072038.

Ruona, Wendy E. A. "Analyzing Qualitative Data." In *Research in Organizations: Foundations and Methods of Inquiry,* edited by Richard A. Swanson and Elwood F. Holton III, 223–63. San Francisco: Berrett-Koehler, 2005.

Ryan, Michelle K., and S. Alexander Haslam. "The Glass Cliff: Evidence That Women Are over-Represented in Precarious Leadership Positions." *British Journal of Management* 16.2 (2005) 81–90. https://doi.org/10.1111/j.1467-8551.2005.00433.x.

Sadker, Myra, and David Sadker. *Failing at Fairness: How America's Schools Cheat Girls.* New York: Scribner's, 1994.

Sanchez, Jafeth E., and Bill Thornton. "Gender Issues in K-12 Educational Leadership." *Advancing Women in Leadership* 30.13 (2010) 1–15.

Sandlin, Jennifer A. "Structure and Subjectivity: Reflections on Critical Research." In *Qualitative Research in Practice: Examples for Discussion and Analysis,* edited by Sharan B. Merriam, 371–73. San Francisco: Jossey-Bass, 2002.

Sayers, Dorothy L. *Are Women Human? Penetrating, Sensible, and Witty Essays on the Role of Women in Society.* Grand Rapids, MI: Eerdmans, 1971.

Schein, Virginia Ellen. "The Relationship between Sex Role Stereotypes and Requisite Management Characteristics." *Journal of Applied Psychology* 57.2 (1973) 95–100.

Scholz, Julia. "Psychologischer Essentialismus Als Relevantes Konzept Für Die Genderforschung [Psychological Essentialism as a Relevant Concept within Gender Studies]." *Journal für Psychologie* 18.3 (2010) 1–12.

Scholz, Susanne. "The Christian Right's Discourse on Gender and the Bible." *Journal of Feminist Studies in Religion* 21.1 (2005) 81–100.

Scott, Halee Gray. "Women Leaders in Protestant, Evangelical Nonprofit Institutions: Individual Perceptions Regarding Congruity between Gender and Leadership Roles." PhD diss., Biola University, 2010.

Shakeshaft, Charol. *Women in Educational Administration*. Newbury Park, CA: Sage, 1989.

Shaw, S. M. "Gracious Submission: Southern Baptist Fundamentalists and Women." *NSWA Journal* 20.1 (2008) 51–77.

Shehan, Constance L., et al. "Feeding the Flock and the Family: Work and Family Challenges Facing Ordained Clergy Women." *Sociological Focus* 32.3 (1999) 247–63. https://doi.org/10.2307/20832041.

Sheppard, Deborah. "Women Managers' Perceptions of Gender and Organizational Life." In *Gendering Organizational Analysis*, edited by Albert J. Mills and Nancy Tancred, 151–66. Newbury Park, CA: Sage, 1992.

Sloan, Diane Kay, and Kathleen J. Krone. "Women Managers and Gendered Values." *Women's Studies in Communication* 23.1 (Winter 2000) 111–30.

Sowinska, Alicja. "Ambiguous Women: Debates within American Evangelical Feminism." *European Journal of American Culture* 26.3 (2007) 167–80. https://doi.org/10.1386/ejac.26.3.167/1.

Sprague, Joey, and Diane Kobrynowicz. "A Feminist Epistemology." In *Feminist Perspectives on Social Research*, edited by Sharlene Hesse-Biber and Michelle L. Yaiser, 78–98. New York: Oxford University Press, 2004.

Stanley, Liz, ed. *Feminist Praxis: Research, Theory and Epistemology in Feminist Sociology*. New York: Routledge, 1990.

Stead, Valerie, and Carole Elliott. *Women's Leadership*. Basingstoke, UK: Palgrave MacMillan, 2009.

Stogdill, Ralph M., and Alvin E. Coons, eds. *Ohio Studies in Personnel*. Vol. 88, *Leader Behavior: Its Description and Measurement*. Columbus: The Ohio State University, 1957.

Stogdill, Ralph M., and Carroll L. Shartle, eds. *Ohio Studies in Personnel*. Vol. 80, *Methods in the Study of Administrative Leadership*. Columbus: The Ohio State University, 1955.

Stolovitch, Harold D., and Erica J. Keeps. *Training Ain't Performance*. Alexandria, VA: American Society for Training and Development, 2004.

Storberg-Walker, Julia, and Laura L. Bierema. "An Historical Analysis of HRD Knowledge: A Critical Review of 'the Foreman: Master and Victim of Doubletalk.'" *Journal of European Industrial Training* 32.6 (2008) 433–51.

Swanson, Richard A., and Elwood F. Holton. *Foundations of Human Resource Development*. 2nd ed. San Francisco: Berrett-Koehler, 2009.

Tisdell, Elizabeth J. *Creating Inclusive Adult Learning Environments: Insights from Multicultural Education and Feminist Pedagogy. No. 361*. Columbus: The Ohio State University, 1995.

———. "Feminism and Adult Learning: Power, Pedagogy, and Praxis." In *An Update on Adult Learning Theory*, edited by Sharan B. Merriam, 91–103. New Directions for Adult and Continuing Education. San Francisco: Jossey-Bass, 1993.

———. "Interlocking Systems of Power, Privilege, and Oppression in Adult Higher Education Classes." *Adult Education Quarterly* 43.4 (1993) 203–26.

———. "Poststructural Feminist Pedagogies: The Possibilities and Limitations of Feminist Emancipatory Adult Learning Theory and Practice." *Adult Education Quarterly* 48.3 (1998) 139–56.

Tokuhama-Espinosa, Tracey. "What Neuroscience Says about Personalized Learning." *Educational Leadership* 69.5 (2012). http://www.ascd.org/publications/educational-leadership/feb12/vol69/num05/What-Neuroscience-Says-About-Personalized-Learning.aspx.

Tong, Rosemarie. *Feminist Thought: A More Comprehensive Introduction.* 3rd ed. Boulder: Westview, 2009.

Trier-Bieniek, Adrienne. "Framing the Telephone Interview as a Participant-Centered Tool for Qualitative Research: A Methodological Discussion." *Qualitative Research* 12.6 (2012) 630–44. https://doi.org/10.1177/1468794112439005.

Trinidad, Cristina, and Anthony H. Normore. "Leadership and Gender: A Dangerous Liaison?" *Leadership & Organization Development Journal* 26.7 (2005) 574–90. https://doi.org/10.1108/01437730510624601.

VanLeuvan, Patricia. "Young Women's Science/Mathematics Career Goals from Seventh Grade to High School Graduation." *The Journal of Educational Research* 97.5 (2004) 248–67.

Vinkenburg, Claartje J., et al. "An Exploration of Stereotypical Beliefs about Leadership Styles: Is Transformational Leadership a Route to Women's Promotion?" *The Leadership Quarterly* 22.1 (2011) 10–21. https://doi.org/10.1016/j.leaqua.2010.12.003.

Weikart, Lynne A., et al. "The Democratic Sex: Gender Differences and the Exercise of Power." *Journal of Women, Politics & Policy* 28.1 (2006) 119–40.

Westkott, Marcia. "Feminist Criticism of the Social Sciences." In *Feminist Research Methods: Exemplary Readings in the Social Sciences,* edited by Joyce McCarl Nielsen, 58–68. Boulder: Westview, 1990.

Westmarland, Nicole. "The Quantitative/Qualitative Debate and Feminist Research: A Subjective View of Objectivity." *Forum: Qualitative Social Research* 2.1 (2001) 223–33.

Wilcox, Clyde. "Feminism and Anti-Feminism among Evangelical Women." *Western Political Quarterly* 42.1 (1989) 147–60.

Wilson-Jones, Linda. "Undergraduate Females' Viewpoints on the Challenges and Barriers Associated with Majoring in a Stem Program at Fayetteville State University." *FOCUS on Colleges, Universities & Schools* 6.1 (2011) 1–14.

"Women in the Labor Force, 1970–2009." *U.S. Bureau of Labor Statistics* (January 5, 2011). http://www.bls.gov/opub/ted/2011/ted_20110105.htm.

Woodberry, R. D., and C. S. Smith. "Fundamentalism Et Al: Conservative Protestants in America." *Annual Review of Sociology* 24.1 (1998) 25–57.

The World's Women 2010: Trends and Statistics. Statistics Division, United Nations (2010). http://unstats.un.org/unsd/demographic/products/Worldswomen/Executive%20summary.htm.

Yoder, Janice D. "Making Leadership Work More Effectively for Women." *Journal of Social Issues* 57.4 (2001) 815.

Young, Richard A., and Audrey Collin. "Introduction: Constructivism and Social Constructionism in the Career Field." *Journal of Vocational Behavior* 64 (2004) 373–88. https://doi.org/10.1016/j.jvb.2003.12.005.

Zikmund, Barbara Brown, et al. *Clergy Women: An Uphill Calling.* Louisville: Westminster John Knox, 1998.

Zinn, Maxine Baca, et al. "Sex and Gender through the Prism of Difference." In *Race, Class, & Gender: An Anthology,* edited by Margaret L. Andersen and Patricia Hill Collins, 147–56. Belmont, CA: Thomson-Wadsworth, 2007.